Plot, Story, and the Novel

Plot, Story, and the Novel

*From Dickens and Poe to
the Modern Period*

ROBERT L. CASERIO

PRINCETON UNIVERSITY PRESS

PRINCETON, NEW JERSEY

To my loved ones

It is nonsense to think only of thoughts and not of words or deeds, since words are only spoken thoughts and deeds are only acted words. They are in fact the most dominant words and the most triumphant thoughts; the thoughts that emerge. . . . Acts . . . are the swiftest thoughts; . . . they are even too swift to be called thoughts. They come from something more fundamental than common or conscious thinking.   G. K. Chesterton, *Robert Louis Stevenson*

The art of storytelling is coming to an end. Less and less frequently do we encounter people with the ability to tell a tale properly. More and more often there is embarrassment all around when the wish to hear a story is expressed.
Walter Benjamin, ''The Storyteller''

❧ CONTENTS ❧

✄ ACKNOWLEDGMENTS ✄

A. Dwight Culler and Charles Feidelson, Jr. encouraged this book when it was first undertaken; they have stimulated its growth by incisively intelligent supervision. Among those whose faith in the book contributed most to its completion are my parents and Aaron Fogel, Geoffrey Hartman, Richard Howard, Stanley A. Leavy, and Allan Trachtenberg; among those whose suggestions and questionings have been most useful are Robert Newsom, Sherman Paul, Mary Poovey, and Seymour Simckes. I must especially single out Catherine Dammeyer and Camille Paglia for the pains they have taken to improve the style of this work.

≥ INTRODUCTION ≤

To plot the story of the intertwined fate of plot and story in the novel since Dickens and Poe is the object of this book.* The story is interesting principally for what it tells of the changing intellectual and moral fortunes and misfortunes of action. If we believe Aristotle, action is the essential necessity of life. "The end for which we live is a certain kind of activity, not a quality. Character gives us qualities, but it is in our action—what we do—that we are happy or the reverse."[1] Walter Benjamin thought that when we lose interest in stories and storytelling we lose the ability to exchange experiences.[2] It is perhaps more significant that when writers and readers of novels lose interest in plot and story, they appear to lose faith in the meaning and the moral value of acts.

Nineteenth-century novelists, heirs of the writers of epic— of the songs of action—more and more made the distrust of action their representational ground. In *A Grammar of Motives* Kenneth Burke declares that "magic, in the sense of novelty, is seen to exist . . . as an ingredient of every human act; for each act contains some measure of motivation that cannot be explained simply in terms of the past, being . . . however tiny, a *new thing*."[3] To a growing number of Victorian novelists and their American counterparts the "new thing" Burke describes began to seem to obstruct novelty. It began also to seem to obstruct the representation of actuality. In some of the most prestigious novelistic fiction of the past and the present centuries, the imitation of actuality becomes opposed to the imitation of acts. The novelists have distrusted action because they have doubted its intelligibility, purposefulness, and morality. The distrust of the imitation of action therefore has become a distrust of intelligibility, purposefulness, and morality altogether. What the novelists troubled by

* Definitions of *plot* and *story* and the reason for their interidentified use here will be found in Chapter One.

plot and story come to value instead of action is quietism, purposelessness, inhibition or suspension of will, passive or static states of mind and feeling, and speculation free of connection with deeds. Whenever we honor such novelists and their work we ally ourselves with this shift in value.

Now the reader will notice a shift here from remarks on literary terms and literary history to remarks on meaning and moral value. It seems impossible to consider plot, story, and their history without considering meaning, ethics, teleology, or human will. This book always compounds these considerations. It is therefore left open to the charge of having tried to survey an unjustifiable number of interrelations. In part this has been done to redress a balance. Modern critics have been stripping literature of its connections with what is allegedly nonliterary. Perhaps the self-containment of literary art—of its genres, archetypal myths, phenomenologies, and deep structures—has by now had its due attention. I am convinced that the most vital element in literature is not its self-containment, but its relation to historical human change—that literary structures are transformed in response to the human metamorphoses they represent. To believe this means to believe a problem in fiction is a problem in life; a formal struggle in one is an intellectual and moral struggle in the other. This book rests on this belief.

The belief cannot be proved. A full justification of its cogency would require a separate book. But since the compound of elements I have mentioned affects the organization and the content of this study, I must address at the start important questions about the material and the presentation. Why, the reader may ask, does a study of plot and the novel pay attention to critical stances not exclusively or specifically addressed to novels? Why does a book on the novel consider historical and autobiographical nonfiction, especially if the close relation of fiction to nonfiction cannot be proved? Why is the literary history in this book not strictly chronological? Finally, is this book a polemic in favor of a certain kind and use of plot and story?

My belief in the direct bearing of literature on life has caused me to debate some of the most current critical procedures—Northrop Frye's, Roland Barthes's, and Edward Said's, for example—whether or not they address the novel only or literature and the literary use of language in general. In such modern criticism, the most powerful tendency is, as I have already mentioned, to question the interpenetration of art and life, to draw strict boundaries between the forms of fiction and fact. Whether or not these procedures directly address plot and story in the novel, the novel is deeply implicated in their ascendancy, for since the Romantic era the fate of novelistic plot has turned upon the attempt by writers and critics to dissociate the signifying structures of literature from what they arguably stand for—especially from conduct and activity in ordinary experience. The respected novelists who have opposed this dissociation have been increasingly in the minority. And novelists such as Dickens and James, whose stature and affinity as *storytellers* have scarcely yet been hinted at, have been made over by modern criticism in the image of their implicit opponents who assume an impassable distance between art and life. It is impossible therefore to recover the truth and value of novelistic story and its intimate relation with experience without pressuring the kind of criticism that emphasizes the artificial nature of narrative and the essential estrangement of art from an external origin or referent.

A challenging pressure on such criticism is perhaps all the present study can achieve because this book is, after all, a strictly literary history, confined to trusting and representing the novel's ties to an external historical reality through the novel's own representations of that vital external dimension. To fully demonstrate this dimension, this book would have had to attempt an historical and sociological analysis of contexts and effects of novelistic narration. This task was beyond me, but I have introduced Chapters Two and Six, which treat historical and autobiographical narrative, partly so that the reader can ponder how it is that narrative problems may well be more than artistic. These chapters represent to some extent the specific external causations, historical conditions, and personal situations (the French Revolution, the decline of fundamentalism, or the loss of religious faith, for example) that produce life's antagonism to plot. Moreover, given the chance to feel the anxiety or satisfaction, the opportunity or loss that writers of communal or personal history experience when they attempt to plot life, the reader may be able to grasp the vital dimension of the "formal" problem—even though it is primarily from within the novel itself, from within the novel's purely literary history, that relations between plot and life are here explored and weighed.

As literary history this study may appear arbitrary to some because it frequently disregards simple linear chronology. Yet although a writer's relation to plot and story is the result of narrative practice in his past and is an influence on the narrative practice of his future, the relevant past and future are not necessarily immediate, and they are not necessarily in his native tradition. Every writer's work is part of a complex constellation of influences that can only be represented by cutting back and forth in time and by comparative English and American references. This does not mean that literary history is also not linear and causal. But the lines are not straight, and the causations often appear as breaks or reversals as well as linear continuities. Of course, the reader should understand that absence of linearity here does not mean I assume history to be either anarchic or unwriteable (assumptions that appear especially in Carlyle and Conrad).

One more thing must be said about continuity and discontinuity in the substance of these chapters. The reader who desires a tidily straightforward history of change will be puzzled to see that the narrative era I am considering is not neatly and cleanly divisible into a "before" and an "after." During the time of Dickens, his "sense of plot" is arguably the norm. But Dickens's time is also Poe's. The antagonism to Dickens's sense of plot is therefore also contemporary with Dickens. The antagonism becomes more normative as we approach the present. But, again because the historical divisions are not patent, even in the era of Lawrence, Woolf, and Joyce when distrust of plot is the prestigious norm, there are signs in Conrad and Faulkner of a renewal of commitment to plot and story.

Thus, this study does not claim that the opposition to plot and story is marked by one decisive decade or by one absolutely unified literary generation. Since this is so, it is possible to argue that in every literary era narrative and antinarrative impulses coexist, so that the conflict over plot and story is atemporal and formal, not in fact timely and historical. Tzvetan Todorov argues this point of view.[4] But if the conflict is always formally characteristic of narrative, the recent historical content of the conflict matters more than its ahistorical aspect. And this content has to do with the intellectual and moral consequences, demonstrated within the novelists' stories, of the possibility or impossibility of plotting life and fiction. For example, as Chapter Five points out, Melville's argument that there is a paradoxical passivity in all action that plotting denies in an unhealthy and vicious manner still has an urgent and practical historical content, meaning, and moral for Americans.

But I have not written overt polemic in favor of the kind of narrative and morality from which, as I argue in Chapter Five, Melville turned away. Personal allegiances and sympathies as well as the challenges to criticism I have mentioned do not stand out glaringly in the text, even though I should like finally to convince the reader that Dickensian and Jamesian plot and story mean more for life and value than, for example, Melvillian narrative improvisation and experiment. But ultimately the reader should be moved to such a belief by the sympathetic attention given to the antagonists of plot as well as to its champions. To those who want obvious polemic I may appear like one of Walter Scott's waverers, ceaselessly shifting sides and switching back and forth among persons and principles of conduct representing different historical eras. Nevertheless, the loyalties of Scott's waverers are finally with one side rather than another. And in the final analysis their wavering sympathies are perhaps more affecting than if they had been outright partisans of just one form of life. In my presentation of the positive and negative sides of the fate of plot and story, I have attempted to make that fate emotionally as well as intellectually and ethically clear. Only through wavering sympathy, wider than an ultimate committed allegiance, can one especially effect this emotional clarification, which is as important as any other.

Having now suggested answers to some questions readers may pose about my presentation, I must glance at two further aspects of the book before providing the story of its story in an outline of the separate chapters. First, each chapter explores some general or theoretical facet of story and plot (such as their relation to meaning or their characterization by reversal or by teleological direction) and simultaneously provides a close reading of a particular case or set of cases in connection with this facet. At the same time, both the general facet and the close reading are placed in the context of the literary-historical narrative dynamic I have described. Second, all the chapters treat both major works and minor or lesser-known texts. This is for several reasons: to be historical rather than canonical; to divert the reader with fresh instances; to stimulate the reader to apply what is said about the major novelists or texts that are included to those that are omitted.

Here then is an overview of the particular chapters. Chapter One raises introductory questions about plot and story. At the same time it considers two cases, Stein's and Orwell's, in order to represent the modern novel's difficulty with narrative. It is all to the point if my readers do not think of Stein and Orwell as conventional novelists or even as novelists at all. By focusing on Stein's and Orwell's distrust of narrative consciousness, on their belief that novelistic story predetermines the writer to lie about life intellectually and emotionally, the dilemma of plot and story in modern writing can best be illustrated.

This skeptical point of view is also a necessary first step in considering what plot is and how it functions. Is it invariably fictive—a lying superstructure erected on top of experience? In the second chapter, plot and story are considered as generalizations about experience, as modes of making experience intelligible or of revealing its truth and meaning. This consideration is tested in relation to three nineteenth-century historical studies, whose authors have especially influenced literary culture. Two of these studies are skeptical that human experience can be rendered objectively and intelligibly through what Ortega y Gasset calls "narrative reason."

But in spite of the skepticism of modern writers and in spite of the skepticism derived from historical life's apparent resistance to storytelling, novelists such as Dickens trust that story not only makes life intelligible but also discriminates our moral values. It does this complexly and arrestingly by disclosing meanings and values through intellectual structures at whose center is the experience of reversal. Chapter Three explores the means by which plot and reversal can make moral as well as intellectual sense. This first of two chapters on Dickensian plot contrasts Dickens's storytelling with Poe's. Although Dickens did not always plot intelligently and Dickensian absurdities of narrative are represented by the weaknesses of *Barnaby Rudge, Nicholas Nickleby* offers a valuable and exemplary instance of plot's powers and uses. In contrast, Poe eschews reversal and moral discriminations, identifying meaning not with content but with the author's cleverly exhibited process of making the story.[5]

The relation of narrative reason and its moral discriminations to significant and willful human action is investigated in Chapter Four by a focus on what is called "the rescue plot" in Dickens and George Eliot. Chapter Five presents Melville as a contrast to these English contemporaries. Melville radically questions the nature of action, and he divorces significance and moral value from plot and from the will's execution of plot in action.

Chapter Six is a further examination of the relation between plot and life outside of fiction. In the second chapter, the general consideration is whether or not plot is an intellectual structure and whether or not such structure is consonant with experience. In Chapter Six, I treat the purposeful or teleological character of plot. By examining autobiographical addresses to the problem of purpose in life, I have presented concrete examples of how life can be plotted with or without teleological concerns.

The seventh chapter, on James, is placed after the studies in autobiography, partly to accentuate the differences between Jamesian narrative and the experiments with story and plot by his younger contemporaries. But the chapter is also a study of key terms I have used so far—*plot*, *story*, and *action*, among others—now in the light of *James*'s use of them. This analysis of James's relation to these terms will freshly illuminate the evolution of his work, which I argue is transformed in his later years by a new commitment to story and action that was absent in his early novels. Although James shares with Dickens the role of hero in this study, Chapter Seven concentrates on James, not on direct comparison of him with Dickens. What links the two novelists is that neither found it possible to avoid the significance and morality of acts and their representation. This chapter also emphasizes James's sense of the relevance of plot and story to "civilization."

The last chapter considers "family plot" and the treatment of the most ordinary human actions of "fathering" and "mothering" in the classics of the modern novel. The family subject in Conrad, Joyce, Lawrence, Woolf, and Faulkner represents thematically their struggle with narrative form, for how these writers perceive family relations controls their narrative practice. I have tried especially to show the relevance of these explorations of family˙ and story to the writers' estimates of life's miseries and satisfactions.

The book ends by reminding the reader of the modernists' divided allegiances for and against plot and story. The novelists' divisions preclude a pat historical conclusion. Since they have not resolved their deliberations on plot, I have not attempted fully to "cover" these deliberations.[6] I regret being able to give the reader only glimpses of the fate of plot and story instead of the full tale or the completed argument. But a sufficient moral conclusion emerges from this unconcluded history and argument. In the following pages it is pointed out that, so far at least, the novelist-storytellers have been committed to plot because they have found it the complement of what they most value. And what they value most is a life more active than contemplative: a commitment to engendering continuities and inescapable, definite meanings; a passionate purpose that rescues life from sterile theorizing as well as from frustration and blankness. The novelists who are uneasy or impatient with story do not value these things very much, or even at all. Their antagonism to story reflects this evaluation. The present investigation of these contrary values and their narrative coordinates is incomplete. But if we have grown increasingly less interested in the acts and values associated with plot and story, their fate is surely great enough to justify even a partial examination.

Plot, Story, and the Novel

ONE
The Sense of Plot

The only thing that is different from one time to another . . . depends upon how everybody is doing everything.
—Gertrude Stein, "Composition as Explanation"

He wanted to sink down, down into the muck where money does not rule. But this baby-business had upset everything.
—George Orwell, *Keep the Aspidistra Flying*

The phrase "the sense of plot" means any complex of attitudes or responses towards plot and story in whoever hears, reads, or tells a narrative of either fact or fiction. Two general attitudes to plot and story have been encouraged by our classic modern novelists. The first is outright hostility. "To pot with the plot," cries E. M. Forster, "break it up, boil it down. Let there be those 'formidable erosions of contour' of which Nietzsche speaks. All that is prearranged is false."[1] The second attitude is wary ambivalence. In all its unease it can be found especially in Conrad, Lawrence, and Beckett. Where is a third alternative attitude to be discovered: an unqualified conviction that plot and story are a cherished necessity of truth and art? The fate of plot and story in the modern novel can be characterized by the absence of this third response, or by unconsciousness or disavowal of it. In James and Faulkner, for example, there is an intense advocacy of plot and story, but it has been neglected and misconstrued. In those who create and interpret the finer examples of the modern novel (up to 1950, at least), what holds sway is a sense of plot either hostile or uneasy.*

* Beckett represents a transition to a postmodern sense that equates plot with purely fictive play. Divorcing plot and story from truth, it is an offshoot of wary ambivalence. We shall see its avatars here in Poe and Wilde.

Our study begins with the sense of plot in Gertrude Stein and George Orwell. Stein, a brilliant narrative theoretician who overturns storytelling, and Orwell, a grudging adherent of story, are both convenient introductions to and characteristic offshoots of the great modern novelists whom we shall consider later. Yet before proceeding at all, we must take time to talk about plot and story, about their definition and character. We must not use these humble words casually or carelessly, as if they named plain, self-evident phenomena. In fact their meanings are intricate and their referentiality rich. Moreover, the locus or ground of plot and story are perplexingly arguable. Is their place only in art, or are they situated in ordinary life? Some working definitions and answers must be proposed. They will be justified afterwards, by the fruit they bear in our examinations of particular plots and stories.

I must first say that *plot* and *story* are used interchangeably here, as they are used interchangeably by the nineteenth-century novelists and by Henry James especially. Ordinary usage of these terms also amounts to a synonymizing of them. When we ask what is the plot of a book or film we are asking about the story. When we ask, "What is the story?" as a slang way of inquiring into what is happening in a given situation, we are asking about more than mere happenings: in effect we are concerned with the *plot* of what is happening. If we consider the use of "story" in journalism, a journalist covers a story, not a plot; but he must plot the story to convey it to readers, and the persons or forces he reports upon are themselves plotting agents. Only accidents seem to be stories without plots; yet they shock and grieve us because they are not synonymous with plotted intentions. The sinister connotations of plot and story—pointing to secrecy and conspiracy or to lies ("A likely story!")—imply an inauthentic, subtly treacherous, or purely fictive reference. Here common usage reflects the debate to be pursued in these pages over the ground of the value and truth of plot and story.

Having identified and interidentified the terms by appealing to their common usage, let us consider what a handbook on narrative can further tell us. "Plot can be defined," the handbook says, "as the dynamic, sequential element in literature."[2] Putting aside consideration of "dynamic" for the moment, let us determine what "sequential" can mean. Is plot the sequential element in narrative? The suggestion is dissatisfying if it means that plot and story are mere successions of events, a meaningless matter of "now this, now this, now this"; but plot and story *are* comprehensible as the sequential element of narration if we open ourselves to the dimension of meaning in sequence and succession. Chronology and sequence are compatible with mind, for mind itself thinks chronologically and sequentially; and succession in thought and consciousness complements intelligible sequences in physical nature. Ernest Fenollosa, writing of nature as a great concourse of plots, reminds us that "perhaps we do not always sufficiently consider that thought is successive not through some accident or weakness of our subjective nature but because the operations of nature are successive."[3] These successions are not random and mindless because it is at least arguable that they are causal; similarly, one thought meaningfully follows another because one thought causes another. Plot and story are significantly sequential and successive insofar as they are the causal and intellectual element in narrative.

Even though plot and story are not simply the intellectual component of narration, the link between sequence and intelligibility in plot and story must not in any way be underestimated. Insofar as a story or a plot records any sequence it solicits memory; it requires an intelligence that remembers what has just been said and what has just happened, and that coordinates remembrance with expectation and foresight. Every plot and story is an intelligence of the world soliciting and stimulating further intelligence; each is thus a muse of memory and prophecy, directing the mind always to look backward and forward. Furthermore, to emphasize the intelligence stimulated by storytelling brings out the way story and plot are essentially relational in character. Thought is successive and causal because it is relational, because it makes relations among phenomena. Since story and plot make relations, a story is called by what it creates and transmits: a story *is* a relation. A story is thus a relating of an intelligence of relations in such a way that further relational thought is incited.[4] Memory and foresight are stimulated to make out, compare, and differentiate the relations that make up the story, and to do the same in regard to relations between the story and what lies outside it.

Because story and plot are the means whereby experience is understood *as* a relation, as a comprehensible or coherent sequence or chain of relations, they make the experience they tell "tell." Their mode of relation makes experience meaningful by opening it to intelligibility. The process whereby plot and story engender meaning and intelligibility can be grasped more fully by considering their connection with time. Often in experience causes and interrelations establish themselves and take effect over an extended period. Likewise in a plot meaning is not disclosed immediately; it takes time for relations to take place. The place relations take is not comprehensible as a sequence of nows, as a continuous immediacy. Thus, plot and story are essentially mediators of experience; like the full expanse of time in relation to the present moment, they are relatively abstract. The dependence of story and plot upon time points up their intellectual function because this dependence emphasizes the abstract and abstracting nature of their mode of relation. For by inspiring memory and foresight, story and plot remove us from whatever is immediately near. They incite relational thought, hence meaning, because they abstract awareness, disengage it from immediacy, and make it consider such prospective things as ends, directions, purposes.

The stimulation of thought about ends, directions, and purposes is the property of what may be called the perspectival elements or functions of plot and story. By means of the perspectival elements, relations are expounded abstractly or, as we say, thematically; by their means relations are unfolded or gathered as sequences, causes, similarities, and differences in a way that equates relations with a purposeful perspective. Now this purposeful perspective is not simply thematic or intellectual. The sense *in* plot is the sense plot makes, and it makes sense emotionally or morally as well as intellectually. Thus, in addition to relations of thought the perspectival function identifies relations of feeling and value. Indeed what is most remarkable about story and plot is the way their perspectives dissolve the differences whereby we usually discriminate thought from feeling, theme from treatment, cognition from evaluation.

Here it is necessary to make the strongest qualification of what has just been said about the perspectival elements of plot and story, lest it be thought that their resistance to temporal immediacy, their thematizing abstractness, or their focus on purpose makes them seem exclusively or primarily abstract. Plot and story must be defined as the perspectival elements and functions of narration that are indivisible from embodiment and representation in action. Any form of telling that does not embody or represent relation as action or that separates the perspectival function from action is the result of a hostile or uneasy sense of plot; it does not amount to plot and story as we define them. Because plot and story, properly speaking, dissolve their perspectives, their thematized relations, in actions, they are indeed the "dynamic" element in literature. They speak their thought, their sense, even their sensuousness as acts and events. It is as if all plot tells us there can be no thought, no intelligibility, without action. And because of this conjunction of action, plot, and thought, I propose that peripety or reversal is indispensable to story, since reversal grounds the intelligibility of experience in an act of transformation and in the significant differences created by transformation that I believe are fundamental to thought. All acts are transformations and differentiations. I follow Kenneth Burke in saying that "the basic unit of action is the human body in purposive motion." But the basic unit implies a realization of the purpose, a transforming of it in such a way that a new creation emerges; a significant novelty and difference are thereby added to experience. Action is to be understood here, in its fullest sense—beyond the basic unit—as an innovating, differentiating creativity or creative force or will whereby purposive motion is made actual or realized. Thus plot and story can be defined finally as the relations or perspectival functions in narrative that culminate—to borrow another phrase from Burke—in the featuring of act.[5]

Now the terms as they have been defined so far clearly result from an approving, positive sense of plot. And the final emphasis on the featuring of act is an attempt to present plot and story not as functions of disembodied thought and of exclusively fictional relations but as phenomena continuous with purpose and activity outside of fiction. The sense of plot is not the exclusive domain of writers: the varieties of the sense of plot—including the positive sense missing in the modern novel—are to be found in what Barbara Hardy calls "the narrative motions of human consciousness." Hardy argues that "in order really to live we make up stories about ourselves and others, about the personal as well as the social past and future." Story and plot in their perspectival functions pervade ordinary cognition: we *think through* them "by telling, untelling, believing and disbelieving stories about each other's pasts, futures, and identities." Moreover, story's featuring of act not only represents life as activity but incites action just as much as plot's relations incite relational thought. "We tell stories," Hardy argues, "in order to change," therefore to propel ourselves towards the creative actualizing of purposive motions.[6]

By positing a directness of relation between narrative motions of consciousness in the novel and in ordinary living we are able to see that changes in the sense of plot, over any stretch of time, make up a continuing argument about the problems and possibilities of human purpose and activity. Only thus is a history of these changes, such as the present one, simultaneously able to be an exploration of story and plot as potential forms of art and an exploration of story and plot as potential forms of life. But to posit these connections touches on a crucial argument in current theories of narrative. The argument can be illustrated if we compare our terms and their characterizations with the treatment of plot and story in the criticism of Georg Lukács and in the theories of the Russian Formalists.

Lukács insists that all literary forms and formalisms are grounded in truths about life. The slowness yet the certainty whereby a story discloses its relations is founded, Lukács argues, on the way we are all ordinarily "called to account" for the tendencies and consequences of our actions. Work too is a fact of life underlying artistic form: "complete personal devotion to a task" is "a dramatization of life in life itself." Thus the sense of plot in life is expressed as work; the more deeply one is "dramatized" by work, the deeper are one's connections with life. According to Lukács, the perspectival and purposeful functions of story and plot are also eminent facts of life. For writers as for everyone, life

> cannot be measured or understood until its stages have been experienced as a movement from and towards a certain goal. These stages and their dynamic interrelations are not purely subjective elements, to be accepted or rejected by the writer at his discretion. Life itself, the categories determining its nature and development, would be distorted if such factors were to be arbitrarily eliminated. . . . Everything in a writer's life . . . is part of, and determined by, the movement from and towards some goal. Any authentic reflection of reality in literature must point to this movement. . . . In all this, perspective plays a decisive role. . . . It is the perspective, the *terminus ad quem*, that determines the significance of each element in a work of art.

In life as in writing, this perspective mediates experience. And without this mediation personal consciousness either daydreams about itself or falsely abstracts and reifies a state

of mind or feeling. The formative choice of an end is a plotting, story-instigating motion of consciousness without
which experience can be neither authentic nor shaped. Thus
Lukács implies that story and plot are not only preeminent
facts of life but the most familiar facts.[7]

In contrast, the Formalists drive a wedge between familiar
life and art, and they use plot for the wedge. To facilitate this
tactic they distinguish *plot* from *story*: "both include the same
events, but in the plot the events *are arranged* and connected
according to [an] orderly sequence" not identical with story
defined as mere chronology. Because plot is arrangement, it
is for the Formalists "wholly an artistic creation"; moreover,
it is "a compositional rather than a thematic concept. Thus,"
the Formalists declared in 1926, "the very concept of plot [is]
changed; plot [is] no longer synonymous with *story*. Plot construction [becomes] the natural subject of Formalist study,
since plot constitutes the specific peculiarity of narrative *art*."
And for the Formalists art is not ever a familiar fact; its function is to estrange us from familiarity, to "defamiliarize" the
actual and the real. Indeed, it is inaccurate to speak of "the
real world"—What, the Formalists ask, *is* reality? What plot
defamiliarizes is prevailing artistic convention, a previously
prestigious and vital but currently decaying form of art. It
also does not respond to either decaying or emerging facts or
forms of narrative consciousness in life.[8]

Thus the Formalist theory of plot and story directly conflicts with Lukács's theory and with my own assumptions.
But I question and challenge the Formalist theory because it
hides not only story's featuring of act but the changing historical content of the sense of plot. The Formalists proclaim *Tris-
tram Shandy* "the most typical novel in world literature," a
novel all plot because it is all defamiliarizing arrangement of
what it "portrays." Following the logic of this, we might approach Gertrude Stein by saying that in spite of her openly
avowed opposition to story, she is all plot anyway because
her writing is all defamiliarizing arrangement. It is true that
Stein believed storytelling is too familiar an endeavor for ver-

bal art to spend its energies on. Yet Stein's opposition to story, unlike that of the Formalists, insistently appeals to reality: story gets in the way of communicating the truth of experience; plot depends upon a sense of history, of time, and temporal experience that Stein thinks no longer writeable because no longer liveable.[9] The Formalist assumption only covers up or contemptuously brushes aside how a writer like Stein believes that in her work the fate of narrative is bound up with the changing fate of human consciousness and action.

The assumptions of a modern artist like Stein thus meet Lukács's or my own insofar as they imply that historical changes in the sense of plot are not merely arbitrary or formal but constitute a living argument about what humanity does or can do. In the words of Tony Tanner, according to Stein's sense of plot, "conventional plot slights reality by its habit of erecting a spurious structure of eventfulness."[10] It is just this alleged slighting of reality that motivates Stein's practice; and the same objection to the same slight can be seen in Forster's shrill *non sequitur* about plot, "all that is prearranged is false." What is curious and especially noteworthy about the Formalist theory and derivatives of it such as Northrop Frye's idea of archetypal literary plots is that they exalt positive senses of plot oddly complementary to Stein's and Forster's modern rebellion. For the Formalist tradition—especially in Frye—avows that ordinary life is essentially formless; it thus slights reality for the truth of plot, whereas the rebellious novelists slight plot for the truth of reality. But both versions of reality are identical, since each argues the stubborn resistance of the actual to plot and story. Both Stein and Orwell believe in and value this stubborn resistance. Since they are the genuine practitioners of narrative, it is high time to turn to them. Far better than any other form of presentation, the drama of the specific practice of the sense of plot in narrative art can establish what plot and story are and what they mean.

Three Lives and *The Making of Americans*, Stein's first published novels, show her already impatient with the idea that

verbal artists must tell stories. Stein believed stories were descriptions or explanations, and although in *The Making of
Americans* she wanted to describe "everything," as soon as
she convinced herself she *could* describe everything, she felt
no impulse to go on. She proceeded instead to write *Tender
Buttons*, whose contents are neither stories nor descriptions.
Stein found stories both too possible to write and too familiar:
why need an artist tell "another story since there are so many
and everybody knows so many and tells so many. . . . What I
wanted to do . . . was what everybody did not always know
nor always tell."

The most significant germ of Stein's discontent with
storytelling in the novel can be found to have originated in
her childhood, in her response to the storytelling of drama.
She early recognized, "nervously," that "your emotion concerning [a] play is always either behind or ahead of the play.
. . . Your emotion as a member of the audience is never going
on at the same time as the action of the play." As Stein saw it,
the perspectival character of plot prevented her from considering what happened on the stage from moment to moment:
it kept her from truly seeing the play until it was "behind"
her. Of course, the bearing and truth of a story are not always
fully articulated until the possible twists and turns of the plot
are at last exhausted. What especially caused Stein discontent
is that, however ordinary storytelling is, the artistic *unfolding*
of plot is apparently *not* ordinary enough. For in ordinary living, in a nonartistic "exposition," Stein experienced in directly unified relation the emotion and action of herself and
other "actors": no matter how stories traditionally unfold
themselves, "there is, there has to be the moment of it all
being abreast." Beginning to write novels, Stein wanted to
express that moment, to get closer to her sense of the immediacy of actual life.[11]

According to Stein, this immediacy is threatened by all so-
called representations, for in itself life *is* and *represents* nothing. Life is presence, complete and self-contained. Representations project life as if it were far, at a distance. But the true,

new business of art, Stein asserts, is to disclose the presence of the "being existing" that is already openly manifesting itself. Thus the task of art is "to live in the actual present, and to completely express that complete actual present." Stories obstruct the complete actual present by busily making and abstracting relations. Stein would say that whoever insists on understanding experience in terms of plot insists willfully upon finding and making abstract relations out of whatever constitutes phenomenal immediacy in order to know—or to make up—the causes or temporal links of phenomena. Her loss of interest in description and explanation fit in here, since they too are intellectual and willful modes of relation. For why, Stein asks, must there always be a relating *of* something, a telling *about* something, rather than the relation or the thing in itself, free of the mediation of story, that instrument of the willful and active making of relations? When for more than thirty years Stein turned away from even the minimal novelistic story or plot of *Three Lives* and *The Making of Americans*, she turned to the idea of relation as storytelling or story-making to the idea of relation itself as an already given presence. To do this she wrote plays she described as landscapes:

> The landscape has its formation and as after all a play has to have formation and be in relation one thing to the other thing and as the story is not the thing as any one is always telling something then the landscape not moving but being always in relation, the trees to the hills the hills to the fields the trees to each other any piece of it to any sky and then any detail to any other detail, the story is only of importance if you like to tell or like to hear a story but the relation is there anyway. [12]

"The relation is there anyway," Stein insists. It is something given, external, independent of what creative or imaginative relational thinking *makes*.

The relation that is there anyway—that expresses the complete actual present—must be there and can be there without inciting memory and intellect to contribute their plotting motions of consciousness, their spurious narrative structurings of life. Another passage from Stein shows her antagonism to story as a relational muse of memory and foresight, of thought and emotion "behind or ahead" of what is always "going on"; and the passage also introduces Stein's attitude towards the featuring of act:

> No matter how complicated anything is, if it is not mixed up with remembering there is no confusion, but and that is the trouble with a great many so called intelligent people they mix up remembering with listening, and as a result they have theories about anything but as remembering is repetition and confusion, and being existing that is listening and talking is action and not repetition intelligent people although they talk as if they knew something are really confusing, because they are so to speak keeping two times going at once, the repetition time of remembering and the actual time of talking but, and as they are rarely talking and listening, that is the talking being listening and the listening being talking, although they are clearly saying something they are not clearly creating something, because they are because they always are remembering, they are not at the same time talking and listening. [13]

This passage implies that the maker of plots or the teller of stories is not creative or "novel" because he is always "remembering" or because by inspiring relational thought he in effect possesses and proposes "theories." By stimulating the "repetition" of what has happened in memory, he produces the confusion of knowledge (the fruit of memory and theory) with "being existing." And here very clearly Stein also has withdrawn from "action" the denotation of conventional doing. When action is defined as "being existing," as "talking and listening," the human body in purposive motion is no longer being thought of as a minimal unit of action. Stein appears to throw together memory, storytelling, and purposive action as uncreative and antivital abstractions, treacherous to the moment of its all being abreast.

How can a person's actions be only abstractions and not bedrock facts of his existence? It is enough for Stein if such a question cannot be answered decisively; and a little consideration suggests that no matter what our assumptions about the featuring of act in daily life or narrative, a decisive answer is at the very least difficult. Stein would argue that because memory defines a man by what he has been and because action defines him by the practical ends and purposes he pursues, by the perspectival functions of his life, both are wrongly reductive of his being. For Stein personal action cannot be reduced to precise definition. Or, if it is accessible to such definition, it is likely to be an action already completed and in the past, fallen into the province of memory and not present in the dynamic and indefinite immediacy of "being existing."

Her depiction of "being existing" is certainly new, but it undoes Stein's novels as novels—at least, that is, from the point of view of any positive sense of plot brought to bear on her books. Stein's motive for this undoing is not a matter of form but of truth. The truth of being as expressed by the lives of *Three Lives* is to be understood as the fact of limitation and of a radical stasis of human character in general and as equally the fact of specifically American character in particular. The lives of Melanctha, Anna, and Lena are not plotted, for the heroines themselves do not plot. Or if they do, what they plot or will remains evanescent, superficial. Their lives are all of a piece, without development in terms of change or transformation; whatever they enact makes no difference *to* them or *for* them. They live out nothing like a narrative motion of consciousness. Instead their lives are continually recurring patterns of what Stein might call intense inward insistence—being as a kind of "being insisting." This insistent inwardness gives the three lives a minimal character that, especially in Lena's case, can scarcely be distinguished from the consciousness of sleepwalkers or the existence of stones. Yet in their smallness and stillness the lives Stein portrays also make limitation and stasis loom beatifically: being existing is indestructible, impervious to the difficulties of outward circumstance, change, "event." Moreover the stasis of being existing is a moment of immediacy perpetually reshaping and reasserting itself; its perpetual reshaping is, oddly, a *process*—even though it does not change or develop beyond itself. *Three Lives* suggests that the truth of all human character is to be found in this particular way of viewing process.

If Stein had not undone her own motions of narrative consciousness she would not have been able to see or to argue her truth. And her truth is finally that in any consideration of vital process a featuring of act is a defeaturing of life. For Stein the meaning and value of life is to be found not in the difference action makes but in the sameness and stillness represented by stance, indeed by a literal standing still. The characters in *Three Lives* and *The Making of Americans* experience life by standing through experience, by standing and withstanding it. Stein adapts her sense of plot to communicate this truth, which is not only a general fact but, she insists, the product of concretely-lived American experience. Stein's renunciation of story and plot is undertaken to complement the collective being existing of Americans. In the following passage her unchecked movement from an American phenomenon to the fate of plot and story emphasizes how a narrative condition is a condition of life:

> I always remember during the war being so interested in one thing in seeing the American soldiers standing, standing and doing nothing standing for a long time not even talking but just standing and being watched by the whole French population and their feeling the feeling of the whole population that the American soldier standing there and doing nothing impressed them as the American soldier as no soldier could impress by doing anything. It is a much more impressive thing to see anyone

standing, that is not in action than acting or doing anything doing anything being a successive thing, standing not being a successive thing but being something existing. That is then the difference between narrative as it has been and narrative as it is now. And this has come to be a natural thing in a perfectly natural way that the narrative of to-day is not a narrative of succession at all as all the writing for a good many hundreds of years has been.[14]

It does of course seem self-contradictory of Stein to appeal simultaneously to standing and, implicitly, to historical change and transformation. But even her idea of change is controlled by her sense that historical transformation in concrete American experience is not identical with change as it is understood in traditional English or European usage. The movement of change in America, even of change in time, is always felt as spatial—indeed, as an unchanging space "filled with moving."[15] The movement of history in America, like the movement of American lives and narration, is thus secondary to the "natural" truth of the still space and stance that hold movement and history within them.

Today, more than fifty years after the ascendency of Gertrude Stein, we have forgotten how plot, story, and the novel—from the time of Walter Scott to the youth of our grandfathers—were considered to be more truthful than fictional. Such was the intensity and strangeness of revolutions and dislocations in the nineteenth century that cultural self-consciousness began to take the form of imaginative stories in novels, "made up" but nevertheless considered to be expressive of the significance of nineteenth-century experience more wholly and truthfully than any other narrations. In Gertrude Stein the sense of plot is still attached to this identification of fiction with veracity, for even Stein's rebellion against plot, story, and the novel persists in equating whatever she writes with truth. And even in a modern sense of plot alternative to Stein's—for example, in the wary sense of plot illustrated by storytelling in the novels of Orwell—there is still the idea that the vocation of fiction is or ought to be the expression of truth.

Thus, at least in the desire to be truthful, differing senses of plot may share, paradoxically, the same aims. And there is another paradox to be noted: in pursuit of truth an ambivalent sense of plot like Orwell's can, in its most negative veerings, seem more adverse to storytelling than Stein's. Indeed, refusing to entangle himself with fiction in any lying sense, Orwell appears not to want to write down anything; he seems to distrust words themselves, as if their merest use is inevitably a temptation towards narrative consciousness. For the most part, all Orwell believes can be truthfully writeable is the embodiment of a special state of mind or feeling that is static, humbly and strongly self-contained, impervious to the world—rather like the states of mind in which Stein's characters stand. And yet unlike Stein or her characters, Orwell is unwilling to entirely let go of the idea that action and the positive sense of plot can embody truth. Unlike Stein he persists in the conventional, referential use of words, risking thereby the temptations to narration stimulated by such usage. We get the feeling that Orwell regrets his desire to renounce the making-up of truthful relations in plotting and plotted terms, and that in penance for his desire he pushes his writing back towards the form of novelistic story. This reluctant push has a triumph in *Keep the Aspidistra Flying*, perhaps the one novel where Orwell finds it possible to be truthful about modern life and to endorse the narrative motion of consciousness. Even in this book, however, it is difficult for Orwell to make this endorsement, which he cannot manage in *The Clergyman's Daughter* and *Coming Up for Air*, novels written just before and after *Keep the Aspidistra Flying*.

We can understand what is at issue in Orwell's difficulty if we recall that the perspectival functions of plot and story highlight purposefulness, which pervades unqualified narrative motions of consciousness. Because of this pervasive purposefulness, we can claim that a novelist's characters insofar as they are purposeful are the delegated plotting agents of their author's own purposeful plotting agency; and presumably both the author and his delegates will want to set up meaningful purposes and to approve their achievement. But we find Orwell's characters cannot plot their lives, cannot purposefully shape them; and to our surprise we find Orwell for the most part presenting this inability as a happiness and a blessing for his characters. Because Orwell so strongly believes that the failure of purpose leads to happiness, he cannot easily sympathize with the kind of alternative represented by *Keep the Aspidistra Flying*.

The happiness that is the failure of plot and purpose is illuminated especially by *Coming Up for Air* and by Orwell's admiration for Henry Miller and Charles Dickens. The hero of *Coming Up for Air*, George Bowling, is a used-up, disillusioned man in his mid-forties who does not mind being used-up or disillusioned. His premature decay has faced him squarely and contentedly with sheer being—with exactly Stein's "being existing." In his encounter with being, Bowling experiences an intense pleasure of relief from desire, will, struggle. He feels carefree, relaxed, tender, lazy—sensations Bowling and Orwell equate with human decency. Nothing obviously or conventionally worldly matters to him. Bowling insists: "I tell you I don't care . . . I only want to be alive. . . . I was alive that moment when I stood looking at the primroses and the red embers under the hedge. It's a feeling inside you, a kind of peaceful feeling, and yet it's like a flame."

Now this peaceful flame-likeness is a state of mind and feeling suspending purposes and the motions of narrative consciousness; its humaneness is measured by its defeat of plot. The social and historical world is full of purposeful plotting motions, but Orwell presents them as identical with inauthenticity and manipulativeness. In a central scene of *Coming Up for Air* Orwell prejudicially identifies modern political ideologies with narrative consciousness. As Orwell sees them, the ideologues tell stories about history that are spurious superstructures erected upon life. The stories are masked forms of aggression and hatred meant to ignore or suppress the carefree, relaxedly pacific core of feeling Orwell suggests is present in Bowling and all of us and is prior to storytelling in the way paradisal innocence is prior to falling. When Bowling is asked to oppose fascism at an antifascist rally, he tries to remind his interlocuter of the wastefulness of the previous war. But "you're thinking of 1914," goes the reply:

> "That was just an ordinary imperialist war. This time it's different. Look here. When you hear about what's going on in Germany, and the concentration camps and the Nazis beating people up with rubber truncheons and making the Jews spit in each other's faces—doesn't it make your blood boil?"
>
> They're always going on about your blood boiling. Just the same phrase during the war, I remember.
>
> "I went off the boil in 1916," I told him. "And so'll you when you know what a trench smells like."
>
> And then all of a sudden I seemed to see him. It was as if I hadn't properly seen him till that moment. A very young eager face, might have belonged to a good-looking schoolboy, with blue eyes and tow-coloured hair, gazing into mine, and for a moment actually he'd got tears in his eyes! Felt as strongly as all that about the German Jews! But as a matter of fact I knew just what he felt. He's a hefty lad, probably plays rugger for the bank. Got brains, too. And here he is, a bank clerk in a godless suburb, sitting behind the frosted window, entering figures in a ledger, counting piles of notes, bumsucking to the manager. Feels his life rotting away. And all the while, over in Europe, the big stuff's happening. Shells bursting over the trenches and waves of infantry charging through the drifts of smoke. Probably some of his pals are fighting in Spain. Of course he's spoiling for a war. How can you blame him?[16]

Here the futile mechanism of society is being blamed for the young man's boredom. But Orwell is also arguing that the youth himself is at fault, even for feeling his life rotting away. He simply will not give himself over to the pleasure of sheer being, as Bowling himself tries to do. And the narrative motions of consciousness are connected with the futile, indecent mechanisms of society and history because they incite habits of thought and feeling, willful manipulations and relations, "the big stuff" of warring ideologies that all prevent being from being an end in itself.

It was by way of Henry Miller and Charles Dickens and by way of a special sense of their narrative procedure that Orwell came to value Bowling's peaceful flame. Orwell identifies Bowling with passive receptivity to experience, and the virtue of passivity is what he finds in Miller, a prophet of the future because

> the passive attitude will come back and it will be more consciously passive than before. Progress and reaction have both turned out to be swindles. Seemingly there is nothing left but quietism—robbing reality of its terrors by simply submitting. . . . Get inside the whale—or rather, admit you are inside. . . . Give yourself over to the world-process, stop fighting against it or pretending that you control it; simply accept it, endure it, record it. . . . A novel on more positive, "constructive" lines, and not emotionally spurious, is at present very difficult to imagine.[17]

Can the passive recording here be combined not only with moral constructiveness but with plot construction? Apparently not, judging from the link between Orwell on Miller and Orwell on Dickens. In Dickens especially Orwell found Bowling's peaceful flame and Miller's idealization of passivity and quietism. Orwell sees in Dickens "a dream of complete idleness," virtually the same state of mind and feeling one experiences inside the whale's belly. The dream of idleness naturally results, Orwell says, from Dickens's "rather negative attitude towards society. . . . [For a Dickens character] there is no objective except to marry the heroine, settle down, live solvently and be kind. And you can do that much better in private life"—by which Orwell apparently means a life hidden away from society and history. The private life imagined by Dickens, Orwell goes on, combines purposelessness with remarkable vitality. And thus it is, Orwell continues— leaping significantly from the subject of idleness to the subject of narration—that Dickens could not write interesting stories, for stories are structures of purpose and action. Dickens is not really interested in those structures, either in direct narrative terms or in terms of work, the plotting perspectival function of life that is "the dramatization of life in life itself." Dickens's lack of interest here "partly accounts for the needless ramifications of Dickens' novels," Orwell says, "the awful Victorian plot."

> The last thing anyone ever remembers about these books is their central story. On the other hand, I suppose no one has ever read them without carrying the memory of individual pages to the day of his death. Dickens sees human beings with the most intense vividness, but he sees them always in private life, as "characters," not as fictional members of society; that is to say, he sees them statically. Consequently his greatest success is *The Pickwick Papers*, which is not a story at all, merely a series of sketches; there is little attempt at development—the characters simply go on and on, behaving like idiots, in a kind of eternity. As soon as he tries to bring his characters into action, the melodrama begins. He cannot make the action revolve round their ordinary occupations; hence the crossword puzzle of coincidences, intrigues, murders, disguises, buried wills, long-lost brothers, etc. etc.[18]

Orwell makes Dickens's plot an excuse, a kind of padding for the novelist's imagining his characters in stasis, standing through their lives "in a kind of eternity," realizing thereby the dream of complete idleness. There may not be any very strong logic in Orwell's argument that a "character" in "private life" cannot be represented in terms of story; but the lapse in logic here is symptomatic of his overriding desire to promote the passivity inside the whale, the not caring about worldliness that Orwell thinks is the only authentic and valuable modern state of mind and feeling.

So far what I have pointed out about Orwell's values and his sense of plot scarcely characterize an alternative to the sense of plot in Stein. Nevertheless, *Keep the Aspidistra Flying*, a novel about the eventually happy *failure* to flee the world and its plots, *is* an alternative, however wary. In this novel, Gordon Comstock, Orwell's delegated plotter, at first decides to "make it his essential purpose not to succeed"; he makes a break for freedom by submerging himself in the "great sluttish underworld" of South London, where society, money, family, even decency, can be escaped. Yet the direction of this break for freedom suddenly reverses itself, becoming constructive and active as if Comstock's commitment to a passive suffering in the underworld were incompatible with life. What brings Comstock back up from inside the whale is his realization that lower-middle-class life, with its mores and money-code symbolized by the hardy aspidistra plant, is not essentially adverse to genuine standards of honor and humaneness. Comstock's final realization comes from his desire for a wife, a child, and a job. But it also originates from the reemergence within him of the narrative motion of consciousness; and there is an intimate relation between the narrative motion and the desire for family and work.

What links plot and story with desire for family and work is the way all three represent our need for novelty and development. In setting out the definitions and characterizations of plot and story, I have adverted to the way plot mediates, postpones, and hides meaning and to the way it makes life "tell" by making a creative difference to experience. This mediating, deferring, and hiding of meaning and this making of a significant difference are all essential to what is ordinarily called the "development" of plot and story. Although Orwell expresses contempt for Dickens's stories, at the same time he faults them for making "little attempt at development." Now Gordon Comstock apparently wants to refuse development altogether; but what brings him up from underground is his discovery that, after all, he desires constructive and adventurous development more than he desires to sink into stasis. The developmental nature of plot means a commitment and openness to change and transformation: we can see this in the way the aspidistra or "the money-life" take on entirely new meanings by the end of the novel. It is the plot that works to differentiate their new meanings from their old; and the greatest difference for meaning and development is made by Comstock when he once more begins to plot his life. He then decides to accept the child his sweetheart has forced him to father. By this "mere" child, by "just" this plot "device," Orwell underlines the way the sense of plot may be creatively developmental, may make a quite literal difference in life, producing something of value that would otherwise be aborted. The child also makes a difference for Comstock in that it inspires in him the desire to be decent and *to act so*, even in terms of taking on a job and "the money-life." Since we shall see later that the parental impulse is a touchstone of the sense of plot in the modern novel, it is not surprising that Orwell has explicitly related Comstock's development as a parent to the desires and motions of narrative consciousness by setting the scene in which he discovers his paternity in a lending library, at a moment when he is being asked by a run of customers to recommend the latest sensational stories and (as the Cockneys say) "*ro*mances." The low-life companions of Comstock's venture in sinking are themselves not interested in saying to pot with the plot; they want to read their lives as elaborate true stories, and Comstock in the end expresses the same desire by siring a family and by exchanging idleness for work.

   In Orwell, sinking underground or, figuratively, under water is an attempt to say to pot with the plots of life and writing, money and work, effort and history. This sinking is endorsed in *The Clergyman's Daughter*, defeated in *Keep the*

Aspidistra Flying, then endorsed again in *Coming Up for Air* and "Inside the Whale." We are left with Orwell's ambivalence, his wary seesawing from a negative to a positive sense of plot and back again. But we can conclude consideration of his case by reemphasizing the motive of his ambivalence. Orwell's sense of plot in the 1930s originates in his shifting estimate of the possibility of forming and transforming *life* as well as plot and story. We can also conclude by noting two ways the prevalent academic interpretation of plot can distort and obscure this sense of the relations between narrative and life. The charge will be made that of course Orwell minimalizes plot because he is a satirist: "the most striking quality of satire is the absence of plot." It is characteristic of "the satiric hero . . . to suffer much and accomplish nothing. His struggle takes no direction, leads to no increase of knowledge or understanding, and never transcends his suffering."[19] Applied to Orwell, we can see at once how misleading this is, for it implies that the satire is directed at the world for not providing knowledge, understanding, accomplishment. In fact the underground men and women in Orwell do not *want* direction or knowledge; they do *not* suffer *insofar as* "direction," the perspectival function and motion of plotting consciousness, is absent. The expectations associated with the generic "plot of satire" are blind to the value for life that Orwell identifies with the struggle *against* plot.

But there is another way of understanding plot, and this way Orwell himself plays into the hands of. The handbook on narrative we consulted earlier tells us that "quality of mind (as expressed in the language of characterization, motivation, description, and commentary), not plot, is the soul of narrative."[20] Now wherever Orwell writes against plotting consciousness, he is suggesting what this sentence states: a division between quality of mind or state of mind and feeling and the action conveying them. And this argues that quality of mind is separable from or superior to the relative coarseness and treacherousness of enactments. But where we believe in quality of mind as the informing soul of whatever is

told, as therefore different from and more valuable than em-
bodiments of mind in practice and product, we are of course
opening ourselves to describing and idealizing thought and
feeling as they are presented in, say, "Inside the Whale." It is
perfectly sound and unobjectionable to do this, but we need
to discriminate the fact that our sense of plot is deeply engaged in what we do. To say that quality of mind, not plot, is
the soul of narrative reflects our modern estimate of the problematic presence, status, and value of plot in narrative as in
life. It is our modern tradition to feel this as a problem, to feel
the sense of plot with decided ambivalence. In the next chapter we will situate ourselves more deeply in this ambivalence
by considering the problem of the relations of mind and narrative to what we call reality or truth.

❦ TWO ❧

Narrative Reason: The Sense of Plot and Historical Experience

Goethe's religion was eminently concrete and devout in its worship of realities. His piety was the piety of truth. He believed in visible fact; he thought reality in itself holier than any fiction could make it.
—G. H. Lewes, *Life of Goethe*

Gone—ah, gone—untouched, unreachable!
A broken bundle of mirrors . . . !
—Ezra Pound, "Near Perigord"

At the beginning of Chapter One the intellectual function of plot and story was pointed out. This is not, of course, their only function; and plot and story must not be identified exclusively with their intellectual component. But the intellectual component's importance in making meaningful sense of whatever plot and story represent must not be minimized. The intellectual perspectival function of plot points out by way of a narrative relation the significant but not immediately apparent relations that abound in experience. The intellectual content of plot and story abstracts us from immediacy by stimulating memory and foresight to make experiences coherent. This coherence is accomplished by a thematizing of our experiences—by a theorizing and generalizing about whatever happens to us. Gertrude Stein associates story's dependence upon memory with theorizing: "intelligent people . . . mix up remembering with listening, and as a result they have theories"; that is, they distance themselves from immediacy by probing, expounding, and proving the truth of theoretical dimensions and accountings of what they think, feel, and do.

Thus story-making or storytelling and theorizing are not mutually exclusive or even necessarily different processes. Plot may be considered a storyteller's way of thinking or theorizing about the experience he represents; it may even be his way of dramatizing and prosecuting theory until he feels convinced that he can substantiate the theory as a truth about life. The same will be true if we think of story as a form of generalization. Of course, only a storyteller with a trusting sense of plot would offer his story-theory or his story-generalization as a reasoning about life that is, in the last analysis, also a definitive truth. This kind of story-theorist would also believe that there is a story and a relation *to tell*, one to which his plotted relation truthfully corresponds, one which is more than merely *made up*. He would believe that although life's story may hide itself in a welter of appearances, it is essentially and objectively there, awaiting representation in the plot. The plot is the storyteller's narrative mode of theorizing and generalizing, in a way that simultaneously presents life's manifold, dispersed phenomena and analyzes and establishes as true life's intelligibility and coherence. This does not mean that this kind of story-theorist passively replicates experience. His story is the fruit of his own active, willed discovery of life's essential structure of meaning. On the other hand, a less trusting sense of plot, in equating story and theory would emphasize the *merely* theoretical, the merely hypothetical, generalizing, and provisional character of story. This alternative sense of plot would probably assume that every theory-story is, in the last analysis, no more than provisionally truthful. To the wary sense of plot experience resists all hypotheses and generalizations, and life evades all attempts to plot its ways.

We can call the intellectual, theoretical aspect of story by the name of "narrative reason." The phrase belongs to the philosopher-historian Ortega y Gasset, and I make use of the phrase for its convenience and because Ortega has made very clear what is at stake both in the connection of story with theoretical reasoning and in the beliefs we may have about

this connection. We cannot prove that the assumptions behind an approving and credulous sense of plot are any more
or less true than the assumptions behind the sense of plot of
E. M. Forster, Stein, Orwell or the Russian Formalists. The
relation of plot and story to fact and fiction remains problematic, a dilemma perhaps only decidable by faith. At the
same time the dilemma presents itself as urgently in need of
resolution. For if all we can tell in terms of plot and story is
merely hypothetical, then, according to Ortega, just because
plot and story are themselves insubstantially theoretical and
exclusively fictive or factitious, we are in a disturbingly pre-
carious condition. For if plot and story have no intimate consonance with truth, if narrative reason is antipathetic or antithetical to actual experience, then Ortega claims that we will
have no experience and no history. Indeed we will lose hold
of reality:

> Man . . . loses himself in the infinite arbitrariness of his
> inner cabalism when he cannot . . . discipline it in the
> impact with something that smacks of authentic, relent-
> less reality. Reality is man's only true pedagogue and
> ruler. Without its inexorable and sensitive presence cul-
> ture . . . does not exist, even—and this is . . . most terri-
> ble of all—reality in [man's] own personal life does not
> exist.

The conviction of inexorable human reality can issue, Ortega
writes, only from the narration of actual experience, of history. "The reasoning, the *reason* that throws light here consists in a narration. Alongside pure physico-mathematical
reason there is . . . a narrative reason. To comprehend anything human, be it personal or collective, one must tell its history."[1] Thus, according to what Ortega says and implies, if
our sense of plot is skeptical or negative, if we distrust narrative reason, we have no teacher or ruler, we will be lost in
infinite arbitrariness, and we will feel that nothing is real.

But surely it could be claimed that narrative reason—the
sense or meaning plot poses as theory and may even substan-

tiate as truth—is itself infinitely arbitrary. What guarantee of
genuine comprehension, not to speak of truth, does the telling of history carry with it? Is it not possible that there are
experiences, even our personal "realities" themselves, that
may be betrayed by the formal structures of plot, story, and
theory? Narrative reason in the nineteenth-century novel was
understood, paradoxically, as the truth of fiction and of fictional storytelling. What grounds did the last century have
for such a belief? Before treating the nineteenth-century
novel, I will explore three exemplary probings of the relations
between life and plot, between nonfictional historical experience and narrative reason. In so doing an attempt will be
made to discover what Carlyle's *The French Revolution*, Ruskin's *The Stones of Venice*, and Pater's *Studies in the History of
the Rennaissance* can tell us about how light is thrown on real
experience by a reasoning that is not physico-mathematical.

    Although Ortega's phrase "narrative reason" will be prom-
inent in this chapter, the emphasis on the theoretical aspect
of narrative reason does not follow Ortega's explicit use of the
phrase, but represents my own development of the phrase's
meaning. And in considering the three histories—which have
been chosen partly because of their influence on the culture
of *novelists*—I will be deliberating the general ability or inability of story and plot to convey the truth of nonfictional experience, while at the same time highlighting the ability or inability of the specifically intellectual, theorizing component of
story and plot to convey meaning and truth in the form of
narrative reasoning. Only Ruskin's *The Stones of Venice* fully
equates story with theory, and equates both with narrative
reasoning that reveals not just *a* truth, or a *possible* truth, but
the truth about historical experience and its structure of essential relations. That Ruskin trusted and used narrative reason in this way is a measure of his remarkably credulous
sense of plot. His credulity appears now, no doubt, to be
naive, antiquated, foreign. Here I make use of his sense of
plot, of course, not to prove that his credulity is right, or that
its operation raises and settles all questions and problems

about the relations of plot, story, narrative reason, and reality. My intention is to probe the explicit and implicit thoughts on story's relation to life in Carlyle, Ruskin, and Pater, not to establish truth where they could not.

A positive sense of plot will not find itself gratified by *The French Revolution*'s version of the relations between life and narrative reason. Carlyle's history is a radically innovative attack on the forms of plot and story; indeed, its presentation of history is worthy of Sterne, and the volume might well be studied in line with precursors and current examples of a hostile sense of plot from Sterne to Stein to Nabokov's *Pale Fire*. Of course the antagonism to plot in *The French Revolution* originates in the desire for truth—the truth of history. But this engenders a result we have seen before: the pursuit of veracity leads to the banishing of story. How can there be history without story? Surely Carlyle is convinced that history is *the* essential category or frame of reference by which man can be known? Perhaps an answer to the second question will explain the first.

In Carlyle the historical way of perceiving man, especially of knowing him in and through revolution, actually seems to free him from definition. Like revolution, history is the trace of man's potential, of what he may be rather than of what he has been. In this way history "reveals" man by emphasizing his potential and his desires, by highlighting what remains humanly mysterious. And thus Carlyle uses history to liberate man from story, from the narrative reasoning that confirms theoretical speculations about what man is or has been. There can be history without story, without narrative reason, if we believe, as Carlyle seems to believe, that the truth of man is his infinite, essentially unknowable arbitrariness of being. In a way, the revolutionary libertarianism of *The French Revolution* is hidden in the author's impulse to liberate man and history from the defining forms and meanings of theory and story.

The germ of the antagonism to narrative reason in *The French Revolution* is sown by Carlyle in *Sartor Resartus*. The fic-

tive Editor of *Sartor Resartus* cannot make sense of the philosophical theorizing about clothes produced by Teufelsdröckh, the Editor's ambiguous subject. We can imagine the
Editor thinking that the reasoning with which to illuminate
the clothes-philosophy would consist of a narration—a story
of the philosopher's life. But when the Editor turns to the
"relevant" autobiographical fragments and texts, he finds
them distributed among bafflingly mixed bags of memoranda
and trash. The relations among these bags' contents cannot
be plotted, cannot be reasoned narratively; the historical personal experience which would clarify Teufelsdröckh's philosophical theory also needs a narrative theory which would
clarify his historical life. Both the illuminating theory and the
illuminating narration evade research. Everything in the "autobiographical bags" is, for the Editor, "without connection,
without recognizable coherence, . . . selection, [or] order. . . .
In all bags the same imbroglio." "If the Clothes-Volume itself
was too like a Chaos," the Editor concludes, the personal history behind the philosophy is "instead of the solar Luminary
that should still it, the airy Limbo which by intermixture will
farther volatilize and discompose it!"[2] But it seems as if Carlyle does not *want* Teufelsdröckh's life to be plotted and
narratively reasoned. The imbroglio of all the bags is the
imbroglio of existence, which must not be *constrained* and
fictionalized by any formalizing organization. In the above
exclamation about the Clothes-Volume appears Carlyle's re-
current imagery of the French Revolution—that indetermi-
nable chaos that the airy mixture of theory (even if appearing
as story) would further discompose and falsify.

   Carlyle knows the possible correlation between theory and
story, narrative reason and plotted reality, and he seems to
prove his knowledge of this correlation by simultaneously
subverting story and all theorizing generalization and generalizing theory about the Revolution. His motive for attack-
ing story and theory together is simple and clear: narrative
reasoning about the Revolution appears to him to stand in the
way of "presencing" the Revolution, that is, of making it im-

mediate and present, of bodying it forth in a vital evocation. The "history" concludes with a paragraph that names the author's intention and the invocational and evocative antinarration it implies. Carlyle asserts that man by nature is definable as "an incarnated Word." At the same time he states how he thinks of his reader as the "not yet embodied spirit of a Brother" and of himself as a disembodied voice. Yet historian and reader can unite spirit with substance insofar as they can make the Revolution a live, immediate presence to each other. This puts the emphasis not on logos, word, or reason but on the incarnational intention. Now such bodying forth might very well be compatible with narrative reason; but Carlyle does not want the Revolution bodied forth either as theory or as story. He wants to incarnate the thing itself. And according to his distinguished reviewer, J. S. Mill, Carlyle accomplishes the incarnation; indeed Mill applauds Carlyle for his presentation, while slurring those who would like theory as well as presence: "How the thing [the Revolution] paints itself in all its greatness—the men in all their littleness! and this is not done by reasoning about them, but by showing them." However, even in spite of his applause, Mill felt troubled by the way Carlyle's presencing of the Revolution made knowledge about it hard to come by: "Except by general principles, how do we bring the light of the past experience to bear upon [a] new case? The essence of past experience lies embodied in those logical, abstract propositions . . . our author makes so light of."[3]

Although Mill's qualification of his enthusiasm seems to appeal to physico-mathematical rather than to narrative reason, Carlyle, as we have said, seems perfectly aware that in historical writing abstract propositions and plot go together, and—for the sake of the Revolutionary presence—must both be expunged. What must go first and foremost is story understood as the chain of causal successions that incites memory, foresight, and relational coherence and that implies development and transformation. For it is these things that stimulate story and theory, not immediate incarnations of experience and not the feeling of the live thing in itself. The only sequence or succession Carlyle allows is a strictly chronological series of *nows*. Thus, for example, we characteristically read of how, on the day of the tennis court oath, "Courtiers . . . look from their windows, and giggle. The morn is none of the comfortablest: raw, it is even drizzling a little. . . . Wild counsels alternate," and so on. And when Carlyle seems to attend to what is not immediate, to that looking behind and ahead we associate with story's incitement of relational thought and temporal mediacy, likely as not we are being deceived. For Carlyle wants to collapse our sense that beginning, middle, and end are stretched out and developed in time; he wants to collapse this aspect of story into yet another immediate presence.

In the chapter called "Mercury de Brézé," for example, Carlyle describes the pathos of the court usher's enslavement to protocol. He tells us that de Brézé, in a clash with Mirabeau, has no future; and he looks quickly back into the usher's life to reinforce the judgment that this moment with Mirabeau is the sum of de Brézé's significant life. Carlyle may be using tellingly relational sequence here; but it is arguable that with de Brézé, as throughout *The French Revolution*, he is subtly orchestrating sequence to make it part of the incarnated state of feeling he identifies with the Revolutionary presence. Carlyle's survey of de Brézé's life shows that it does not develop or change: the apparent extension of de Brézé's life in time is in fact the author's intension. It is something not successive and developmental, but very like that vital stasis of continual presence we find in Gertrude Stein's version of life.

For its own life as story, narrative reason depends upon far more than a sequence of nows. Without a virtual theorizing of causes, without an hypothesizing and substantiating of development and transformation in experience, plot is crippled. Carlyle seeks to cripple it because he does not want to betray the Revolution, which, as he sees it, is life understood as a perplexing, indecipherable, and timeless urgency. The Revolution is present, Carlyle asserts, "as a rage or as a terror

. . . in all men. Invisible, impalpable; and yet no black Azrael, with wings spread over half a continent, with sword sweeping from sea to sea, could be a truer Reality."[4] By its paradoxically invisible and impalpable immediacy alone, we can understand how such a presence could baffle narrative reason.

That Carlyle does not believe we can speak about the causes of the Revolution or of any of its sequences is especially resistant to the characteristic reasoning of story. "Actual events are no wise so simply related to each other as parent and offspring are," Carlyle wrote in "On History" in 1830; and in *The French Revolution* even a complexity of causal relations is eschewed. The reader does not learn, for example, why the Parlement of Paris refuses, at just that time in French history, to register the King's tax-edicts of 1787; nor why a noble as important as the Duke of Orléans takes so forceful a part in the Parlement's rebellion. Carlyle's interest lies not in asking how or why or when precisely this or that happened. For him, in an extraordinarily literal way, the facts speak for themselves. For Carlyle to suggest and argue causes would be to implicate himself and the Revolution in theory. This might distance the Revolution from us by allowing us to think about it or to manipulate it intellectually rather than to feel its presence.

Finally, for Carlyle the most treacherous aspect of narrative reasoning about the Revolution would be its assumption that the Revolution changes in time and is to be understood in terms of development. René Wellek points out several startling truths about Carlyle the historian. Carlyle "ignore(s) or neglect(s) the pastness of history"; he finds in Kant what he supposes to be sanction for wanting "to sweep away the illusion of Time, to rend it asunder, to 'pierce the Time-element and glance into the Eternal.' " For Carlyle, the Revolution is the Eternal showing itself in time. Indeed, Wellek points out that Carlyle the historian has "a metaphysical conviction of the fundamental unreality of time which makes for a static view of the world."[5] When we put this "static view" together with a remark on Carlyle by George Levine, we can fully understand how little Carlyle's convictions about life, time, and Revolution complement narrative reason. According to Levine, "Whatever really moves on the surface of [Carlyle's] prose is likely to be regarded contemptuously as ephemeral since all movement is in the physical world and therefore merely an appearance. Instead of movement toward developing meanings there is repetition."[6] What relevance can narrative reason have in the absence of causes and developments and in the face of an absolute, urgent but imponderable presence?

But those who have read *The French Revolution* will strongly object to how the book has been looked at so far—and will object especially to a paradoxical equation of Revolution with stasis. They will assert that Carlyle at least provisionally theorizes about and plots the revolutionary experience, that he gives it a story that makes it considerably more intelligible than the vivid but imponderable presence that has been so far described. Indeed, it will be claimed that the story of *The French Revolution* is obvious: Carlyle represents a cycle of alternating critical and creative moments and epochs; he shows how an age of paper or theory or sham, set aflame, gives birth to a creative life-phoenix in a constantly recurring Saint-Simonian dialectic or in a constantly recurring providence of death and rebirth that is God's plot for the universe. And it might be argued that although this story does *not* emphasize the intellectual theorizing or generalizing organization or relations of plot, since we have claimed that one of plot's perspectival functions is moral, is not *The French Revolution* a specimen of *moral* narrative reason? Now it is admissible that Carlyle is thinking about alternating cycles and that his thought is a moral speculation; yet it must still be claimed that his history is not communicated in terms either of narrative intellectual reason or of narrative moral reason. In his assertion of the alternating cycles of sham and reality, Carlyle is offering us a moral intuition. He has no intention of representing that intuition through any narrative motion of consciousness, for like the necessary black angel of the Revolutionary presence, the intuition and the moral it expresses cannot be plotted. Wellek again provides an appropriate comment here. He points out Carlyle's debt to sources in English literary historiography, which was more an occasion for ethical contemplations than for historical research. "Never able to keep consistently to the historical point of view . . . [Carlyle] always introduced a set of ethical standards which are not derived from history itself."[7] The phoenix-story is an intuition about noumenal reality, an unmediated transcendental moral insight not derived from history and resisting the very name of story. And, it may be added, Carlyle has the courage not to pretend that his intuition is a narrative reasoning.

At the same time, Carlyle wants to vindicate his opposition to the plotting of history; he wants both to idealize his revolutionary antinarrational intuition and to make the intuition take on a kind of fleshly clothing that is not identical with story. He does this by making Mirabeau the essential hero of *The French Revolution*. We must understand Carlyle's Mirabeau as an anti-muse of plot, story, and theory. For Carlyle this hero must incarnate a reason and a morality suitable to a reality whose imbroglios cannot be plotted. And not surprisingly, in this light Mirabeau is presented as a man who will have nothing to do with theories, those superstructures that like story and along with story may be treacherously erected upon life:

So blazes out, farseen, Mirabeau's Life, and becomes ashes and a *caput mortuum*, in this World-Pyre, which we name French Revolution. . . . A man who "had swallowed all formulas": who, in these strange times and circumstances, felt called to live Titanically, and also to die so. As he, for his part, had swallowed all formulas, what Formula is there, never so comprehensive, that will express truly the *plus* and the *minus* of him, give us the net-result of him? There is hitherto none such. Moralities not a few must shriek condemnatory over this Mirabeau;

the morality by which he could be judged has not yet got uttered in the speech of men. We will say this of him again: that he is a Reality and no Simulacrum.

For this assertion of Mirabeau's eminent Reality, there is of course no narrative reason, either intellectual or moral: Carlyle himself has swallowed all formulas and all ways of making formulations. That the hero, like the historian, is free of organizing theories means of course that he is in and of the presence of the Revolution. Carlyle's passage goes on to make much of Mirabeau's visionary capacity, a power of physical and prophetic sight that frees the hero from dependence upon theory and narrative reason:

> Whoever will, with sympathy, which is the first essential towards insight, look at this questionable Mirabeau, may find that there lay verily in him, as the basis of all, a Sincerity, a great free Earnestness; nay call it Honesty, for the man did before all things see, with that clear flashing vision, into what *was*, into what existed as fact; and did, with his wild heart, follow that and no other.[8]

How does Mirabeau *see* what is going on, rather than reason about it, rather even than do anything but see? As soon as he enters Carlyle's pages, Mirabeau is the luminous representative of all-intuiting vision: "Count Mirabeau has actually arrived. He descends from Berlin, on the scene of action; glares into it with flashing sun-glance; discerns that it will do nothing for him." With such confidence and vital vision Mirabeau "sees-by-seeing" throughout the history. Expelled from the Assembly of the Noblesse of Provence, he "stalks forth into the Third Estate." He apparently has no qualms, and he knows entirely and immediately what he is doing. Already he has become "a world-compeller and ruler over men," a commanding force of nature: "wild multitudes move under him, as under the moon do billows of the sea." By the time of the procession of the Third Estate, he is called the King of Frenchmen: here we are first told that he is "a man

not with logic-spectacles; but with an eye!" This "eye" enables Mirabeau to cut through and past words, discourse,
theory, formulations, and their like instantaneously: just by
seeing de Brézé, Mirabeau knows his shamming unreality.
Likewise he *sees* what facts in France are tending towards Reality and life and which are tending towards Sham and death,
without the need of analysis, without the need to tax his
memory and foresight by looking beyond what is present,
without the need to test his own hypotheses, generalizations,
or theories against the developing meaning of the speculation
and activity of others. Carlyle's practice as an historian is an
attempt to see just as he believes Mirabeau saw. He invites
his reader to look along with him at realities and shams, intuiting them immediately, not narratively reasoning about
them. We might here raise a consideration relevant to plot
and story, even though it takes us beyond our focus on narrative reason: Carlyle's heroicizing of Mirabeau's (and his own)
intuitive sight is a last blow at story because it strikes at the
significance of action. In *The French Revolution* the featuring of
act is replaced by a featuring of sight that reasons—if it reasons at all—without the forms of reason or action. Thus for
Carlyle, the Revolution, with Mirabeau as its figurehead, is
finally a way of intuiting the world, not a way of analyzing,
plotting, and acting in the world.

But we must not do *The French Revolution* any injustice. We
have been reading it partly in light of a positive sense of plot,
whose assumptions Carlyle brilliantly resists. The resistance
derives from his sincere belief that narrative reason is not
writeable because causes and moral insights are intuitional
rather than demonstrable. This is especially true of narrative
reason in regard to the Revolution. For finally we must emphasize that *The French Revolution* is not a conventional plot or
story, because Carlyle sees his subject as an astounding, indefinable vital force and chaos of energy. To say this does not
contradict what we have said about the absence of development in Carlylean "history." The chaotic energy does not develop, but repeats itself; its force is both a process and a static

constant. Yet because the energy is demonic and anarchic, it cannot be *articulated* as reasoned story or as clear-cut action; it can only be felt and "presenced," and its bearings only intuited. In fact, in the face of the chaotic energy, even Mirabeau's and Carlyle's ability to differentiate between Reality and Sham is subverted. Carlyle not only knows that intuition is faith but that there is after all a considerable burden of faith accompanying an ideal of direct and unmediated sight. In the last analysis Mirabeau fails fully to see; and so does Carlyle. And this failure of the sight and insight that distinguishes Sham from Reality means blind surrender to believing in, trusting, and sympathizing with a chaos that apparently works creatively even when it leads to mass murders and the tanning of human skins. Evidently one must trust that the revolutionary force is creative, even though it blurs the distinctions between truth and error, destruction and creation.

A clearer and more conceptually determined plot, story, or narrative reason would have diminished the influence in Carlyle's writing of the chaotic, irrational, indeed Dionysian, force of the Revolution.[9] To oppose Dionysus—understood as the very force and essence of history—would mean to assume that plot and narrative reason have a real status in history, or that they are the means by which historical matters are best comprehended or differentiated. Opposition would also assume that an historian needs plot in order to achieve a quasi-rational stance, a posture of distance that will keep him from such immersion in his subject that it will seem unintelligible. Finally an historian may need plot as a quasi-empirical form to avoid the abstract presentness that, it is arguable, results from Carlyle's presentational mode and from his moral intuitionism, his "divinatory method."[10] But *The French Revolution* resists all of these assumptions, for they originate in a trusting sense of plot and narrative reason. The novelty and power of *The French Revolution* derive from just this resistance, which it carries out in the name of experiential truth.

Perhaps the nineteenth-century novelists influenced by

Carlyle would have been shocked by this reading of him. It may be that the young Dickens saw in Carlylean narrative the breakdown of all distinctions and the antinarrative impulse a modern sense of plot is practiced to see; it may be that Dickens copied this breakdown in *Barnaby Rudge*. Yet in spite of *Barnaby Rudge*, which I will discuss later, Dickens has an essential commitment to story and narrative reason that may have moved him to risk some skepticism in the face of Carlyle's implied claim that truth and story are at odds. It is likely that Dickens would not have been as wary of logic-spectacles as is Carlyle—and as are even many Dickensians. For Mirabeau no doubt theorized about his own experience; and that theory became the story or plot of his life as he told it to himself and as he put it to the test of action. A man may see only when he has once worn, at least for a time, spectacles of the theorizing and storytelling kind; moreover, a man's acts more than his insights may constitute his significance and alone tell his life story. This is what Dickens the storyteller may have thought; but we can put Dickens aside and say ourselves that, had Carlyle set out to reason narratively about the revolution, to tell an articulated theory-story about it and to plot its events more emphatically as a developing action, he might have better revealed even the Dionysian thing in itself.

Nevertheless, no matter what Carlyle *might* have done, the modern sense of plot finds itself at home wherever the status and truth of what history reveals remains problematic. Carlyle's close associate, J. A. Froude, sounds especially modern when in "The Science of History" (a lecture of 1864) he approvingly reiterates Napoleon's question, "What is history but a fiction agreed upon?" For Froude—and for us too, no doubt—history supports whatever theories are brought to it, and supports them all indifferently. In contrast, *The Stones of Venice* attempts to prove the falseness of Froude's kind of viewpoint. Ruskin presents the rise and fall of Venetian life as a drama, a three-act structure with strictly delimited beginning, middle, and end. The sense of drama in Ruskin's book depends upon the author's alliance of plot and theory. And the causal theory about Venetian rise and decline, the plot line of the history, Ruskin argues, is the objective shape of the past embodied and still present in the stones of Venice's buildings. These buildings are themselves the definable and definite acts incarnating the theories, motives, values, and struggles of those who erected them. Carlyle's incarnation of the inarticulate is repeated in Ruskin; yet in Ruskin plot and story make the stones finally clearly speak the Word.

To a modern sense of plot, Ruskin's claim that his story is both theoretical and actual seems unjustifiably self-assured. Ruskin does not stop at suggesting that stories may tell *some* of the truth about their subjects. He presents *The Stones of Venice* as if it were not tentative or provisional; it is the story that is *there*, the set of relations that is *there*, and he has found a mode of narrative reason exactly communicating both. So Ruskin can say confidently, for example, that 1300 is "a kind of central year about which we may consider the energy of the Middle Ages to be gathered; a kind of focus of time which . . . is to my mind a most touching and impressive Divine appointment." And if this seems subjective and tentative, we may consider the following confident assertion: "I date the commencement of the Fall of Venice from the death of Carlo Zeno, 8th May 1418; the *visible* commencement from that of another of her noblest and wisest children, the Doge Tomaso Mocenigo, who expired five years later."[11] No modern sense of plot feels comfortable with these razor-edge turning points presented as real and absolutely certain events.[12] It is especially difficult for a modern sense of plot to see these turning points as the effect of the practice of superior virtue or extraordinary vice bearing in upon a culture. But these turning points, their causes and effects, are Ruskin's theory-story— one which makes both narrative intellectual reason and narrative moral reason an inexorable pedagogue.

Unlike Carlyle, Ruskin does not present the reader with mere intuitions about the past. Ruskin's commitment to narrative reason is the foundation of his certainty about history, and this commitment means a slow, painstaking exposition, development, and interconnection of causal relations in experience. For Ruskin narrative reason can reveal truth only if story and plot are like a glass through which we must see darkly, paradoxically as the only way we can see clearly and directly. *The French Revolution* wants both to idealize and embody revelation without any reserve, without any intervening glass—whether in the form of logic-spectacles, of causations in the phenomenal world, of sequential narrative suspense and narrative order. *The Stones of Venice* trusts the darkened optical glass of plot and story without suggesting an antagonism between narrative and revelation, even though Ruskin can sound at times remarkably like Carlyle. Ruskin always speaks of *reading* architecture, painting, and sculpture; the stones of Venice are for him a book. The only way finally to read this book is through a power of sight much like that which Carlyle assigns to Mirabeau. Ruskin narratively reasons (and moralizes) *The Stones of Venice* partly to communicate both the ideal and the possibility of such sight, which he thinks is the specific function of art to develop. He asks how the truth that art communicates is to be ascertained and accumulated. And he answers:

> Neither calculation nor hearsay,—be it the most subtle of calculations, or the wisest of sayings,—may be allowed to come between the universe, and the witness which art bears to its visible nature. The whole value of that witness depends on its being *eye*-witness; . . . All its victory depends on the veracity of the one preceding word, "Vidi."
>
> The whole function of the artist in the world is to be a seeing and feeling creature. . . . It is not his business either to think, to judge, to argue, or to know. . . . There is . . . no great workman in any art, but he sees more with the glance of a moment than he can learn by the labor of a thousand hours.

Yet Ruskin does not reveal this truth about the artist until the start of his third volume. He has to prepare for even this statement by a most reserved and un-Carlylean sequence of analysis. Ruskin makes clear that Mirabeauian sight can come to anyone who is not "a great workman in any art" only as it comes to him and his readers: through the extended mediations and relations of story.

Let us take a closer look at *how*, according to Ruskin, narrative reason, or theory-story, can disclose truth or can convince us of such things as the causes and effects of the transformation of Gothic life and art into Renaissance life and art. *Is* the "optic" of narrative reason compatible with authentic sight and insight? Or is there not, as Froude would have said, an impassable gap between history, the thing in itself, and any theory-story about it? Ruskin did not openly broach these questions. I would argue nevertheless that they engaged him and that he left an implicit answer to them towards the end of *The Stones of Venice* in the course of describing a Byzantine mosaic picture of olive trees in the dome of St. Mark's.

My primary reason for offering a mosaic picture as an analogue of Ruskin's understanding of how narrative reason works lies in Ruskin's notion that the Byzantine artist best portrays the thing in itself (in this case the olive tree) by having ideas about it. Indeed the artist portrays or relates the tree through an already abstracted comprehension of it, and he also portrays both his comprehension and the tree simultaneously. In this way, by its intermixture with ideas, the artist's sight is a "darkened" glass. Narrative reason works in exactly this darkened way: it starts out with an idea in order to portray an empirical reality, and it works to present and to justify the complementary relation of the idea and the reality. This idea or abstracted comprehension is "theory," in the sense that equates theory with a more or less verified or verifiable explanation accounting for phenomena. Like a narrative artist, Ruskin's mosaicist is explaining what he pictures *as* he pictures it. Indeed he must also explain it to himself *before* picturing it. This means that the picture is the result of relational thought; and theory is, of course, a kind of relational thought or account. The mosaicist's theory of the tree is his explanatory relation or account of the tree's characteristics and forms; it is also his explanation of the olive tree's relation to other trees. Hence what the artist portrays is an abstract network of ideas, relations, and ideas about relations. Pervaded by relational explanations and accountings, the artist's picture, like narrative reason, communicates the thing in itself by having ideas about the thing.

The Byzantine mosaicist is thus a storyteller as much as a visual artist. His picturing, as Ruskin describes it, is his form of narrative reasoning. And when Ruskin himself sets out to describe an olive tree in order that we can judge the mosaic representation by the thing itself, even his description of the tree is a bundle of relations: in "telling" "the notable and characteristic" features and effects of the olive, he has already seen it along with other trees, and he is implicitly making out its relations with them:

> It has sharp and slender leaves of a greyish green, nearly grey on the under surface, and resembling, but somewhat smaller than, those of our common willow. Its fruit, when ripe, is black and lustrous; but of course so small, that, unless in great quantity, it is not conspicuous upon the tree. Its trunk and branches are peculiarly fantastic in their twisting, showing their fibres at every turn; and the trunk is often hollow, and even rent into many divisions like separate stems, but the extremities are exquisitely graceful, especially in the setting on of the leaves; and the notable and characteristic effect of the tree in the distance is of a rounded and soft mass or ball of downy foliage.

Now the mosaicist of St. Mark's has to represent this tree while he is working under a number of contextual constraints: the locale of the representation, the mosaic's decorative function, and so on. But in spite of the constraints, the artist's intention above all is to tell the truth of the tree. And in Ruskin's description of how the mosaic is accomplished, we can see how the picture of the tree is also a reasoned and reasoning narration of it:

> There is to be an olive-tree beside each apostle, and their stems are to be the chief lines which divide the dome. [The mosaicist] therefore at once gives up the irregular twisting of the boughs hither and thither, but he will not give up their fibres. Other trees have irregular and fantastic branches, but the knitted cordage of fibres is the olive's own. Again, were he to draw the leaves of their natural size, they would be so small that their forms would be invisible in the darkness; and were he to draw them so large as that their shape might be seen, they would look like laurel instead of olive. So he arranges them in small clusters of five each, nearly of the shape which the Byzantine give to the petals of the lily, but elongated so as to give the idea of leafage upon a spray; and these clusters,—his object always, be it remembered, being *decoration* not less than *representation*,—he arranges symmetrically on each side of his branches, laying the whole on a dark ground most truly suggestive of the heavy rounded mass of the tree, which, in its turn, is relieved against the gold of the cupola. Lastly, comes the question respecting the fruit. The whole power and honour of the olive is in its fruit; and, unless that be represented, nothing is represented. But if the berries were colored black or green, they would be totally invisible; if of any other color, utterly unnatural, and violence would be done to the whole conception. There is but one conceivable means of showing them, namely, to represent them as golden. For the idea of golden fruit of various kinds was already familiar to the mind, as in the apples of the Hesperides, without any violence to the distinctive conception of the fruit itself. So the mosaicist introduced small round golden berries into the dark ground between each leaf, and his work was done.[13]

The picture is a narrative reasoning because it avoids a presentational immediacy; instead it represents the tree by explaining and mediating the olive's relation to laurels, lilies, and other fruit- or berry-bearing trees. It thus depends upon memory and comparison, and it "writes" them both into the manner of the representation. Especially in regard to the representation of the fruit, one has to read the picture conceptually or theoretically. The gold color is accounted for by the tale the color tells: it says that the olive fruit is the power and honor of the tree and is therefore essentially gold, even if it is not gold to the eye. Here the insight of the account is more essential than physical sight; and it is the insight available only to the optic of narrative reason, whose focusing idea or conception of the tree makes the tree present "in itself."

Both the mosaic and Ruskin's description of it are likenesses of story's way of plotting or representing life. Like the mosaic in relation to its subject, story abstractly theorizes about life in order to represent its most tellingly notable and characteristic features, its essentials. The narrative of *The Stones of Venice* works like the Byzantine mosaicist's design: it makes the Gothic and Renaissance "things" all the more present to us because the story, instead of just showing or intuiting the stones, tells us about them. And it tells us about them in a way that leaves no room for arbitrariness in understanding what the stones mean. According to Ruskin's practice, as a kind of theoretical expression—as narrative reason—story and plot intensify and define our seeing of reality. Ruskin's sense of plot assumes that story is what we see and that it sharpens our sight as well as stimulates our ideas the more we see it.

But it is not a matter of sight only. In relation to Ruskinian sight and the optic of narrative reason we must not forget the relation of story to the featuring of act. Carlyle uses Mirabeau's "eye" to cast suspicion on the importance and the articulating capacity of acts. Does Ruskin use narrative reason to make us see theoretically in order to identify the discoveries of theoretical contemplation or speculation with action? Although Ruskin makes the process of narrative reason a purposeful motion of consciousness, hence suggesting it as an action in itself, we must remember that he makes consciousness dependent upon acts that purposefully realize and externalize consciousness in the world. The stones of Venice incarnate not just what Venetians thought or felt but how they enacted thought and feeling. Even the olive tree mosaicist must act, not just by doing his representational work, but by choosing a mode of representation that is honest. The honor of the tree and the honor of the artist's truthfulness are both at stake in the actual picturing of the tree whereby the artist in fact *acts out* honesty. One of Ruskin's implicit contentions about the vice of Renaissance life, of course, is that it divorces contemplation from the actual world and from defining enactments of value. For example, Ruskin claims that a Renaissance artist picturing an olive tree would not have bothered to look at one; he would have painted his own idea of a tree, asserting a vague contemplation or imagination as truth and thus opening all truths, all things and deeds, to an indecipherable arbitrariness of speculation. The only thing revealed by such speculation is the inflated subjectivity and ego of the speculator. The shrinking from testing out thoughts by deeds of course protects the vanity of the thinker: his thoughts cannot be proved, but neither can they be disproved. For Ruskin, the narrative reasoning of experience defines us by revealing not only our sights and thoughts but by putting their cogency and value, their potential freedom from arbitrariness of definition or meaning to the proof of action.

But let us return to the purely theoretical aspect of narrative reason for a final comparison of the relation of life to the sense of plot in Ruskin and Carlyle. Carlyle wants to have much less to do with narrative reason than Ruskin because he thinks it may obscure the amoral vitality of the Revolution, his symbol of life. But Ruskin, like Carlyle, is also interested in amoral vitality. He is groping towards a new morality, dissolving the notions of "virtue" and "vice" and substituting the notions of "life" and "death." *The Stones of Venice* is obviously the embryo of *Unto This Last*: already "life" for Ruskin has become the one indicator of value, and whatever in human experience or art "tends toward" life is seen as ethical. Venice's fall is really not the work of "pride"; at least, in order to talk about pride, Ruskin goes on to demonstrate that pride is "sinful" because it betrays vitality. Renaissance art turns its back on "the imperfection essential to life"; and it embodies "an unwholesome breadth or heaviness, which results from the mind having no longer any care for refinement or precision, nor taking any delight in delicate forms, but making all things blunted, cumbrous, and dead, losing at the same time the sense of the elasticity and spring of natural curves." For Ruskin, it seems, story is the narrative-reasoning form of refinement and precision, of natural elasticity and "spring." It is thus suited to represent the life force that Carlyle thinks is incompatible with clear intellectual design or clear demarcation of things in their sequences, causes, and acts.

I have shown *how*, according to Ruskin, narrative reason discloses truth. I have not shown, nor can I show, that narrative reason *does* disclose truth. Ruskin himself does not demonstrate conclusively that the Byzantine artist could not have made his mosaic out of purely abstract elements, controlled by a purely abstract idea having nothing to do with actual trees. Perhaps the Byzantine had no sense at all of the olive's real nature; perhaps Ruskin had no sense at all of the way things happen in history. There is perhaps no definitive matching of narrative reason with what it reasons about and no basis for a sense of plot not suspicious of its own arbitrariness. And Ruskin began to suspect his own story. In 1864 in a letter to Froude, he endorses "The Science of History," and restates its thesis in his own terms: "There is no law of history any more than of a kaleidoscope. With certain bits of glass—shaken so, and so—you will get pretty figures, but what figures, heaven only knows. . . . The history of the world will be forever new. The wards of a Chubb's lock are infinite in their chances. Is the Key of Destiny made on a less complex principle?"[14] The story of *The Stones of Venice* is presented as a kind of law: if men feel and act "thus," then historical results

will follow "thus." Yet in 1864 Ruskin confesses that his particular story, and story itself, is arbitrary reason.

The way Ruskin writes about "life" in *The Stones of Venice*
perhaps undermines the definitiveness of representation his
historical plot intends to honor and embody. He attacks the
Renaissance for "squaring, counting and classifying" virtues
and putting them into "separate heaps of firsts and seconds."
But does he not show the same tendency in his own practice
of narrative reason? He does not doubt his sense of "life" as a
value distinctly opposing modern tendencies toward spiritual
death. But if virtues cannot be "squared and counted" because life cannot, then how can life be narratively reasoned?
Squaring, counting, and classifying are differentiating activities. As we have stated in the first chapter, story in all its
aspects defines experiences by relating them through difference as well as similarity. Since differentiation is also a form
of making relations, we may say that plot and story are the
precise recording or tracking of an innovative difference, of a
development that is a creative transformation of what had
existed prior to the difference. The acts that narrative relations represent are themselves creative by virtue of making a
new difference in experience. But what is the fate of narrative
reason if, to a potential storyteller, it appears that life's differences are "fictive," are only fabrications of the mind? It seems
very difficult for a narrative writer, even one with a hostile
sense of plot, to give up differentiations; Carlyle's intuition of
what is sham and what is authentic keeps *asserting* their differences, even if the Dionysian life-chaos seems finally to defeat Mirabeauian insight and to make everything unintelligi-
bly indistinct.

Now in Walter Pater's *Studies in the History of the Renaissance*
we find narrative reason especially challenged by the author's
sense that the differentiations upon which we base our sense
of "telling" significance is illusory and factitious. Consequently Pater's book breaks down apparently unquestionable
distinctions. The most obvious subversion concerns love, insofar as love is understood as an energy opposed to death.

Pater realizes that Botticelli sees Venus in one of her essential aspects as cold and deathlike. The stories of Abelard and Heloise and of Amis and Amile in the first essay of Pater's book are examples of eros mingled with death. But the merging in love of these apparent opposites is not a new idea. Pater makes use of it merely to prepare and to buttress a collapse of distinctions more original with him, more central to his work: a subversion of the usual distinctions between historical epochs. He wants us to understand that experience is not defined by sequence, succession, and significant innovation; and he blurs the boundaries delimiting historical phases, so that he can also blur the successions and differentiations of story.

Pater's book tacitly rebukes Ruskin for thinking of the historical thing in terms of relations and delimitations. Even in the opening lines of "Two Early French Stories," the blurring is already at work: "The history of the Renaissance ends in France, and carries us away from Italy to the beautiful cities of the countries of the Loire. But it was in France also, in a very important sense, that the Renaissance had begun." If there was *a* Renaissance, Pater is asking, if it is *a story* to be told, where is its beginning, middle, end? What distinguishes its different and special character from anything before and after? Indeed, it turns out that the essential character of the Renaissance is a resistance to all such definite distinctions: in fact the privileged epoch of "Renaissance" is anywhere we find such resistance. Pater is discovering that the Renaissance, like Carlyle's Revolution, is omnipresent presence (if we have the eyes to see it); and it is a way of seeing that confounds the distinctions we associate with narrative reason. In describing a series of Leonardesque drawings of John the Baptist, Pater is fascinated by the indistinctness of the subject and of the parts of the series. He realizes that in these pictures "the ostensible subject is used, not as a matter for definite pictorial realisation, but as the starting-point of a train of sentiment subtle and vague as a piece of music." None of these pictures has a discrete frame or a definitive outline. It is the same with Pater's "history." "Two Early French Stories" studies the Renaissance insofar as it has already taken place in the Middle Ages. The Middle Ages turn out to be a time in which the pagan world partly comes back to life; and, as Pater goes on to show, the Renaissance reoccurs through the Enlightenment figure of Winckelmann because Winckelmann revives paganism. History—and plot and story—are emblematized by these unions and echoing repetitions, "subtle and vague as a piece of music."

In the Paterian assertion of the essential indistinctness of being and in the consequent identification of history, story, and narrative reason with vague music, there is an important moral impulse. At the end of "Winckelmann" Pater wonders how art can represent men and women in the "bewildering toils" of "the magic web" of biological necessity and at the same time "give the spirit at least an equivalent for the sense of freedom." The subtle vagueness, the blurring of distinctions, promises Pater this equivalent of freedom. For all distinctions or differences are felt by him as limits, exclusions; "the Renaissance" means the continuous enlarging of human potential, hence it means the human freedom attainable by the breakdown of limits. If "the Renaissance" has no discrete boundaries in time, then its essence is both a collapsing of differences and at the same time a coupling of them, a kind of wedding of disparate and disjunct ideas and persons, experiences and things. For Pater, the only "history" or story worth bothering about occurs only where this coupling is present. And here is also the way of release from the toils of the magic web.

History or story releases us from the toils of the web if it can break down exclusive or definitive statements or truths. In that case is it history or story? The "Renaissance" occurs wherever there are "no fixed parties, no exclusions" and apparently whenever there are no fixed enarrable outlines in theory or in life—when narrative reason is shown to be itself a limitation. And just as consciousness is to be renascent when the limiting operations of narrative reason are broken down, the definite and defining actions on which narrative reason founds its theorizing are also broken down. Consciousness is to be reborn by a special kind of shrinking from concrete action, from any humanly defining commitment to events and their outcomes. In a passage more central than his "Conclusion," Pater describes this shrinking from commitments and acts in Botticelli's Madonnas:

> Perhaps you have sometimes wondered why those peevish-looking Madonnas, conformed to no acknowledged or obvious type of beauty, attract you more and more, and often come back to you when the Sistine Madonna and the Virgins of Fra Angelico are forgotten. At first, contrasting them with those, you may have thought that there was something in them mean or abject even, for the abstract lines of the face have little nobleness, and the color is wan. For with Botticelli [the Madonna] too, though she holds in her hands the "Desire of all nations," is one of those who are neither for Jehovah nor for His enemies; and her choice is on her face.

Her choice is not to adopt limiting or defining alliance with Jehovah or his enemies; and her choice is not only on her face but in it; it is somehow the face or the body itself.

Pater's reading of Botticelli's Madonnas suggests that the human body is wholly self-adequate: for its justification it need not incarnate the slightest seed of spirit. Nor is it the body in purposive motion, the basic unit of action, that matters here; rather it is the body shrinking from the alleged limitations of purpose and act. In this self-sufficient shrinking from a "higher," purposeful call, the human body is Pater's essential historical ground; and he sees it, like his version of history, as subtle and vague, mysteriously indistinct. This body thinks, to be sure; and it is both subjective and objective. But the business of art, of narrative reason, of story, and of history is now to refuse the promise of an articulation of anything beyond this body or to emphasize any defining and

limiting intention in the body's "bewildering toils." As a result of Pater's refusal to make the narrative motion of consciousness more important than that fleshly ground, the
body (which for Pater blurs love and death and even sexual
difference), freedom appears within "the web" of biological
necessity. For we are liberated by this focus on the body from
what Pater suggests is an arbitrarily imposed, coercive,
purely *cultural* necessity of making even the body tell itself as
story.

For Pater the theorizing, logos-bearing nature of narrative
reason especially bruises and deflowers flesh. To focus on the
body's glamorous web thus amounts to freedom from
theories or stories that bind the body's and the mind's moments into purposefully linked successions of thoughts and
acts. This focus bears startling fruit in the life of the hero of
Pater's one novel, *Marius the Epicurean*, which can be viewed
as a kind of extended illustration of the earlier *Studies*. At the
end of his life Marius, whose body is all eye—a new version
of Mirabeauian or Ruskinian perfection of sight and insight
("revelation, vision, the *seeing* of a perfect humanity, in a perfect world . . . he had always set that above the *having*, or
even the *doing*, of anything")—cannot see how his life's moments cohere or tell as plot and story. Those moments await
"some ampler vision, . . . as the scattered fragments of a
poetry, till then but half understood, might be taken up into
the text of a lost epic, recovered at last."[15] But there is no recovery of the epic story that can plot the moments; Marius's
mind at the end of experience, in spite of its many impressions, is still curiously a tabula rasa, a mind whose narrative reasoning seems not yet begun.

This narrative blankness worries Pater more and more in
his maturity, and we must of course remember the possibility
suggested by *Plato and Platonism* and by *Greek Studies* of a
Paterian rapprochement with history.[16] But in *Studies in the
History of the Renaissance* the desire for the ultimate epic—for
the fulfillment of narrative consciousness—is not apparent.
There Pater finds satisfaction in "the scattered fragments" of

the body's and the mind's vague and subtle moments. Indeed, after 1873 Pater elided the word *history* from his book's title, thereby accurately showing how to his mind "Renaissance" means resistance to story—acceptance that the links among the fragments do not matter. In "The School of Giorgione" he proposes the idea of drama too as a composition of discrete moments rather than a plotted interrelation of history or experience:

> It is part of the ideality of the highest sort of dramatic poetry, that it presents us with a kind of profoundly significant and animated instants, a mere gesture, a look, a smile, perhaps—some brief and wholly concrete moment—into which, however, all the interests and effects of a long history have condensed themselves, and which seem to absorb past and future in an intense consciousness of the present.

"Exquisite pauses in time," Pater calls these instants. But where is the "long history?" How is it available or relevant? Pater turns his back on it. He identifies the pictures of Giorgione's school with the scattered fragments of poetry. And "although its productions are painted poems, they belong to a sort of poetry which tells itself without an articulated story." For Pater life essentially tells itself without an articulated story, and "the Renaissance" is the moment—any moment—of our consciousness of the inadequacy, irrelevance, and limitation of telling life by means of narrative reason.

What do we learn, finally, from Carlyle's, Ruskin's, and Pater's examples of the relation of narrative reason to real experience and historical truth? On the basis of *The Stones of Venice* we can believe that narrative reason by its blend of theory and story is a finer reason than any other because it discloses the truth of life both concretely and abstractly. But when we weigh Ruskin's doubting of his own theory-story together with the fortune of narrative reason in Carlyle and Pater, our positive sense of plot is shaken. At most we can think of theory-as-story or story-as-theory as "just" theory, as mere unverifiable hypothesis. In the last analysis, according to our three authors the stories we tell, the theories whereby we plot and reason narratively, are arbitrary and are not our "rulers." Carlyle tells us we can and ought to see reality intuitively, without the unreliable discourse of narrative reason, because nondiscursive, nondifferentiating Dionysian force rules us. Ruskin admits life is not clear in the way "the darkened glass" promises to make it. And according to Pater, the foundation of history, the body that resists plot, is or ought to be our true pedagogue; and a life's momentary sights and insights may suffice for satisfaction even if they are not coherently interrelated. The conviction these writers may well leave us with, then, is that plot, story, and narrative reason are fictions, elaborate evasions, artificial discourses pretending to theorize definitively about the vital spiritual and material forces that may very well rule our lives because stories, plots, and narrative reasonings do not.

❧ THREE ❧

Plot and the Point of Reversal:
Dickens and Poe

> The descent
>   made up of despairs
>   and without accomplishment
> realizes a new awakening:
>   which is a reversal
> —William Carlos Williams, *Paterson*

I have been gathering examples of story congenial to a negative or at least a wary sense of plot, barely illustrating an alternative sense or any grounds for an alternative. It is time to change direction. I have held back positive consideration of plot and story in the hope that their strengths will now become more apparent. Not that we are to be free of doubts about the truth, meaning, or usefulness of plot; but by turning to the function of *peripety* or *reversal* in story, we approach ground on which a confident sense of plot can trust the truth of narrative reason in both its intellectual and moral functions. We also approach ground on which narrative reason is shown to depend upon an alliance of significance or meaning with the featuring of action. But one might wonder how a focus on peripety can be an approach to a trusting sense of plot if reversal represents what Aristotle implies by peripety: the terrible, untrustworthy instability or mutability of experience. My answer is that, at least as Dickens—and his great predecessor Scott— use reversal, peripety's representation of the instability of life incites the clearest and most persuasive reasonings and moralizings of experience. At the same time, the earnest use of reversal in Scott and Dickens testifies to action as the origin of development, of novelty, and of creativity. Scott and Dickens make us feel that when in story—or in life—we experience reversal, even if this means the over-throw of the purposes of our heroes or of ourselves, we face in surprise and wonder the radical fact of a new difference in experience, a creative development. If reversal in Scott and Dickens annihilates one purposeful motion, another purpose appears in its place.

Thus, through these novelists we see the primacy of action at work in the world as both transformation and transforming force, not, we might add, in the way Carlyle views his ver-sion of peripety, the Revolution, as a chaotic static presence, but rather as a definable change. Peripety seems to define the transforming action it represents; where it is used to at-tenuate or confuse definition or difference or where it is used as mere narrative decor—as an artificial trick or "twist"—we shall find ourselves in the presence of story and plot doubting and undermining themselves. With reversal, as with any of story's elements, a negative sense of plot can work its own distrustful way. The distrust, of course, can issue in brilliant results, as is the case with Poe, whose power and originality depend upon the joining of story with a witty flaunting of peripety. This flaunting lends itself to a modern sense of plot far more than to a sense of plot like that of Dickens, and in this respect Poe is a playful ally of the hostile and wary senses of plot. Dickens and Poe are in fact great antagonistic con-trasts as storytellers, and a focus on their use of plot-reversals best defines their implicit antagonism. Whereas Poe's bril-liance results from his subversion of the dependence of plot on reversal, Dickens's brilliance results in large part from his cherishing of the experience of reversal and of its structural analogue in story, the point of peripety. The modern sense of plot, especially as it shows itself in the critical interpretation of literary storytelling, is strongly shaped by its response to peripety and is deeply implicated in the contrasting uses of reversal represented by Dickens and Poe.

In considering Dickens's use of reversal in the novel we are taking up issues of literary influence and critical evaluation.

We cannot dissociate Dickensian story and its use of reversal from Scott; moreover, Scott's influence on Dickens and Victorian plotting reminds us of Orwell's description of the Victorian plot as "awful." All the "melodrama" and "machinery" Orwell associates with "the awful Victorian plot" derives from Scott, and Orwell's use of both words results from the effect of the continuously surprising and ensnaring peripeties upon which both Scott and Dickens base their stories. Does this indeed make their stories "awful," a complex mechanical muddle? I believe that Dickens plots badly only when he is attempting to prove his talent by resisting Scott's form. Indeed Carlyle's *The French Revolution* and Dickens's *Barnaby Rudge* ought to be understood as two examples of the sense of plot dominated by a jealous hostility to Scott. This means that they are texts dominated by a resistance to yoking together story and plot with the experience and the structural form of reversal. For Scott chooses for his subject, for the keystone of his stories, the fact of a great reversal in human consciousness and human affairs—the English Revolution and Civil War—and the effect it works for more than a hundred years on the daily lives of men and women. This historical reversal is for Scott "the thing in itself." According to Scott, what we are results from the fact and the understanding of the human transformations that have preceded us. The sense of actuality or reality that rules "the infinite arbitrariness of our inner cabalism" originates in reversal, which for Scott bears profoundly on the intelligibility of experience and on any considerations of morality. And of course for Scott's sense of plot, it takes the passing of time to both accomplish and understand reversal; indeed in Scott as in social revolution, time itself is reversal's essential medium. Hence, for example, in *The Heart of Midlothian* the turnings of time and experience represented by the plot finally give us the definitive moral measure, the sadly but inevitably diminished stature of Jeanie Deans's heroic effort to save her sister from death. Here reversal is the ultimate instructor of narrative moral reason. And along with its moral disclosures,

reversal also reveals the purely intellectual coherence of the
way Effie Deans's son, a follower of Rob Roy, finally kills his
father and, fleeing to America, settles with Indians. For this
fate of the son is no random and inexplicable melodramatic
accident; it articulates in its own small way the continuing
fortunes of the tribal life that the English Revolution began
utterly to abolish. It is the English Revolution and *its* historical reversal that makes intelligible the only *apparently* way-
ward and insignificant life of the lost boy. These turnings
make experience "tell" for Scott. And of course for Scott,
men's actions, above all, bring them to telling points of reversal, just as the reversals of experience bring men to the point
of their most telling acts. But when we look to *The French Revolution* and *Barnaby Rudge* we find both narratives stamped
with resistance to Scott's assumptions about the instructive
nature of peripeties.

   Barnaby Rudge does indeed have an awful plot; Dickens's
sense of plot, having built so brilliantly on Scott's in *Oliver
Twist*, *Nicholas Nickleby*, and *The Old Curiosity Shop*, is undone
temporarily when it competes with Scott in a representation
of the era portrayed in *Guy Mannering*. It is undone because
Dickens abuses reversal in *Barnaby Rudge*, especially when he
attempts to divide his plot from his theme: he has written reversals resolving his plot's conflicts and events into his story,
and at the same time has emphasized aspects of the story that
leave crucial elements of his plot unexplored and inert. He is
forcing a division between what happens and reasoning
about what happens, requiring his story and his action to be
merely an excuse, a convenience on which to string imaginations and contemplations that undergo no significant transformation or development. To modern criticism this divorce
of theme and plot (which I see as a forcing of self-
contradiction upon the perspectival functions of story and
plot) is congenial. We find one of the most intelligent modern
interpreters of *Barnaby Rudge* stating that the novel's true
theme is the unresolvable conflicts of fathers and sons, representing "contradictions which, continuing without resolu-

tion, make existence intolerable. . . . Nowhere in *Barnaby Rudge* do we find anything that genuinely suggests reconciliation."[1] This is a way of saying that the conflicts of Dickens's plot do not tell us anything but that they are conflicts. In fact his plot tells us much more; but it is as if Dickens, as much as his critic, wants to ignore what the plot tells: he wants to thematize deadlock, even though his story tells of resolution. And the way Dickens can separate the theme from the plot's events, making the plot look like muddled machinery, is by misusing, or by not using at all, the experience and form of reversal.

Before we embroil ourselves in the complicity of modern criticism with its separation of theme and plot and its simultaneous evasion of reversal, let us look more closely at the absurdities occasioned by Dickens's abuse of reversal in *Barnaby Rudge*. This abuse I believe is the result of Dickens's attempt to fight off the influence of Scott's storytelling practice. One of Scott's principal uses of reversal lies in his placement of the wavering figure at the center of his novels (most of which are named generically for the figure who embodies "wavering"). The theme of all Scott's novels has been identified as the search for a way to balance the attractions and claims of differing historical forces when those differences appear in revolutionary conflict.[2] For Scott's heroes, the way of achieving this balance is through their unstable mediocrity, their constant wavering. By his own instability the hero can find out which changing historical forces he should lend himself to and which to abandon in order in the end to achieve independent and balanced maturity (and relative modernity). The plot of this kind of hero's story must also be a continuous wavering, a constant reversing of expectation, allegiance, awareness. Together the wavering hero—and the complex wavering plot—finally enable history and the personal story to make intellectual and moral sense. Of course, the wavering of both hero and plot is a form of constant reversal: the plot fits the theme, its reversals eventually showing how it is that balance can be achieved by the hero's openness in fronting the turns and counterturns of experience and judgment. And the reader too must be kept wavering, so that when the plot reveals and articulates the character's final form and his final historical position, the revelation will seem the just result of all the story's elements and of Scott's disinterestedness.

Now Dickens, by transforming the wavering hero of Scott into Barnaby Rudge, gets rid of wavering altogether. Most of the plot takes its bearing from the fact of Barnaby's idiocy, which Dickens describes with relentless pathos. Barnaby does not have enough sense to waver. Insofar as he stands at the book's center, one cannot gauge with disinterested judgment the value or importance of what happens to or around him. Yet if Barnaby did have wavering sense, the reader could only be as bewildered as he is. For in this novel Dickens has not only banished reversal as constant wavering but he has gotten rid of the idea that history is significant as a turning point in human affairs. What significant reversal in human consciousness and action is represented by the Gordon Riots and 1780? Dickens does not know and cannot say. He uses the idiot Barnaby as a symbol of the urgent incoherent popular needs of England in the 1770s, but he cannot define those needs. In *Barnaby Rudge* history is the projection of private mania or personal hatred and spite; it is thus a tale signifying nothing, or a word masking a kind of noumenal inarticulateness or madness.[3] If we ask if 1780 is for Dickens a turning point in Protestant and Catholic relations in England, we get no answer. Dickens can scarcely be dramatizing Protestantism through the shrewishness of Mrs. Varden, just as he can scarcely be dramatizing Catholicism through Lord Gordon's imbecility. The Catholic-Protestant donnée of the plot has no content after all: the Catholic Geoffrey Haredale works for the emancipation of his coreligionists only offstage; in the story itself his conflict with John Chester results not from religious differences but from the fact that Chester once stole Haredale's only love. Dickens writes the historical religious content into the plot, and almost immediately writes it out. Just as he will not use Scott's wavering hero to make his story tell, so he is not using any demonstrable historical turning point, any significant human reversal and transformation, to make his plot make sense.

In fact in the plot of *Barnaby Rudge* Dickens has imbedded reversals that *do* make sense of what happens, but since he wants to thematize an idea of unresolvable conflicts, he ignores the telling turning points of his story. Mrs. Varden does surrender her religious mania to the cause of domestic peace; the Chester-Haredale hatred reverses itself through the love of their children. Dickens seems merely to mention these turns, however. And the most significant reversal of all, made use of only to be brushed aside by the author, is Gabriel Varden's reversal of the sentence of execution handed down against Barnaby. The theme of "unreconcilable" contradictions and conflicts is built on the antagonism between Hugh "the centaur," the uncivilized man, and his unacknowledged father, John Chester, the civilized man. But by Gabriel's reversal of Barnaby's sentence, the plot tells us what Dickens does not want to consider—that the contradictions are resolvable. By reversing Barnaby's fate, Gabriel Varden, the middling man of the middle class, obviously stands for the possibility of enacting a reconciliation of the natural man (Barnaby and Hugh) to civilization, without suffering contamination by the unnatural diseases of civilization (typified by John Chester, Geoffrey Haredale, and Mrs. Varden). But Dickens in effect throws away his own tale, refusing to articulate what the plot's reversal accounts for. Thus the story of *Barnaby Rudge* seems to be a forced relation of fragments, events, and motives that make no sense. We never know, for example, the motive or meaning behind the murder committed by Barnaby's father. Does this murder also illustrate the "irreconcilable" conflicts? But Varden shows that the conflicts *are* reconcilable. Is the primal murder, which in fact causes Barnaby's idiocy, to highlight for us the inevitable bad effects of bad deeds? But Varden subverts such a logic of effects. The more we ask questions about the plot the more we feel the plot as an encumbrance. And this results from Dickens's rejection of the compositional logic of wavering. In the end one remembers *Barnaby Rudge*, as Orwell would have said, "statically": Hugh and Barnaby and Dennis the hangman have no development, they go on and on in a kind of eternity because Dickens cannot "bring his characters into action" without involving them in a story that, by virtue of his own neglect, looks a mechanical mess.

Yet the absence of narrative reason and of significant reversal in *Barnaby Rudge* is highly unusual for Dickens; I have been forced to explain the novel's uncharacteristic absurdity of plot by positing a competition with Scott that has bad effects on Dickens's form. Elsewhere Dickens plots brilliantly, does not separate story from theme, and makes reversal the heart of his narration. But while the Dickensian sense of plot is *not* represented by *Barnaby Rudge*, modern criticism has been willing not only to overlook this fact but to applaud and to justify Dickens for just the kind of bungling that is rare in his storytelling. The traditional charges against Dickens's plots have always emphasized their absurdity, their artificial and implausible contrivances, their divagation from the way things happen in ordinary reality. Modern criticism takes these negative charges and writes them all positive: Dickens is great, it is said, because his sense of plot is absurd and because his kind of story has nothing to do with real happenings. It is especially important to our analysis that this kind of justification of Dickens during the last twenty years belongs to the guardians of the interpretation of literary plot and that theirs is a kind of interpretation that significantly undervalues—and in truth overlooks—the importance of peripety.

The criticism I speak of believes that all plot in literature is myth, that all narrative reasonings "displace," by means of a distorted repetition, a handful of archetypal mythic stories. This is the criticism of Northrop Frye and his school. We can see at once that just by its notion of "displacement" such criticism can easily lead to the separation of theme and plot: the author's plotted events may be treated as distortions of an archetypal story whose theme in turn may be read back into the fiction at issue with a kind of casual dismissal of the particular plot of the fiction as well as of any particular thematics in conflict with the alleged archetype. And there are other misleading results of the sense of plot belonging to this prestigious critical method: for example, it upholds our now apparently inveterate tendency to distinguish "eventfulness" or "external" incidents and something opposed to them, something "deeper" or more artful, a symbolic or purely speculative action rather than a literal one. Prestigious as this method is, since I believe it stands in the way of a genuine appreciation of Dickensian plot and action and since we are about to consider the successful waverings of *Nicholas Nickleby* as a marked contrast to those of *Barnaby Rudge*, let us consider what Northrop Frye tells us about plot and peripety in general and about Dickens and *Nicholas Nickleby* in particular.

In "Dickens and the Comedy of Humours" we find Dickensian plot justified because of its absurdity:

> We notice in Dickens how strong the impulse is to reject a logicality inherent in the story in favor of impressing on the reader an impatient sense of absolutism: of saying, in short, *la fatalité, c'est moi*. This disregard of plausibility is worth noticing, because everyone realizes that Dickens is a great genius of the absurd in his characterization, and it is possible that his plots are also absurd in the same sense, not from incompetence or bad taste, but from a genuinely creative instinct. If so they are likely to be more relevant to the entire conception of the novel than is generally thought.

Frye goes on "to explore a little the sources of absurdity in Dickens, to see if that will lead us to a clearer idea of his total structure." He shows how a Dickens plot differentiates two embryonic societies, one characterized by spontaneity and beneficence and the other by an insistent exercise of pedantic and parasitic humors. At the end of a Dickens novel this second society has consolidated itself and is blocking its rival. Then "a twist in the plot reverses the situation." The genial, generous, and lovable humors smash the blocking forces. "Once again in literature," Frye notes, "the hidden world is the world of an invincible Eros, the power strong enough to force a happy ending on the story in defiance of all probability." Dickens's Eros is "a designing and manipulating power." And, Frye contends, if Dickens's Eros-originated plotting seems absurd to us, we must remember that

> in literature it is design, the forming and shaping power, that is absurd. Real life does not start or stop; it never ties up loose ends; it never manifests meaning or purpose except by blind accident; it is never comic or tragic, ironic or romantic, or anything else that has a shape. . . . The silliest character in *Nicholas Nickleby* is the hero's mother, a romancer who keeps dreaming of impossible happy endings for her children. But the story itself follows her specifications and not those of the sensible people. The obstructing humors in Dickens are absurd because they have overdesigned their lives. But the kind of design that they parody is produced by another kind of energy, and one which insists, absurdly and yet irresistibly, that what is must never take final precedence over what ought to be.[4]

Of the two remarkable assumptions these excerpts evidence, the first is Frye's assertion that "real" life is blind shapeless accident. Frye's sense of plot differs from, say, Stein's or Orwell's, because it ostensibly delights in narrative form, and it certainly believes story is true to what we may imagine or desire; but it is also clearly a modern sense of plot in that it divorces empirical reality from story's form or shape. No story *as story* is true for Frye. The second assumption in the excerpts does not show itself as clearly as the first. It is glimpsed in the claim that a Dickensian dilemma is reversed by "a twist in the plot." What does it mean to speak of reversal as "a twist"? It sounds like "the twist" is a convenience, a mechanical contrivance for the assertion of the absurd forming and shaping power that is invincibly there anyway, twist or no twist. For Frye "the twist" is implausible and does not grapple with or express any realities other than our imagination's desire.

When Dickens uses reversal as a convenient twist he plots badly, as in *Barnaby Rudge*. But in fact, unlike Frye, Dickens usually does not demean reversal to the status of a convenience because he believes in the power of reversal to focus the particular narrative reason and moral of a particular, undisplaced plot, and because he wants his readers to feel that the action pointed up by reversal is a hazardous, crucial, and "real" development for his readers as well as for his story's characters. It is not merely imagination or desire that are at issue. In his use of reversal Dickens is much closer to Aristotle than to Frye, who uses the terminology of the *Poetics* but then shortchanges peripety. When Aristotle speaks of reversal and recognition as the soul of plot and as the mark of the superior dramatist he is favoring the power of the turning point to engage the audience. They are engaged, thrilled with pity and fear, because the reversal ensnares them, making the audience believe that what is happening on stage is happening literally or "really," not just in imagination. Dickens wants his turning points to have the same effect; indeed he goes farther than Aristotle, for while Aristotle seems to consider drama finally as a deflecting substitute for action, Dickens seems to want to use novelistic story to incite readers to imitate and reproduce the acts he represents.

Whatever their differences, however, both Aristotle and Dickens appear to value peripety's potential for erasing the boundary between literature, imagination, and real life. Frye does not favor this. As *Anatomy of Criticism* puts it, literature's "relation to reality . . . is neither direct nor negative, but potential." If the emotional effect of peripety is to substitute a "direct" relation for a "potential" one and to thus break down the boundary between literature, imagination, and "real life," then criticism must reconstruct the boundary. For Frye calls "the sense of the sharply focussed reproduction of life in fiction" the province of what he terms "critical natu-

ralism," a criticism of " 'effects.' " "We need to move from a
criticism of 'effects' to what we may call a criticism of causes,
specifically the formal cause which holds the work together."
Dickensian reversal is "effect," "twist"; but the formal cause,
the unifying agent of the story and the true province of interpretation, is, apparently, the underlying plot-myth of the
work. Dickens writes "not realistic novels, but fairy tales [or
myths] in the low mimetic displacement." To make much of
reversal is to make too much of Dickensian "effect."

Yet without reversal and its effect, Dickens seems to claim,
we know or recognize nothing significant about our experience, nor do we even know that we are actors. Again like
Aristotle, Dickens understands that reversal and significant
recognition go hand in hand—though for Dickens "recognition" means far more than the literal recognizing of persons.
Moreover, when Aristotle gives examples of peripety he uses
the verb *mellein*, "to be on the point of doing something."
Thus the reversal, as Dickens sees it and as I understand it,
emphasizes "doing" as much as "point." Finally, what the
reversal tells us as knowledge and as a featuring of act is generally for Dickens (and perhaps also for Aristotle) a thrilling
and novel revelation, a recognition not available to us otherwise or before. Frye, on the other hand, transforms Aristotle's
"point" of recognition into epiphany, "the symbolic presentation of the point at which the undisplaced apocalyptic
world and the cyclical world of nature come into alignment."
The epiphanic point reveals the mythic world—for example
the paradise of absurdly designing Eros—but our recognition
of this world is a discovery without surprise, without the
shock of experiencing a novel turn. Because the mythic world
is undisplaced and has its origin in imagination and desire
and because it is a nonpragmatic human universal, the reader
knows it before he sees it; and the revelation comes as a
featuring of seeing, not of doing. According to Frye, no point
of reversal inciting both novelty of awareness and action can
be important for a nonnaturalistic criticism which believes
that

the profoundest experiences possible to obtain in the arts are available in the art already produced. . . . The culture of the past is not only the memory of mankind, but our own buried life, and study of it leads to a recognition scene, a discovery in which we see, not our past lives, but the total cultural form of our present life.[5]

For Frye, revelation and recognition do not go hand in hand with any feeling of reversal. In contrast, I believe that a point of reversal suggests a radical overturning of expectations, a new awareness in time of a new fact in time, or of a fact so extraordinarily presented as to strike one as surprisingly and perennially new. From the point of view of archetypal criticism this idea apparently belongs to direct experience, to precritical naïvete, not to criticism and to literature more properly considered. It is apparently naive to treat the "twist" of a novel like *Nicholas Nickleby* as interesting in its own right, as offering surprising, perhaps as yet unrecognized human intelligence or news or as instancing the creativity of desire or imagination transformed into external, purposive, and pragmatic act.

Nevertheless, Dickens is guilty of this naïvete. He gives us the sense that a novel is new, that a novel's plot is new, because he believes human experience in some way is always new. This means he feels sharply the instability and inconsistency of experience, that he feels (*pace Barnaby Rudge*) life is always wavering, always at the point of peripety. Generally Dickens starts out plotting a story by reversing in some way the assurance we feel about what it is to be human or natural. He himself seems to feel "reversed": in each story he approaches daily life as if he were a stranger, having to find out where he is and what the people of the place are like. This approach issues in a new or freshly felt sense of humanity or nature. In response to such novelty the reader is likely to resist any reversal of his expectations. When *Nicholas Nickleby* begins with Squeers and Dotheboys Hall, the reader squirms: There are not people or institutions like this, are there? But to be insistently confident about human nature or reality may lead to just the lack of grasp on it that uneasy readers accuse Dickens of having. By leaving open the possibility of a deep, essential turn of awareness, one begins to see what Dickens is talking about and how authentic his perceptions are. But although he cultivates the surprising inconstancy and novelty of experience, Dickens uses reversal, both as phenomenon and as form of story, to make a clear narrative reasoning about life. In Dickens's major work the uncertainty of experience does not throw us into a permanent state of unknowing. Epiphany, recognition, cognition seem possible to him in the greater part of his practice only through and because of the use of the point of reversal. Moreover, for Dickens reversal significantly engages the reader's attention when Dickens does not attempt to separate plot and theme, when he does not assume that a particular story with its particular turns is ruled by an underlying extricable fairy tale or myth arbitrarily forcing the turns upon the story.

In one last preparatory step towards *Nicholas Nickleby*, let us consider what a genuinely Dickensian sense of plot makes of Dickens's storytelling, of mythic plots, and of points of reversal. In his introduction to a 1907 Everyman edition of *Nicholas Nickleby*, G. K. Chesterton finds it possible for "literary shape" and theme to come directly from the elements of the plot at hand and for critical naturalists to sort out the feeling of unity these elements express. For Chesterton (and for common sense?) unity is felt and known in literature and outside it without appeal to an underlying myth-cause. Moreover, the critical naturalist may comment on an art work's "sharply focused reproduction of life" and at the same time talk about a mythical pattern or force felt in and through the immediate "effects." Thus, Chesterton at once points out the romance plot of *Nicholas Nickleby* and goes on to identify the questing hero and the other characteristics of "every pure romance." But his penetration to the archetype results from his conviction of the presence of the archetype as a fact of life. His archetypal criticism is simultaneously naturalistic criticism. He thinks of romance, and he thinks of it as affecting a reader in an immediate way. This immediate and indeed urgent impact of romance on the reader has to do with its ability, as Chesterton says, to foreshorten existence and to bring it "to a point—to the point." He asserts this in the opening paragraph of his commentary on *Nicholas Nickleby*:

> Romance is perhaps the highest point of human expression, except indeed religion, to which it is closely allied. Romance resembles religion especially in this, that it is not only a simplification but a shortening of existence. Both romance and religion see everything in an abrupt and fantastic perspective, coming to a point. It is the whole essence of perspective that it comes quickly to a point—to the point. For instance, religion is always insisting on the shortness of human life. But it does not insist on the shortness of human life as the pessimists [do]. . . . Pessimism insists on the shortness of human life in order to show that life is valueless. Religion insists on the shortness of human life in order to show that life is frightfully valuable—is almost horribly valuable. Pessimism says that life is so short that it gives nobody a chance; religion says that life is so short that it gives everybody his final chance. In the first case the word brevity means futility. In the second case the word brevity means opportunity. . . . All this is equally true for romance. Romance is a shortening and sharpening of the human difficulty.

The description of Dickensian plot in this appeal to romance is especially faithful to Dickens's novels and to the experience of reading them because in the main Dickens makes use of his elaborate and complicated plots for the sake of a maximum of abrupt points and perspectives. The points that for Dickens are essential to narrative reason and that open up the romantic and religious perspectives are points of reversal. (And it is reversals that Chesterton is implicitly thinking of here—as we shall see later.) Just as the stories of

Greek tragedy are for Aristotle most powerful when they shorten and sharpen the human difficulty by bringing experience to the turning point, so too are plot and story for Dickens. In Dickensian narration it seems as if men and women in story and in life cannot recognize themselves, each other, or the actions engaging them without experiencing peripety. The awful Victorian plot is the sort of plot that tells nothing because its turns, if it has any, are carelessly made to tell nothing. But the great Victorian plot—preeminently the great Dickensian plot—reverses the expectations of both the characters and of those reading or hearing the story because it assumes that knowledge, life's value, and the featuring of act are available only through the abrupt and fantastic perspective described by Chesterton.

Now that we have considered the bearing of Scott's reversal-filled stories on Dickens and narrative reasoning and the bearing of modern criticism's evasion of peripety on the understanding of Dickensian plot, we can look closely at Dickens's use of reversal in *Nicholas Nickleby*. It must first be noted that the reversals that develop Dickens's story do not separate the intellectual and moral aspects of narrative reason. And Dickens's characters, his delegated plotting agents, also move the story's development along by hazarding a series of moral ventures that stimulate some crucial turning point of action, which itself creates intellectual and moral recognitions. Dickens dramatizes recognitions that are literal and personal, but he usually combines reversal and recognition in another way. His plots create recognition scenes *for the reader* that are only secondarily the discovery of the literal relations among persons in the story. Primarily, recognition scenes in Dickens make the reader grasp the unity and relatedness of human experience and moral concern that bind the characters and their activity into one single narrative.

Dickens begins almost invariably with a mystery—with an unintelligible reversal, we might say—because he does not want the reader to ask who originally killed or abandoned whom but how the disparate persons and actions of the story interrelate—how they are coherently connected. The principle of coherent connection is what we refer to in common usage as theme, and it is also that theoretical part of narrative reason we have discussed. As I have suggested earlier, theme is the theory whereby an author explains and accounts for what he is talking about, whereby a storyteller, as Henry James says, "prosecutes those generalizations in which alone consists the real greatness of art."[6] Dickens insistently uses reversal to enable his readers to prosecute those generalizations with him; the reversals therefore usually precede—or are inextricably connected with—the gradual disclosure of the unifying theme. But for Dickens the theme is not just intellectual; it embodies a pressing moral insight. The reversals disclose this moral insight, and they do so aided by the moral choices and acts of the characters. Dickens's plots are a kind of curious moral allegory in which the turns of plot rather than the allegorical personifications move the intellectual and the moral design along. The design itself awaits the end of the story for its disclosure; some nearly final turning point of action signals the death of the story and reveals its intellectual and moral principle of life. The retardation of the disclosure results from the fact that almost up to the end of the story the characters have no certainty about what kind of willful exertion and what kind of moral action will ensure the achievement of happiness. Throughout the story, will and action and crucial points of peripety are moral experiments—the characters must gamble on which way to follow and which way to turn. When the reversals and their effects are sorted out, the plot amounts finally to a resolution of moral uncertainty. Thus, the moral and thematic perspectives of the plot, the actors' hazardous moral ventures, and the story's reversals are bound up together as an invariable condition of the sense of plot in Dickens.

Now the theme Dickens is most interested in exploring in *Nicholas Nickleby* concerns the contemporary state of marriage, which Dickens sees as his character Squeers sees nature. "It is a blessed thing . . . to be in a state o' natur," says

Squeers, but "natur . . . is more easier conceived than described." Similarly, it may be a blessed thing to be in the state of matrimony, but in *Nicholas Nickleby* matrimony too "is more easier conceived than described." Indeed it is so difficult to describe that state, which seems to Dickens to have undergone in modern times a mysterious transformation of character, that at first Dickens seems to be telling a story about something very different: until late in the novel it looks as if he is pursuing a thematic consideration of the appropriateness or the prudence of the hero's need to strike out, even violently, against his enemies.[7] But this thematic intention turns out to be a kind of feint of narrative reason, a false perspective. Eventually the thematic perspective comes to a turning point at which the reader can look back and see the novel's earlier phenomena and events fall into a more compelling thematic arrangement and coherence than is supplied by the focus on prudence or aggression. The reader has been on a road the reversal transforms, a road the reader sees clearly and all the more compellingly because of the new vantage point the reversal provides.

The true theme, the essential narrative reasoning, of *Nicholas Nickleby* is an argument that modern marriage is what Dickens calls "a system of annoyance." The turn revealing the theme is found in Chapter 45. As he tells Squeers, Ralph Nickleby has decided "to wound" Nicholas "through his own affections and fancies." The novel makes clear that wounding others this way preoccupies a large number of persons and that married men and women can use their marriages especially as a system of such wounding. Ralph himself formulates and names the system; wanting to strike at Nicholas through his affection for Smike, a boy Nicholas has befriended, Ralph concocts a tale whereby Smike will be turned over to a flunky of Squeers, who will claim to be Smike's father and will take him from Nicholas. According to Ralph's lie, the alleged father thinks his son Smike is dead until the alleged father's estranged wife confesses on her deathbed that the boy has not died. "And this confession,"

Ralph tells the factitious father, instructing him in the plot, "is to the effect that his death was an invention of hers to wound you—was a part of a system of annoyance, in short, which you seem to have adopted towards each other." At this point in the story we recognize that the system of annoyance is not a mere imaginary or singular case but a precise naming of all the cases of marriage appearing in *Nicholas Nickleby*.

In 1838 such cases were not new either in literature or experience. But Dickens presents them with an intensity of concern, of fear even, that is—and remains—new. He wants these marriages to be accepted as representative of an actual contemporary historical condition, not as stock jokes one can laugh at in easy recognition of literary convention. Dickens wants us to feel that our assumptions and expectations about marriage are complacent and blind and that they need the illuminating shock of reversal. The marriages he exhibits embody a will to throttle or manipulate any persons in their sphere in order to defend against the personal emptiness of the spouses and against the social and moral emptiness of the larger community of spouses.

Characteristically marriage in *Nicholas Nickleby* unites two persons by being a constant safeguard against each spouse's knowledge that his self is a nullity. In the marriage of the Mantalinis, the husband demonstrates his intimacy with his wife by speaking of her in the third person when he speaks directly to her. This means that, in order to feel loved by her husband, Madame Mantalini needs to have herself dramatized by him, even if no one else is present. She needs her husband to "put her on"; his impersonal personal treatment of her motivates, manipulates, and controls her entirely—and gives her an ego we feel she would otherwise not have. If Mantalini does not give her a self by "putting her on," she is empty, she wants to commit suicide. And the same is true for him: *he* threatens suicide if she does not stimulate him to play his role. But these ego roles are substitutes for a vacuum; the threat of suicide always draws the spouses back together, for the loss of one partner would expose entirely the emptiness of the other. Nevertheless, as oddly life-preserving as this system is, the Mantalini marriage is always a system of annoyance because for each spouse the means of expressing self and of "making" love is to push the other toward suicide. To those inside it, the system becomes a system of pleasure *and* annoyance, of extreme coercive manipulation, of the will of one partner to harass and throttle the life of the other as a perverse demonstration of love. And it is not only the comic Mantalinis who exhibit this pattern; Dickens shows that society itself—the spousal community—perversely stimulates the self and "lovemaking" by making men and women in effect suicidal.

If this is the truth about modern marriage, Dickens asks, what is to be done in the face of this system of annoyance? He accompanies with a question both his attempted reversal of our assumptions about marriage and the reversal in the plot that makes us see the force and density of the system as the novel's true theme: Can a genuine and decent human success in life and marriage be achieved in a world—a real world whose deep structure the novel's narrative reason represents and discloses—pervaded by systems of annoyance? Nicholas Nickleby and his sister Kate become the symbols of this question, and the emotional effect of the reversal of our sense of the theme of *Nicholas Nickleby* is to draw us more deeply into the search for a way to enact an answer. Our interest in the plot is especially intensified by Nicholas's and Kate's quest (as if it were ours) for conditions and persons who can succeed in making a freely chosen, vital marriage, even in such a world. However, there seems to be very little opportunity in *Nicholas Nickleby* to form life in a way that escapes the system.

The Browdies of Greta Bridge come close to embodying the positive ideal of marriage that Dickens's plot is in search of. They do not marry for the sake of mutual annoyance or for the sake of hiding from and reinforcing personal emptiness. Nor do they seem bent on annoying others systematically, as is the case with the Mantalinis, the Knags, and the Wittitterleys, who try to force the system on other men and women in their spheres. Nevertheless the Browdies are provincial: their marriage would not survive the personally nullifying effects and the stimulation to systems of annoyance exerted by money and sham in London, where Nicholas and Kate must make their way. It is true that one finds an example of a good city marriage in the Kenwigses. But just as the hulking Browdie would never knock down Squeers (as he should), so Kenwigs would be even less likely to knock down his wife's uncle, a variation of Squeers named Lillyvick. The Kenwigses love and respect each other, their children, and their neighbors; but they worry and nearly destroy their happiness just to please an exponent of the system of annoyance like Lillyvick. Nicholas and Kate thus have virtually no models to inspire their search for a way out of the system. Yet as the story unfolds Dickens demonstrates more and more the desperate need to get out. For the wages of the system of annoyance are not just a threat of suicide but suicide itself, finally carried out by Ralph, the formulator of the system. In another of the novel's most significant reversals, Ralph discovers (on the point of carrying out his plot against his nephew Nicholas) that Smike is his very own son—that his own estranged wife lied, telling Ralph that his son was dead, an invention of hers to wound him. The plot Ralph makes up as a fiction to hurt Nicholas with turns out to be the plot of his real life—a reversal Dickens uses both to make us see the wages of the system and to make us feel how Ralph's own novelistic fiction is the servant of strange but actual truth. Ralph wounds his own affections, not Nicholas's. But Ralph's suicide (in an attic Smike remembers as his boyhood home) does not issue from remorse; it is itself a grimly surprising turn because Dickens presents it as an act of fury and spite. Ralph hangs himself as a way out of coming to grips with the failure of his life, with his own emptiness. He is blindly repeating in his willful death the disabling fatality of the system of annoyance. Nicholas and Kate must escape repeating it in their own lives, or else they will risk both a cultural form of suicide and suicide in fact.

We have seen how reversal in *Nicholas Nickleby* points out

the plot's intellectual and moral narrative reasoning. By effecting a turn of our attention to the theme of marriage as a system of annoyance, Dickens's use of peripety gathers the diverse phenomena of his novel into an especially significant and intelligible whole. This wholeness addresses our intellectual response, but the reversal that reveals the intellectual unity of the novel also stresses the urgency of the marriage theme's moral claim on our attention.

We must now consider finally how Dickens uses reversal to point up the hazardous but telling nature of action. Nicholas and Kate do in the end manage to find their appropriate spouses in Madeline Bray and Frank Cheeryble, and although Dickens scarcely describes these latter two characters, we must understand that their personal quality is the same as the hero's and heroine's. We must also understand that escape from the system is a moral venture, a hazard that features its own act because the system provides no models for acts that challenge it. Much more important than the personal objects of Nicholas's and Kate's choice is the brave, risky action of the choosing. "Happiness and misery are realised in action," Aristotle writes, "the goal of life is an action, not a quality." Dickens's sense of plot endorses the *Poetics*—although Dickens always manages to define a quality and imitate an action at the same time. Now the accurate final choosing of spouses by Kate and Nicholas could not have been possible without the insight provided—to both characters and readers—by reversals along the way; and the choice itself is a reversal that checks the power of the system of annoyance.

Let us turn to the widowed Mrs. Nickleby, allegedly "the silliest" character in his story, to show how Dickens combines in her case too the moral hazard or venture whereby a character challenges prevailing convention and enacts a significant reversal in his own life. Mrs. Nickleby does what her children do: she confronts the system of annoyance and makes an escape from it, surprisingly changing her life as well as our expectations about her and making us recognize that she is con-

siderably less silly than she has seemed to be up to the point
of reversal. Mrs. Nickleby's decision at this crucial turning
point strongly demonstrates how our acts shape us for better
or worse and how what we choose not just to think but to do
damns us or saves us. Late in the novel, in Chapter 49, the
widow discovers she has a final chance for marriage. One day
while in her garden she finds herself the target of a barrage of
phallic-shaped vegetables coming at her from over the garden wall. The assailant shows himself and proposes love, if
not exactly a wedding. Unlike Kate Mrs. Nickleby will not
shrink in embarrassment from her suitor's erotic aggression;
and she refuses to believe he is mad. Dickens wants to in-
struct, as well as to amuse here. He wants the reader to consider with Mrs. Nickleby that the gentleman is not mad, at
least not merely because he is aggressively and directly erotic.
The good marriage has to include something of that direct
force. Without it marriage might be the kind of beneficent yet
rather impersonally sterile and sad alliance it is in that oddly
married couple, the Cheeryble brothers. The Cheerybles are
not *dei ex machina*, incidentally, as much as they are contribu-
tions to the marriage theme, qualifications of the reader's
surmise that maybe the only ideal kind of marriage in this
world is an unqualified system of benevolence. But Dickens's
story insists that the ideal kind of marriage would not depend
on unqualified benevolence anymore than it would depend
on what the alleged erotomaniac finally represents.

The suitor makes a last assault on Mrs. Nickleby in coming
down the chimney of her house and embarrassing the family
with a pair of legs in the fireplace. At this point Mrs. Nickleby
makes her choice:

Kate, my dear, . . . you will have the goodness, my love,
to explain precisely how this matter stands. I have given
him no encouragement—none whatever—not the least
in the world. You know that, my dear, perfectly well. He
was very respectful, exceedingly respectful, when he declared, as you were a witness to; still at the same time, if I

am to be persecuted in this way, if vegetable what's-his-names and all kinds of garden-stuff are to strew my path out of doors, and gentlemen are to come choking up our chimneys at home, I really don't know—upon my word—I do *not* know—what is to become of me. It's a very hard case—harder than anything I was ever exposed to, before I married your poor dear papa, though I suffered a good deal of annoyance then—but that, of course, I expected, and made up my mind for. When I was not nearly so old as you, my dear, there was a young gentleman who sat next us at church, who used, almost every Sunday, to cut my name in large letters in the front of his pew while the sermon was going on. It was gratifying, of course, naturally so, but still it was an annoyance, because the pew was in a very conspicuous place, and he was several times publicly taken out by the beadle for doing it. But that was nothing to this. This is a great deal worse, and a great deal more embarrassing.

She rejects her suitor because he offers her, finally (and "naturally so"?), annoyance entangled with and taking precedence over gratification. Her choice is both very funny and very touching. Had she been thoroughly silly or mad, she would have married him. Indeed from the point of view of the prevailing system of annoyance, she *ought* to marry him. But she still has enough hold on sense to see both his lack of sense and the ultimate if socially unacknowledged destructiveness of the system. This is, in fact, the first time in the novel she confronts a reality that is not a matter of conventional appearances. This is the first time she stops daydreaming: she does not give way to wish fulfillment. The rest of the novel shows her children also keeping closely in touch with a more telling reality than conventional and accepted appearances and systems. "The silliest character in *Nicholas Nickleby* is the hero's mother, a romancer who keeps dreaming impossible happy endings for her children. But the story itself follows her specifications and not those of the sensible people."

Is this not simply untrue? In rejecting her suitor Mrs. Nickleby makes sense. This turning point in her life shows how the story itself is a sensible investigation of the pursuit of marriage in the real world. And it is the venturous *act* of making sense, the hazardous choice transformed into a purposive deed that is emphasized by the turning point. This is no mere "twist" in the plot. On the point of choosing her future and her fate, on the point of making a mistake we might well expect her to make, Mrs. Nickleby shortens, sharpens, and resolves her human difficulty by an act that tells its sense in the form of the abrupt change of perspective brought about by a reversal.

But just as we have already seen writers who believe action is an obstacle to truth or significance, we must certainly acknowledge that there are writers who resist the association of plot, story, and reversal—who do not believe in peripety's essentially telling nature. Such a writer is Dickens's great contemporary Poe, whose sense of plot is distrustful and wary (like the modernists), yet also playful and proud of its factitious, fabricating power (like the postmodernists), and proud too of its power to fabricate brilliantly without using peripety. We can most distinctly gauge Poe's achievement (and perhaps a peculiarly American sense of plot that he helps initiate) by comparing his response to reversal with that of Dickens. And the first way we might compare the two is to remind ourselves that a wavering, reversal-filled plot gives us, through its development, a sense of continuous surprise and novelty. Reversal seems to be an avoidance of repetition; it keeps us from thinking that the points of revelation repeat themselves. In Stein, for example, the repetitiousness of the style and of the effect of the complete actual present absorbs surprises, turns, reversals. In a story, this absorption of reversal by repetition can make the story seem strictly and purely linear or circular. Indeed if we imagine a Dickensian plot, we would picture an intricately coiling, uneven maze of design—a not very symmetrical labyrinth of turns and counterturns. But when we compare the Dickensian labyrinth-plot to plot in Poe, we find in the American something like an attempt to tell a story without turnings, to make a labyrinth that is a single straight line.[8]

Why would Poe want to straighten out the unstable wavering of story line—to reverse reversal? In a story, peripety places those it affects at a turning point at which they enact something surprising. The turning point thus creates a novelty; even if it sparks a recognition, a strange new sight of the already familiar, the revelation creates a different vision of what had already been known or present. Now we might expect a suppression of or indifference to reversal in plot to accompany the absence or blurring of differentiations. And in Poe a suppression of reversal does accompany his blurring of the significance of differences (in a manner we considered earlier in regard to Pater)—especially of those between life and death or between ideas and matter. In contrast, in the turnings of the Dickensian plot the reader feels an urgent struggle of the forces of life, whether physical, spiritual, or moral, against radically different forces of death. This is another way Dickensian reversal is a differentiating function. But Poe insists to his readers that differences are illusory, and because of this insistence the stories are made out of repetitions. From the start to the finish of each tale the apparently disparate phenomena are presented as repeated variants of each other. Death and life are *not* opposites in Poe's stories; they are states reiterating each other in grosser or finer tones. How frequently Poe's characters are dead and alive at the same time and in a way that makes the two states indistinguishable! "Loss of Breath" represents death-in-life comically; "The Facts in the Case of M. Valdemar" sees it as ugly; "The Fall of the House of Usher" and "Ligeia" treat it poignantly and ambiguously. Poe's stories likewise confound the difference between matter and spirit, flesh and idea, as in the case of "Bon-Bon," or in Roderick Usher's ability to paint ideas, or in the way Usher himself seems an idea embodied as

acutely sensitive flesh. Since there is an absence of differentiation in the world Poe represents, why, he seems to ask,
should he make a significant use of reversal, a structure of
story that seems to argue the reality of differences?

I have been suggesting that Poe needs a special nonwaver-
ing form of story to complement a thematics arguing the il-
lusoriness of differences. But there is a more substantial reason for Poe's contrast with Dickens in respect to reversal.
Even in spite of *Eureka* Poe's theories about the interidentity
of matter and spirit, of gigantic life-volition and gigantic
death, are narrative reasonings consistently undermined by
their author. He tends to use his ideas as tools or devices of
narrative construction rather than as truths he is compelled to
reveal. For Poe story is preeminently a fiction, a fabrication;
and far more than he wants to reveal ideas or incite terrors he
wants to exhibit the wit and mastery that accompany a new
kind of story line. We have only just begun to see (for example, in "How to Write a Blackwood Article," "Some Words
With a Mummy," or "The Man That Was Used Up") Poe's
comic self-parody of his famous "ideas," of his claim to deep
metaphysical truth.[9] Poe is therefore not using his ideas even
to initiate a reversal in the reader's consciousness of life and
death, intellect and matter. He uses these ideas because they
are especially convenient for a desire to tell stories in a
proudly original way—in a way that subverts the interde-
pendence of plot and peripety. And he wants above all to call
our attention to his method and manner, which highlights
the remaking of story's maze of plotted design in the form of
a single, straight line. William Carlos Williams was the first to
perceive that Poe was more committed to a new general narrative method than to any specific narrative reasoning:

> Of . . . the Tales, the significance and the secret is: au-
> thentic particles, a thousand of which spring to the mind
> for quotation, taken apart and reknit with a view to em-
> phasize, enforce and make evident, the *method*. Their

quality of skill in observation, their heat, local verity, being *overshadowed* only by the detached, the abstract, the cold philosophy of their joining together.[10]

"The Man of the Crowd" is both an exemplary justification of Williams's summary and a convenient illustration of how Poe's cold philosophy of narrative joinings eschews reversals. Furthermore, "The Man of the Crowd" tells us about Poe's negative relation to the featuring of act. Although Poe uses his stories to highlight a method of construction, the construction is a mathematical contemplation or ratiocination, a narrative reasoning curiously more a method than a content, and a method that is hostile to active doing. No less than Carlyle's Mirabeau or Pater's Marius, Poe's constructions are favorings of a kind of intellectual sight and insight transcending empirical praxis—though we must stress that in Poe what is seen (identities of life and death, for example) seems less important than the method of seeing. For most of the ten pages of "The Man of the Crowd" the narrator's method of seeing is to sit at a table, contemplating the personal and social types passing outside his window. He knows them all thoroughly, just by watching them pass. At one point, however, his curiosity seizes on a mysterious old man, whom he goes out into the street to follow. He wants to discover what strikes him as singular about this subject. As the narrator tracks the old man for almost two days through the labyrinth of London, the reader looks forward to a significant peripety, a sudden, striking revelation. Yet the narrator breaks off his hunt:

> He noticed me not, but resumed his solemn walk, while I, ceasing to follow, remained absorbed in contemplation. "This old man," I said at length, "is the type and the genius of deep crime. He refuses to be alone. *He is the man of the crowd*. It will be in vain to follow; for I shall learn no more of him nor of his deeds."

This is obviously an epiphanic point of recognition, yet it also subtly rebukes the need for a revelation in terms of reversal. The narrator finds what he wants to know—or as much as he can know—by stopping dead, by no longer pursuing his subject through a labyrinth. Indeed the labyrinthine turns *make no difference* to knowledge. And Poe makes it clear that none of us are more or less skillful at knowing than is his narrator. One "solves" a human mystery by sitting at one's still point of observation. Moreover there are truths too deep for knowledge or for stories; in the case of "The Man of the Crowd," this truth is "the essence of all crime," forever undivulged. But what *can* be known can be known from the start. Like his narrator in "The Man of the Crowd," Poe gives up the active pursuit of his *ostensible* subject to remain absorbed in the contemplation of what he already knows. His knowledge or truth is not to be revealed at a particular and significant turning point or even at the story's end. The only significant truth is identical with the path of the solution, the path being not a winding way but a short straight line—a point without a turn. The story's particular truth or moral— that some secrets (crime's, for example) do not permit themselves to be told and that the man of the crowd is a criminal—needs no plot and no reversal intervening between it and its expression; moreover, this truth or moral is revealed by the stopping short of action.

Of course Poe's method of narrative reasoning, with its curious new emphasis on method for its own sake and with its witty flaunting of reversal, is writ most large and most dazzlingly in "The Murders in the Rue Morgue." This story gives us two kinds of expectation about storytelling, two senses of plot, playing them off against each other to the detraction of one. The discredited sense of plot is Dickensian, and is shared by the police and the narrator. They expect that the secret of the murders will be disclosed through a revelation provided by some stupendous turning point. In fact the narrator and the police like the populace at large consider the murders in themselves to be an astonishing reversal, crime on the point of divulging its essence of horror. But insofar as the murders are seen as a turning point in criminal annals, the onlookers are blinded. They expect a solution must entail a perplexingly turned labyrinthine search and revelation.

Dupin represents the sense of plot that can dispense with the turns. The turns suggest layers of truth, a privileged or secret focus, an epiphanic moment revealing a definitive essence behind a deceiving appearance. This suggestion, Dupin declares, as he plots against the reversals of plot, is a trap. "As regards the more important knowledge, I do believe she is invariably superficial. . . . By undue profundity we perplex and enfeeble thought." Peripety promises depth; the point of reversal speaks for a profundity revealed by the turn. Yet this promise in fact baffles truth by inciting mystery and "profound" ingenuity. Ingenuity is superficial: Dupin says this and so does Poe in the method of his narrative constructions. To prove ingenuity superficial Dupin, like Poe, uncoils the maze of design, makes it a straight line by the cold philosophy of *his* joining together the simple and obvious appearances and facts. The detective goes straight to the point; indeed, he barely "goes," for it is apparent to him almost at once that an orang-utan has been the murderer. The wit of this storytelling method is its method of adding two and two when the sum is obvious and needs no discovery. To solve the mystery Dupin needs only to repeat what has happened, not to develop it; he needs only to resist what is identified as a conventional but perverse desire to come to truth by wandering a circuitous and reversal-pointed path.

Like Dupin Poe creates stories by defeating interest in their slow indirect circuitousness. Dupin's analytic intellectual penetration combines "the creative and the resolvent" so as to make the imagination a breathtaking intuitional power, *ahead* of all the instructive developments and surprising turns we associate with plot. And where there is apparently development and surprise in Poe—as in the novel-length *The*

Narrative of Arthur Gordon Pym—these too are used to emphasize the cold philosophy of Poe's Dupinesque story-making. One does not read this story in fear or suspense or surprise but in the hope that it will go on entertainingly repeating itself, keeping Pym precariously balanced between life and death, always at the edge of an adventure which looks new, yet which turns out to be only a copy of one he has just had. In a sense nothing *happens* in Poe's and Pym's world—there is nothing there but an exciting sameness; a constant fusion of life and death, of activity and passivity, of adventure and blankness.

Pym's dilemmas of course are all manifestly contrived in a way insured to strain the reader's credulity; but Poe wants the strain, for it calls attention to his own insistent forging of Pym's situations. The forging is the reality that counts. Such an insistent self-exposing method of narrative construction takes one far away from the element of reversal in plot as Dickens makes use of it. It makes us think that in telling stories Poe is putting on an act: the featuring of act in him becomes the deliberate factitiousness of role-playing. The role is that of "author," and we are to applaud the purely fictive tricks the role asks of the actor. Whereas Poe plays with reversal as with all the elements of plot, Dickens uses reversal only so that reversal will use him—as if the turns of the actors and the action need him to set down what they disclose. And what they disclose, at the level of both content and form, is not merely fiction, not a self-referring aesthetic display. In the end it is Poe, not Dickens, who uses plot as mere machinery, and Poe who is essentially the performer.

Although the last paragraph of Pym's narrative has the effect of a major peripety, nothing is revealed, and the narrative just breaks off. Poe gives us the final turning, the sudden appearance of the white giant in the mist as a self-contained mystery, as a kind of beautifully meaningless structure or geometrical artifice. From this point one returns to the more characteristic and self-consciously humorous Poe—the one who adds the concluding note, saying that Pym has come

back and that Peters lives in Illinois. In effect Poe ends by ex-
hibiting peripety—what another sense of plot would consider
an essential formal element of plot and story—as if it were a
fossil form of storytelling. And if we do not want to figure the
final turn of Pym's narrative as a breaking off that accentuates
the straightness of this story's line, we might say that Poe
uses the fossil of reversal as decoration: the maze of
peripeties becomes in Poe an arabesque, a lovely echo of
what story has been. Even in the pathetic shudderings of
"Ligeia" we see the playful transformation of reversal into
arabesque written into the detail of the wavy lines of the
decor of the gold chamber wherein the heroine confounds the
differences among will, life, and death. Again this is Poe's
way of emphasizing elements of plot as calculated fabric and
decor, not as earnest forms of revelation.

Perhaps the general relevance of comparing storytellers by
their sense of plot's response to peripety can best be under-
lined if we consider how and why makers of plots have had
an inveterate sense of their stories as labyrinths. One senses
an almost primitive insistence here, and at least one modern
anthropological study confirms the sense. In *The Gate of Horn*
G. R. Levy has written a study of the survival of cave religion
and cave ritual in Europe from paleolithic times to the time of
Aristotle.[11] The paleolithic cave ritual, Levy writes, enacted
the communion of power shared by men and the animals
they hunted. The form of worship that guaranteed the community of power was the ritual approach by men, through a
deliberately constructed labyrinth, to an image of divine
power at the labyrinth's end. In a strikingly obvious way
primitive men did not build the cave passages as straight
lines. The galleries took purposely winding paths, and were
full of turns. The reason for this remains mysterious. Perhaps
the windings imitate the path divine power takes on its way
to earth; or they may imitate roadways between the worlds of
life and death; or they may even represent the awesome differences between divinity and mortality, life and death.
When the paleolithic cave religion resurrected itself in the

form of the Eleusinian mysteries it also gave birth to the drama as Aristotle knew it. In her summary of the *Poetics*, Levy does not explore a question her thesis makes rather obvious: when Aristotle theorizes about peripety in relation to dramatic plot, is he remembering the tradition of a necessary ritual turning point in the labyrinth? Even in Chesterton's remarks on romance, religion, and *the* point in Dickens, the idea of the labyrinth is imminent. Chesterton asserts that every romance needs three characters: a Saint George, a lady, and a dragon, characters who continue the mythic life of Theseus, Ariadne, and the Minotaur.

In the final analysis, we might say that for Poe the idea of the plot as revelatory labyrinth is naive and primitive. He plays with this naïvete; certainly his sense of plot is less negative or wary than it is playful. But for all of Dickens's playfulness, there is none to correspond with Poe's where peripety is at issue. Unlike Poe, Dickens suggests in all earnestness that by the turns of story and storytelling we can reconcile ourselves to life's most serious difficulties. Early on in *Nicholas Nickleby* the hero is in a stagecoach accident, and he and his fellow passengers get over their shock by listening to a pair of tales narrated by the travellers in the group. These stories are ostensibly "told against each other," but they address themselves to the same question. Since life is full of pain and annoyance, they ask, would it not be wise to renounce it—either by way of ascetic religion or by despair and suicide? Both stories make out good cases for these negative solutions—and then suddenly reveal grounds for happiness and renewal, so that asceticism and despair look foolishly grim. The reversals at the heart of these tales are vehicles of the hope and the affectionate human decency that all of *Nicholas Nickleby* is intended to make a positive claim for; they are also the signs and promises of the creatively developing nature of life understood as purposeful action. Poe has no need for or interest in such signs and promises—for one thing because his sense of life as simultaneously a process of death makes a resistance to despair and suicidal impulse rather pointless. But most of Dickens's questioning about what is human does not interest Poe because Poe wants to tell stories for the sake of their inward coherence—their mathematical fitness of proportion, their brilliant repetitions and redundancies, their mazes restructured as straight lines or as decorative "twists"—rather than for their ability to comment on life as we normally experience its terrors and pleasures outside of fiction.

Of course the attenuation of the structure of reversal in Poe's stories is also a reversal in the English tradition of the sense of plot. And we would claim, finally, that while Poe frees story from dependence on reversal, we cannot free the story of Poe's career from a reversal that is a matter of history, not a mere matter of plotted form. Williams argues that Poe's apparent idiosyncrasies are a logical response to his American ground: his innovations, his mathematical coldness, his straightening of the labyrinth are his way of asserting the originality of American experience in relation to what has preceded it. And D. H. Lawrence believes that Poe's " 'morbid' tales . . . need to be written because old things need to die and disintegrate, because the old white psyche has to be gradually broken down before anything else can come to pass."[12] In this light Poe's work weakens reversal in storytelling at the same time as it represents one of the significant turning points in our consciousness.

FOUR

The Featuring of Act as "The Rescue": Story in Dickens and George Eliot

> The food of hope
> Is meditated action; robbed of this
> Her sole support, she languishes and dies.
> —Wordsworth, *The Excursion*

I have been arguing, according to the assumptions of a positive sense of plot, that plot and story make sense of life by reasoning about it with an intellectual and moral narrative reason that is attached to a ground not merely speculative. This ground is action; and I follow George Herbert Mead's belief (in his *The Philosophy of the Act*) that intellectual and moral perspectives are "unified through action, [which] is essential to the verification of hypotheses." For Mead, in relation to ideas, action has "consummation value."[1] Here too action is assumed to have this value, but I see its value as not only consummatory but initiatory. For it is my belief that narrative reason is instructed by reversal; that reversal is the product of change and novelty; and that novelty and change—the agents of action—testify to the reality of purposeful and intelligible motion in the world. In the case of Mrs. Nickleby, intellectual and moral reasoning is verified and consummated by action; but in the case, say, of the *reader* of *Nicholas Nickleby*, action is instructive, is the first (as well as the final) teacher and arbiter of ideas. Action is of course a creator of something more than ideas; in *Nicholas Nickleby* it fashions personal happiness and a community alternative to the system of annoyance. Of course a writer with a sense of plot like Poe's would object to tying narrative reason to action or to the happiness of the actor. For a thinker like Dupin, action has no

"consummation" value. And we must grant Poe what he instances: according to his sense of plot, narrative reason may
indeed be divorced from action. Poe reasons narratively, but
in a purely contemplative way, detached from representation
of a *bodily* purposeful *motion* of consciousness. This is the
kind of detachment we have suggested leads to the divorce of
plot and theme. In Poe's case, in *Pym*, for example, the events
of the story are not thematized; rather, the artist's manipulations of the events—his sense *for* them as inspirations of
artifice—is put forward as the thematic center of interest. The
plot, representing events not telling in themselves, shrinks in
importance in relation to the author's highlighting of his own
performance of those events.

We have seen the same divorce of narrative reason and action in Carlyle, although without the emphasis on the
writer's proud performance. Separating narrative reason
from empirical praxis and action, Poe takes pride in pointing
out how his ratiocinative mechanisms transcend the empirical. In contrast Carlyle takes no pride in narrative reasoning
divorced from action; he uses narrative reasoning for one
end: to point out the need for an insight and morality—
Mirabeau's—that transcends the need for action *and* for narrative reason. Carlyle thus uses narrative reason solely to
humble it, to expound a meaning and an ideal that negate its
importance as a vehicle of thought and an imitator of action.
This goes much farther than Poe, who humbles only action.
But both Carlyle and Poe stand on the other side of the assumptions of a positive, and we might now say, Dickensian
sense of plot. The latter does not use narrative reason to
humble it, to represent the essential meaninglessness or distance from meaning of the world. To this positive sense of
plot all reasonings are initiated and consummated by practice
and action; indeed, for this sense of plot, practice and action
rescue life's meanings from indeterminacy. For Dickens, action (as Mead would say) consummates meanings by connecting signs and their referents in such a way as to articulate

relations and to create or recreate them by a novel, practicable determination of them.

In Dickens—and in the general Victorian address to story represented by Dickens—plot imitates action and action imitates Dickensian plot because both are seen by the novelist as agencies of rescue. Plot and action rescue life from chaos, from inhibition of desire and utterance, from indeterminacy of meaning and relation. This means that plot and action rescue life from unhappiness, for Dickens identifies unhappiness with chaos, inhibition, and indeterminacy as much as with the obvious social misery of exploitation and poverty. So much does Dickensian story feature act as creative rescue that even evil is turned into some form of good by virtue of its translation into action. Since Dickens believes that by actions the truth of men's inner potential and of their hidden relations is defined and externalized for good or evil, the act in the Victorian plot represents the making of a novel difference in life, *for* life—a difference that creatively determines and fixes meaning.

But if representation of the Victorian plot is divided between Dickens and George Eliot, then the featuring of act and plot as creative rescue from chaos or indeterminacy of meaning is more difficult to assert as characteristically Victorian. For George Eliot opens up a quarrel with Dickens relevant to the featuring of act, a quarrel that strongly conditions the modern sense of plot. We can illustrate this modern sense of plot toward which the treatment of action in Eliot is tending by invoking the brilliant French narratologist Roland Barthes, who is closer to Eliot (and certainly closer to Poe and Dupin) than to Dickens. In Barthes's *S/Z* we find that to plot and enact a story or to tell the story of plots and enactments is to be undone, is to initiate an act and to simultaneously subvert and even destroy the significance and creativity of action. For Barthes any storyteller represents life in terms of such a paradoxical simultaneous instigation and undoing of acts and events. Story may posit a differentiation of creativity and

destructiveness—it may posit and represent some version of
a rescue of the former from the latter—but as Barthes learns
from Balzac's *Sarrasine*, both action and differentiation are
self-undoing and negating in a way appropriately symbolized
by being-castrated and castration.

According to Barthes, the narrative form of a rescue of life
from meaninglessness or from relative absence of meaning
must inevitably undergo a humbling of its intention, a subversion of the capacity of narrative to be meaningful. Barthes
himself undoes the *featuring* of acts in plot by making acts one
linguistic code among many (hermeneutic, symbolic, seman-
tic, cultural). By this undoing, he also reminds us how little
relevance "action" in the novel has to action in the actual
world. "Imagine the disorder," he exclaims,

> the most orderly narrative would create were its descrip-
> tions taken at face value, converted into operative pro-
> grams and simply *executed*. . . . What we call "real" (in
> the theory of the realistic text) is never more than a code
> of representation: . . . it is never a code of execution: *the
> novelistic real is not operable*.

For Barthes a series of actions in a plot is "description," is
the arbitrary "unfolding of a name"; the code of acts does not
feature acts but the seeking of names, "a labor of the classification of language—a *maya* activity, as the Buddhists would
say." Is there not in George Eliot, in *Middlemarch* especially,
already an immanent foreshadowing and appreciation of
such statements? George Eliot uses narrative reason to arrive
at meaning and the representation of action, and yet she then
humbles narrative reason by using it also to portray the
evanescence of meaning, the nominal and yet essentially indefinable nature of action. For Eliot the rescue is finally not
practicable. And based on this judgment of the impracticable
nature of the rescue, the dissociation of the novel from Dickensian story and plot that George Eliot endeavored to carry
out is still, vis-à-vis prose fiction, the principal project of
modern criticism of the novel. We need only look to J. Hillis

Miller's recent readings of *Middlemarch* to see how cogently Eliot can be made to underpin a Barthesian sense of the novel's version of action.[2]

Now Dickens would not have been astonished at Barthes's sense of plot as if he had never considered the multiplicity and self-referentiality of codes by which writing and reading are accomplished. (He has left us his meditation on these things in *Our Mutual Friend*.) But it is doubtful that he would have thought acts in the plot of a novel were on an equal footing with its other elements or that he would have thought of acts or purposive deeds as synonymous with castration. Dickensian plot seems to be always a search for a way whereby "the novelistic real" and the "purely" nominal may be imagined to be and may become operable as action; story in Dickens insists that it represents the real world in order that it can ultimately comment on and honor its own code of acts— as it comments on and honors acts in the world outside the text—as more significant than the *maya* activity of nomination. But there is no doubt that a shift away from just this featuring of acts, from an interest in their defining capacity or their paramount importance for the instruction and consummation of narrative reasonings, caused Dickensian plot in its author's last ten years to decline in the estimate of readers and other novelists. We find a novelist like D. H. Lawrence, for example, pointing to George Eliot as the major revisionist of the senses of plot and action because she *internalizes* action: "You see, it was really George Eliot who started it all. . . . It was she who started putting all the action inside. Before, you know, with Fielding and the others, it had been outside. Now I wonder which is right?"[3]

It is perhaps by the internalization of action, a step that ultimately makes action imponderable or makes it at best an arbitrary and unfixed sign in an unending series of metonymies, that George Eliot most undermines Dickens's sense of plot. Of course the impulse orginating this internalization is an appeal to reality. Is there "really" and plausibly, George Eliot wonders, any one way of truthful narrative reasoning about character, action, experience? Are narrative reasonings not always infinite and arbitrary, incapable of resolution either by thought or action? Indeed, George Eliot also wonders if there is a genuine difference between action and suffering, doing and refraining from doing. Is the difference itself not nominal (as narrative reasonings are nominal); is it not inexact and misleading to call action in both the real world and in novelistic representation creative or the only measure of creativity? And it is not only action that is imponderable. Are the characters of real or fictive men and women significantly differentiated or not? Is there not an internality of experience, an always constrained potential or intensity of feeling not expressed by action that is most synonymous with life? Because of its insistence upon such questions, the Eliotic plot, we might say, constrains itself from reaching (certainly from enacting) an answer. And this self-constraint has a powerfully ironic result: George Eliot makes such questionings the ground of the plausible "realism" of her novels, yet the persistent cultivation of the questions verges on an unintended result for the realist tradition. It results in an emphasis upon the novel as preeminently a special kind of discourse which, as Barthes puts it, "has no responsibility" to the real after all. George Eliot's questionings of Dickens's stories for the sake of realism brings the novel to the brink of the dissolution of realism, to "the *maya* activity" of linguistic classification we find later in Stein, in Woolf, and in the Joyce of *Finnegans Wake*.

Now "which *is* right," Dickens or George Eliot? Even in *this* age of criticism let us risk repeating Lawrence's naive question. Are the acts and the rescuing power of acts represented by the Dickensian sense of plot unrealistic, implausible, merely an unfolding of names—"right" only as such? If we cannot establish scientific exactitude on this point, perhaps we can at least recover Dickens's intentions for featuring acts as fruitful arbiters of meaning and happiness; perhaps we can keep his sense of plot distinct from that which is now more in vogue. To do this we shall compare two roughly complementary sequences from *Bleak House* and *Felix Holt the Radical*. I suggest *Felix Holt the Radical* documents—much better at least than "The Natural History of German Life" or than any of G. H. Lewes's criticism—George Eliot's quarrel with Dickens's way of plotting life and meaning and of featuring act. This novel exhibits similarities to *Bleak House* which indicate that George Eliot set out to rewrite Dickens's story as a way of confronting his sense of plot with her own.[4] Her motive for the confrontation is like Carlyle's and Pater's or Stein's and Orwell's—an opposition to traditional plotted form for the sake of fiction's claim to truthfulness. She seems to have intended to illuminate by her work's contrast Dickens's narrative sensationalism and his inability to control his *"animal* intelligence, restricted to perceptions"[5] with any plausibly plotted experience.

The resemblance between these novels is not limited to the prominence in both of a disputed inheritance mired in Chancery. The study of Mrs. Transome seems most closely to connect George Eliot's novel with that of Dickens, for like Lady Dedlock this proud and aristocratic lady needs to suppress a guilty past and suffers at the mercy of a cold and unscrupulous Chancery lawyer. George Eliot seems especially to want to criticize the implausibility of Dickens's Lady Dedlock, particularly on the grounds of an absence of credible and normative psychology in her. We can imagine Eliot criticizing the pure fictitiousness of Dickens's story in the following way: "Dickens makes Lady Dedlock all but innocent of her own sin, first by stressing her continued fidelity to a lover who deserted her twenty years before—and by asking us to believe in her continuing remorse for an incident so long buried; then by conveniently keeping her ignorant of the fact that her innocent child by her lover still lives; and finally by portraying the lawyer who tortures her as a morality-play fiend without humane affections or connections. I will not so manipulate the story of my version of Lady Dedlock. Realistically I imagine her living in full knowledge of her illegitimate child; plausibly I imagine the lawyer to be both her former lover and

her present neighbor and business manager. I see their passion, true to the nature of things, as long since over. In this I
have a more lifelike donnée and more potential genuine pity
and fear than Dickens could achieve."

Yet there are deeper motives for an appeal to lifelikeness
and plausibility than those revealed by this monologue. To
clarify and illustrate the differences between Eliot and Dickens, I will now give summaries of segments of plot from each
of the novels. These summaries will reproduce in detail how
the stories unfold purely as sequences of act in order later to
discriminate Dickens and George Eliot as imitators of action.
In saying that I present "pure" sequences of act, I mean that I
am presenting what happens without any appeal to theme,
since we want to see if acts in Dickens and Eliot are presented
as agents of meaning in themselves. This is in line with my
assumption that action may initiate meaning as well as consummate it. We will want to see how the acts are featured by
their authors, how and to what extent they are made to represent the rescue of life's meanings from indeterminacy, from
confusion and inhibition of utterance, from unhappiness.
Both sequences dramatize rescue as action and act as rescue.
Here then—with apology for its necessary length—is what
happens in chapters 54 through 59, the three installments of
Bleak House that narrate the last days of Lady Dedlock's life:

> Inspector Bucket of the London detective force must
> reveal Lady Dedlock's past to her husband because a
> crowd of blackmailers, threatening to expose her to the
> public, demand that the old baronet pay to keep them
> quiet. The blackmailers include: a usurer who once was a
> creditor to Lady Dedlock's long-lost lover, Captain
> Hawdon, and who has now discovered Hawdon's love
> letters in the rubbish of a rag-and-bone shop where
> Hawdon had been living; an absurd independent minis-
> ter now married to the nurse of Lady Dedlock's bastard
> child Esther Summerson; and a Mrs. Snagsby, the wife
> of a stationer to the Courts, who participates in all this to

spite her husband, since she believes Hawdon's old friend, Jo, the crossing-sweep, was Mr. Snagsby's illegitimate son. Bucket has also had to prepare Sir Leicester for the suspicion that his wife has murdered the family lawyer, Tulkinghorn, because he knew her past. But the detective can now relieve Sir Leicester of this suspicion; he has lured Lady Dedlock's discharged French maid, Hortense, to the house; and once the blackmailers go, he arrests *her* as the murderess. These exposures stun Sir Leicester. Left alone in his library, he suffers a stroke and collapses.

Another suspect has already been arrested for the lawyer's murder: George, a former army officer, and once an intimate friend of Hawdon's. Long ago George ran away from home and never returned, and it turns out that his mother is Mrs. Rouncewell, who keeps house for the Dedlocks at their country estate. The mother has steadily hoped to be reunited with her son; but George, ashamed of his youth, has refused to return. In prison he also refuses to be represented by any lawyers because Tulkinghorn has tried (unsuccessfully) to extort from him information about Hawdon's love affair and because George has also seen the fruits of Chancery practice: he runs a fencing and shooting gallery in Soho, and two victims of the Court's legal fraudulence have died on his premises. But his friends will not allow him to go unaided. The wife of an old army mate has done her own detective work, and has found out George's mother. She brings her to London from the country house, and reunites mother and son. Yet George remains in prison, since all this occurs just before Bucket arrests Hortense.

It so happens that Mrs. Rouncewell has received an unsigned letter (sent by Hortense) accusing Lady Dedlock of the crime. From the jail she has gone to her mistress, showing her the letter and asking her—without making any accusation—to help secure the release of the returned prodigal. And Lady Dedlock has endured another upsetting visit. The first man to notice a similarity between Lady Dedlock and her bastard daughter was a silly lawyer's assistant named Guppy. Gambling on the resemblance and expecting eventual profit from it, Guppy proposed to Esther. She rejected him. He did not really accept the rejection until he saw her disfigured by an attack of smallpox. Stirred by shame at his own behavior, Guppy has now turned up to tell Esther's mother that her past is public: he has just seen the blackmailers leave the house. In despair, Lady Dedlock runs away without attempting to see her husband.

Not until hours later does an old maid cousin discover Sir Leicester's stunned body in the library. He regains consciousness, but is frenzied. He cannot speak, yet wants desperately to see his wife. He tries to write inquiries about her on a slate, but learns he is partially paralyzed. Finally Bucket returns from committing Hortense and freeing George. He understands he must follow Lady Dedlock and rescue her—perhaps from suicide. Looking for a helpful clue, he stops in her bedroom, where he finds a handkerchief with Esther's name on it; he realizes she must be the illegitimate daughter (he has not heard her name, even from the blackmailers). Esther may help in winning Lady Dedlock back to her home, so Bucket sets out to find her. He succeeds, although in doing this he loses more time.

Waked out of sleep, Esther goes with Bucket first to the police station where he files a description of Lady Dedlock as a missing person and then to a Thameside spot where the river is dragged for drowned bodies. This check turns up nothing, and Bucket and the girl set off for St. Albans, the village outside London and the site of Bleak House, the home of Esther's guardian. Bucket surmises that Lady Dedlock wants to see her daughter. But there is a complication here connected with the handkerchief. Near Bleak House are located a miserable band of brickmakers, who are from time to time the objects of avowedly charitable evangelical missions. Very early in the story Esther found herself dragged along on one of these missions by a particularly outrageous dogooder. She had at that time left her handkerchief in a brickmaker's hut, and this handkerchief had later come into the hands of Lady Dedlock. It may be, Bucket thinks, that Lady Dedlock went first to the brickmakers rather than to Bleak House to learn of Esther's whereabouts. And she has been there. But the brickmakers sullenly refuse to be helpful; they will only say that Lady Dedlock has proceeded north. Bucket and Esther move ahead as day dawns in heavy snow, sleet, and fog; with Esther close to collapse, they push through this bad weather until past nightfall. Then Bucket begins to lose his confidence. He announces in the middle of the night that they must turn around and go back to London, following the track not of Lady Dedlock but of one of the brickmaker's wives who was missing from the cottage and whom they first thought had been sent by Lady Dedlock back to London with a message for Sir Leicester or for Esther.

But Sir Leicester has received no message. Mrs. Rouncewell's reunion with her son encourages his hopes. He regains enough speech to declare to the household his forgiveness of his wife. As his daylong watch stretches into the early hours of the next morning, Esther and Bucket reenter London. The track of the brickmaker's wife has led them to Chancery Lane and the vicinity of the courts. Esther, terrified by being farther from her mother than before, recognizes Allan Woodcourt, a young surgeon, in the street; she allows him to join the search. Esther really loves Woodcourt, but she has refused to admit this to herself, especially now that she is disfigured; she has decided, instead, to marry her old benevolent guardian, Jarndyce.

The surgeon, who has just come from tending wards

of the court, accompanies Esther and Bucket to Snagsby the law-stationer's, for a policeman has seen the brickmaker's wife with Snagsby's servant Guster. It happens that Guster periodically falls into violent fits of hysteria, and she is in one at the moment. The jealous Mrs. Snagsby, thinking that the visit had something to do with the infidelities she ascribes to her bewildered husband, has made the girl senseless with fear of punishment or dismissal. Woodcourt manages to calm her, and secures the message Guster has in fact received. It is a statement of remorse, and it announces Lady Dedlock's intention to be lost to the world. Where then is the brickmaker's wife? She has asked directions to a wretched burial ground nearby—the place in fact where Esther's father (though this is unknown to Esther) is buried in a pauper's grave. The pursuers follow her there, and they see a woman lying in the snow and refuse on the steps of the graveyard. Yet it is not the brickmaker's wife but Lady Dedlock. She had the day before changed clothes with the other woman in order more effectively to lose herself. Esther recognizes her mother, but Lady Dedlock is dead—as we are told—"of terror and her conscience."

So much then for a summary of the content of six chapters of Dickens's novel—six chapters out of sixty-seven. These chapters do not unravel the plot to its end, since the novel has yet to narrate the close of the monumental case of Jarndyce and Jarndyce, the death of Richard Carstone, and the resolution of Esther's love for Woodcourt.

Now the parallel sequence of chapters 44 through 50 in *Felix Holt the Radical* gives us Lady Dedlock's "descendant," Mrs. Transome, meeting her nemesis:

Felix Holt the Radical is in prison, awaiting trial on a charge of manslaughter. He had tried to control an anarchic riot of workingmen on a national election day, but his attempt had in fact made him appear as one of the leaders of the uproar. The riot issued in two deaths. One of the dead men was the last of a line of claimants to the estate of Harold Transome, a Radical candidate in the election. His death makes way for the rightful claimant to the estate from a collateral line: a poor Dissenting minister's daughter, Esther Lyon, who has fallen in love with Felix, though she scarcely acknowledges this to herself.

While Felix is in prison, Esther has gone to live in Transome Court. Harold and his mother know they must resign their estate to her, and have chosen to befriend her. Esther has always dreamed of such an inheritance. When Harold begins to fall in love with her it seems that Esther will have the opportunity to become a great lady without, after all, needing to turn the Transomes out of their hereditary home. But a prison interview with Felix reminds her sharply of her love, especially since Felix remains undaunted in the social and moral idealism she loves him for. At the trial Felix defends himself (he distrusts the honesty of the legal system, and he has distrusted the honesty of the elections); Harold Transome, hoping to please Esther, gives testimony in Felix's favor; and Esther suddenly and dramatically steps forward to testify to the goodness of Felix's intentions. But he is found guilty and sentenced to four years in prison.

However, a number of the county leaders, including Transome, have been stirred by Felix's predicament, and they put aside political differences to meet and to secure him a pardon. Transome is followed to this meeting by the family lawyer, Jermyn, against whom Harold has started a Chancery suit for mismanagement of the Transome estates. Harold is prosecuting this suit partly out of spite because Jermyn has not helped him win the election. Now Jermyn has in fact mismanaged the estate, and has lined his pockets with income from it. But frustrated and violent, Jermyn intends to goad Harold into giving up the suit, if need be, by revealing Mrs. Transome's past. At the close of the public meeting Harold, infuriated by Jermyn's pursuit of him, strikes Jermyn in the face with a whip. Jermyn blurts out that he is Harold's father. Harold, Jermyn, and Mrs. Transome are now publicly exposed.

Returned to Transome Court, Harold tells Esther that a family disgrace makes it necessary for him to resign the estate at once; he also resigns any personal claims he has made upon her, if that is her desire. To Esther the great estate now represents only an inheritance of pain and moral mediocrity; she can think only of Felix. She has no assurance of a life with him in the future, but although she makes her choice in the dark, she chooses to give up her claim. Her choice is reinforced by a last interview with Mrs. Transome. "The dimly-suggested tragedy of this woman's life, the dreary waste of years empty of trust and affection, afflicted [Esther] even to horror." With this, Esther returns to her father's humble house.

Where shall we begin to discriminate assumptions about story, plot, and rescuing action as they appear in these two novelistic sequences? Three things strike us immediately. First, on the surface at least, Dickens's sequence seems to dramatize a defeat of rescue, whereas Eliot's dramatizes a success—the pardon that rescues Felix. How does this appearance square with our thesis that the rescue is a positive for Dickens and at best a wary ambivalence for Eliot? Second, there appears to be no equivalent in Eliot's story of Buckets and French maids, Snagsbys and Gusters, stray handkerchiefs and similar confusing particulars. Dickens seems to be simultaneously insisting upon the relevance of every detail to his plot and to his characters' actions and upon the allowance of no arbitrariness of detail. Thirdly, Eliot seems far more plausible than Dickens; in her we see the apparently greater normativeness of psychology and experience. To have Lady Dedlock, in clothes underlining her degradation, end at the grave of the lover she has thought dead for twenty years: is this not a most strained coincidence, a manipulation of Lady

Dedlock's meaning, and a forcing of action to speak authoritatively and without arbitrariness about her? If Dickens wants to feature the place of action in plot, should he not at least make his action plausible?

Since we come back to the issue of plausibility, perhaps we can best examine the phenomenon of action in both writers by focusing on their plotting of coincidences—for coincidences seem, at least to many readers, the greatest strain upon plausibility in the summarized chapters from *Bleak House*, where they stare out at us far more obviously than in the chapters from *Felix Holt the Radical*. Both novelists seem to make use of coincidence to argue that human connection and interrelation are life's most important facts. But Dickens seems to want to exaggerate integrations by making his story complexly bristle with coincidences; of course he would have defended his practice by claiming he modelled it on life. On the other hand, George Eliot appears to play down or to oppose coincidence and plotted complexity even at the same time as she uses them, for this seems to her to be more responsible to what is real. *Up to a point*, this strategy or responsibility to reality in George Eliot is a featuring of action. For action is purposive creative motion, and when Eliot presents coincidences at first sight as accidents but upon reflection as intellectually and morally purposeful motions and relations, she is using plot's representation of action as an agent that rescues life's appearances from their lack of connection and their arbitrariness of meaning.

But there is a curious, emphatic, and highly characteristic qualification of this featuring of the rescuing agency of plot in Eliot. She gives with one hand and takes away with the other. She plots to reveal accidents as somehow purposefully creative, but she also makes them seem incapable of being principal or enduring agents of meaning. In Eliot there is an arbitrary relation between what is done and narrative reasonings about what is done that always threatens to return action to the form of accident. And this constant threat to the significance of action, which in its turn threatens to return meaning itself to the form of accident or to mere nomination, is also offered by Eliot as most plausibly representative of "the real." Although we may not see much of accident and coincidence in the summarized chapters, their content is deeply threatened by accident and coincidence. The realism of George Eliot ultimately depends upon periodic strenuous exertion against this threat and also upon periodic capitulation to it. Those who find her representation of life most plausible find it so because she presents actions and the narrative reasonings they stimulate as unclear, unresolved problematics of experience.

Whenever Eliot uses plot, narrative reason, or action she uses them to mean something that humbles them, something that means the resistance of life to imitation, explanation, or consummation. Even the normative psychology we associate with Eliot is a form of narrative reasoning about life; and Eliot uses this, but also casts it in doubt. Perspectives on or of the self do not *consummate* themselves in the certainty of a normative psychology in Eliot any more than life-perspectives consummate themselves in clearly definable action in her work. In Eliot's sense of plot there is a connection between praxis in general and practical jokes—a connection that is ominous because the practical joke, though purposeful, is also dangerously close to contingency and seems invariably to become accident. Through the practical joke Eliot can portray experience itself as a prank, an intention "to mean" that is co-opted by resistance to meaning. For example, the riot that leads to Felix's imprisonment is the result of a prank. Workmen at the election cuff and goad each other: it is "fun . . . in danger of getting rather serious." The ensuing uproar *is* serious, and accidentally overtakes Felix to whom

> pressed along with the multitude into Treby Park, his very movement seemed . . . only an image of the day's fatalities, in which the multitudinous small wickednesses of small selfish ends, really undirected towards any larger result, had issued in widely-shared mischief that might yet be hideous.

The passage implies that movement directed purposefully and unselfishly towards larger results is not fatal but creative, and that it is hence significant action. In Eliot meaning re-sults—is rescued from indeterminacy—when coincidences or "sports" are disclosed as the adjuncts of purposes and deeds that make a significant and certain difference to their con-texts. But how truly and lastingly is this significance estab-lished?

If we examine the roots of the revelatory explosion between Harold and Jermyn, we will find at first a chain of events that Eliot demonstrates is accidental and coincidental in appear-ance but purposeful in fact. The conflict between the un-known father and the bastard son begins with Esther's knowledge of her right to the Transome estate. This knowl-edge is caused by the accidental discovery by Felix of a lost wallet and the accidental discovery of another heir to the Transome estate by the man who loses the wallet. The wallet belongs to the valet of a local Tory landowner; the valet is (by the way) an old friend of Esther's dead unknown father, a captain named Maurice Christian Bycliffe. At the captain's death the friend received tokens of Bycliffe's marriage to Esther's mother, a Frenchwoman. For his own personal rea-sons the valet now calls himself Maurice Christian, and he carries Bycliffe's mementos on his person. Christian belongs to a large, boorish retinue of servants addicted to pranks. He has been sarcastic about his fellow servant the butler, and the butler wants revenge. One afternoon the butler discovers Christian asleep on the estate grounds, and he thinks it a good practical joke to cut off part of the sleeper's coat. In this part, which he tosses into the shrubbery, are the mementos and a wallet belonging to Christian's master, who is the Tory candidate for parliament. Felix finds this fragment and its contents; he brings them to Esther's foster-father Lyon be-cause as a Radical Felix does not want to visit a Tory house-hold. Subsequently, the minister's questioning alerts Chris-tian to the possibility that Bycliffe's heir is alive and has a claim to the Transome estate. But yet another accident and prank must intervene before the Bycliffe heir is found. Chris-

tian happens to play a joke on the other heir, Tommy Troun-
sem, the idiot who will die in the riot. In the course of the
joke he learns that Jermyn employed a second lawyer to help
administer the Transome estate. Christian looks up this
lawyer, puts information from him together with what he already knows about Bycliffe, and then sells what he knows to
Harold. The information frees Harold from dependence on
Jermyn, and frees him, besides, to start the law suit against
the man who is his father.

Now we may certainly accept this as George Eliot's elabora-
tion by means of coincidence of the rich interconnections of
experience's threads; and we can certainly see that she is attempting to show that whatever happens, even sheer accident, is pervaded by an intellectual and moral purposiveness
that will bend coincidences to its own ends. This purposiveness is natural and plausible, not mysterious; the natural
political divisions of the county, for example, get mixed up
with the return of the wallet, and hence ordinary politics
reveal Esther's background. We may say that George Eliot
attempts to *naturalize* coincidence by rescuing it from its
arbitrary accidental quality. By naturalizing coincidence, she
makes it plausible—real—in essence continuous with
genuine action.

But once her plot has moved forward to rescue life from indeterminacy of relation, Eliot's story moves back on itself,
humbling its shaping and reasoning power, returning what it
represents to indeterminacy. The meaningful agency of action is threatened, for Eliot presents it as a purposive motion
that bears no discernible fruit, that creates no defining, fixed
transformations. Uncertain in its effects, action again becomes unknowable and indefinable; it seems to make even
less a difference to life than coincidences or pranks. When
Felix is being rescued from prison, Eliot pointedly makes this
genuine act of rescue (purposeful, deliberated, not a practical
joke) merely the background of the undoing of the Transomes. Just when Harold and the landowners are repeating
their author's form of naturalizing coincidence by making

sense out of the nonsense that has engulfed Felix, Eliot shows their action broken in upon by the meaningless, wasted, and hence "coincidental" life that Mrs. Transome's old relation to Jermyn represents. What looks like a creative rescue action for Felix is also uncertain. Liberated from imprisonment, Felix—as we shall see—is delivered over to another form of constraint, as if the rescue made no difference, was not meaningful. And whereas the accidental revelation of kinship between Harold and Jermyn seems creative in itself—the making or re-making of an important relation—the tie is made only to be at once unmade. Harold Transome discovers his real father, but the discovery intensifies Harold's immobility and isolation. Esther, newly seeing the connection between the Transome estate and the Transomes' misery, resigns her inheritance. But what she exchanges the inheritance for is nothing as definite as action: it is the hope of uncertain future creativity and satisfaction. This is also Felix's "gain" in exchange for prison. As for Lady Transome, she becomes more isolated and more dreary and immobilized than she has yet been.

The actions of Eliot's characters do not express what they are intended to express. In compensation for this, it appears that an inhibition of action is accompanied by an enlargement of vision: it makes the characters see more than they saw previously. Harold sees his relation to Jermyn; Esther sees in Lady Transome a person she may come to resemble. But what is seen impresses us as relations that are virtual rather than real. The reader, like Eliot's characters, sees a sign of relation and its referent, but does not see a further actual relation that realizes the connection between the two. In Eliot's world relations are more virtual than actual: they are glimpsed or named, hypothesized rather than substantiated. And this is true of relation in two senses: as connection among persons and events and as narrative reason. Like relation, action and meaning in Eliot are evanescent glimpses, hypotheses whose substantiation seems now imminent, now receding. This virtuality of action and meaning is emblematized in Eliot's way of presenting the self as also a curiously virtual rather than actual nature or identity. She wonders how the self establishes its characteristics and its meanings: Is it through deeds, through feelings, through externalizing utterances and expressions, through identity with others? And she asks, in what way is the self identical with others? Certainly not through its acts, since, in general, acts in Eliot are no more determinately meaningful than those we have described. In Eliot, the self is (at the very least) double, and it is always anxiously constrained from an imagined full utterance: if it expresses itself in sympathy, it cannot express itself in action; if it commits its meaning to action, it loses the meaning of its feelings. As an internalized arena of reflection, the self repeats the condition of action and meaning as Eliot usually presents them: as a continuous interweaving of significance and arbitrariness, a paradoxical indeterminate or virtual determination.

The self in Eliot is "plausible"—and "normative"—because it is an unclear, unresolved problematic. We can see this in Chapter 49, in Esther's interview with Harold just before she leaves Transome Court. Esther wants to know if the public meeting has rescued Felix; but she must restrain her curiosity, since her love for Felix in effect injures Harold. She feels herself very different from Harold, so different that he repels her. Yet *is* she, the Transome heir, different from Harold? And is *he* so different from Felix, especially since he has just done more practical good for Felix than Felix has in fact yet done for anyone? Does action define the differences between the two selves meeting each other? Are Esther and Harold not identical in their inner potential for action and feeling, for bearing good and bad fruit? Why then is each self—as an arena of sympathy and of anxious restraint of sympathy, of simultaneously determined and indeterminate character— not identical with the other but rather its antagonist?[6] The questions are not to be resolved.

As Esther sat . . . along with the empty chair which suggested the coming presence, the expectation of his be-

seeching homage brought with it an impatience and re-
pugnance which she had never felt before. . . . Harold
appeared.

He had recovered his self-possession since his interview with his mother. . . . He had been occupied with
resolute thoughts, determining to do what he knew that
perfect honour demanded, let it cost him what it would.
. . . It is true he had a glimpse . . . of reward; but it was
not less true that he would have acted as he did without
that hope or glimpse. It was the most serious moment in
Harold Transome's life: for the first time the iron had en-
tered into his soul, and he felt the hard pressure of our
common lot, the yoke of that mighty resistless destiny
laid upon us by the acts of other men as well as our own.

When Esther looked at him she relented, and felt
ashamed of her gratuitous impatience. She saw that his
mind was in some way burdened. But then immediately
sprang up the dread that he had to say something hopeless about Felix.

They shook hands in silence, Esther looking at him
with anxious surprise. He released her hand, but it did
not occur to her to sit down, and they both continued
standing on the hearth.

This scene epitomizes George Eliot's sense of plot, her
curious way of featuring act and of internalizing action in the
self. The silence and constraint in which both figures remain
standing typifies how George Eliot presents action and self as
at best the stress of a potential—a possibility or virtuality of
meaning or realization rather than a definite, externalized
release or "rescuing" fulfillment of them. Moreover, the act
"realized" is described as a hard pressuring yoke: an act,
then, is scarcely more valuable or creative than an accident.
Action also seems to obstruct the sympathetic identification
of one self with another, for Esther and Harold can be intimate only in a speechless and motionless state of restraint. In
the preceding passage it is action and definition of self—
exteriorization of self through action—that is being held at

bay as a threat. Consequently, in silence and stillness, in internality, there is perhaps as much meaning, and more, as in externalizing articulation and motion.

The difficulty this virtuality and internality poses for meaning, for any narrative reasoning that does not check meaning's confident motions, may be exemplified by a comparison of the final states of Mrs. Transome and Felix. The two characters are supposedly different, since we can call the first a failure, the second a success. Yet this difference is indeed nominal—for what meaning can we assign it? Why is Felix happier in *his* hap than Mrs. Transome in hers? Mrs. Transome's last punishment is the lonely and monotonous existence that finds no outlet in action. Her life is ultimately no more significant than a prank, an arbitrary purposeless happening. The older woman's entrapment "afflicts Esther to horror." Surely a significantly active life would rescue Mrs. Transome from despair. Yet the wisdom of the novel, identified with Felix's speeches, is to accept this horror as identical with the fruitful order of things. If Eliot's characters believe that they can enact their lives and rescue them from indeterminacy of meaning and of fulfillment according to plots they willfully fashion and execute, their stories show that this belief must be modified or given up by even the best of them. The plotting motion of consciousness is an arbitrary actor and signifier; its externalizations meet an arbitrary fate and do not consummate perspectives and meanings. Felix understands this, and knows that, in spite of his virtue, his future will be brought to birth as an immobilization rather like Mrs. Transome's. So his plan and plots do *not* feature acts, only the constraint and doubtfulness of acts. They also feature the virtuality rather than the realization or consummation of meaning. He will do work that is "small" and "close at hand." He tells Esther:

> As to just the amount of result [a man] may see from his particular work—that's a tremendous uncertainty. I put effects at their minimum, but I'd rather have the minimum of effect, if it's of the sort I care for. . . .

Where great things can't happen, I care for very small things, such as will never be known beyond a few garrets and workshops.

So much for the result of action. Is the cause not the same as the result? The initiation of action, whether it be the riot, the rescue, Esther's resignation, or Felix's work, is also "a tremendous uncertainty"—in its own way an accident or coincidence. Among the small things close at hand is another uncertainty, the self. Felix's garrets and workshops, like the silent room in which Esther and Harold speechlessly face each other, are symbols of the interior space of the self, an at once damnable and blessed uncertainty for Eliot similar to that of action. The presentation of life as such uncertainty is the final fruit of Eliot's attempt to naturalize coincidence and to put the action "inside"—her attempt to rescue life from meaninglessness by featuring act and her undoing of the rescue simultaneously by featuring the reality of arbitrariness and indeterminacy. Barthes tells us that the novelistic real is not operable, cannot be put into practice; *Felix Holt the Radical* leaves us wondering whether practice is operable or other than arbitrarily significant within the real itself.

But we must turn back now to Dickens, for what George Eliot presents as reality and what she makes of action and its creative rescuing agency is shaped by her antagonism to his rendition of life and to his plotting of life's form. Dickens does *not* naturalize coincidence in his story; he points up strikingly grotesque accidental interrelations in order to stress the literal nature of coincidence because for him this will make it possible to feature action and rescue. For Dickens, coincidence simply does not threaten action, plausibility, or meaning. But what is especially coincidental in Dickens? In his kind of story, coincidence (however it may appear in our summary), has less to do with action, with accidental events, than with character. Dickens's sense of plot relies upon a notion that small groups of separate characters or persons are somehow all the same character or person. Dickens sees character as an aspect of literal coincidence; and his characters themselves, in shock and wonder, recognize the ways in which they are practically each other.

To speak of coincidence in Dickens is thus to speak of exact agreements among events or persons rather than, as in Eliot, of accidental agreements. Where there are exact agreements we feel the presence of meaning—a realizing rather than a virtualizing of significance. Dickens uses the coinciding of identity to represent movement towards the realization of meaning in the lives of his characters. We may consider the apparently individuated or differentiated character of Esther Summerson in order to see how her differences from others break down. In a chapter prior to those summarized, Lady Dedlock searches out Jo, so that he will show her her former lover's grave. In doing this she disguises herself as her maid Hortense. Tulkinghorn sees her in this disguise and to make sure he has seen rightly, once she is discharged, he pays Hortense to undergo a meeting with Jo. Jo identifies Hortense as the lady he showed the grave to. Then Hortense speaks and shows Jo her hand, and Jo has to admit she is different. Yet he remains rather obstinate about his impression: "It is her and it ain't her," he says.

A little later he falls sick. Under Tulkinghorn's direction, Bucket has been moving Jo out of London; in a delirium caused by disease Jo has wound up at the brickmakers' cottages in St. Albans. Esther hears of this, and she and her maid, Charley, go to help him. On the way Esther feels something uncanny: "I had for a moment an undefinable impression of myself as being something different from what I then was." In Jo her feeling finds an immediate response:

> The boy staggered up instantly, and stared at me with a remarkable expression of surprise and terror.
> "The lady there. She's come to get me to go along with her to the berryin ground. I won't go to the berryin ground. I don't like the name on it. She might go a-berryin me." His shivering came on again, and as he leaned against the wall, he shook the hovel.

"He has been talking off and on about such like, all day, ma'am," said Jenny the brickmaker's wife softly. "Why, how you stare! This is *my* lady, Jo."

"Is it?" returned the boy. . . . "She looks to me the t'other one. It ain't the bonnet, nor yet it ain't the gownd, but she looks to me the t'other one."

Jo goes on to ask Charley, "Ain't the lady the t'other lady?" And he then exclaims: "If she ain't the t'other one, she ain't the forenner. Is there *three* of 'em then?" Intentionally or not, Esther has already partly answered Jo's question by feeling that she is both herself—and a different being.

Esther is in fact at least "three." When she sees her mother's body, she is asking in her own way, "Ain't the lady the t'other lady?" "I saw before me, lying on the step," she insists, "the mother of the dead child." She means the brickmaker's wife, whose dead baby she had covered with the significant handkerchief. But these words suit Lady Dedlock as well, for part of her tragedy had been the belief that her child died at birth. And in a very damaging way Esther has taken to heart her godmother's conviction that she would have been better off unborn. Esther lives as a kind of self-repressing spectre, as if she had survived the end of her own life. So Esther does discover the mother of the dead child (herself) at the end of the chase. And the uncanny interidentity of Lady Dedlock, Hortense, and Esther extends itself: Esther is also like Jo, the diseased orphan, and like Guster, the Snagsby's hysterical orphan maid. It is arguable that there is a similar interidentity for each of the characters in *Bleak House*.

This literalizing of coincidental identity in Dickens means that Dickens plots in order *not* to "put all the action" inside. If the Dickens characters feel the need to resolve conflicts within themselves, they discover—as the reader discovers—that the conflicts are not imponderable and inexpressible but defined in others who are outward personifications of the conflicts they feel within. For Dickens individuation is in effect illusory, and thus the only way for persons to resolve conflicts among the "others" who are simultaneously themselves is through an action that represents in a literal external event—a rescue event—any one individual's attempt to rescue his life from a predicament. If this predicament is, for example, that the character cannot establish his purposes, cannot mean in life what he intends fully to mean, then the rescue can effect this meaning; for Dickens insists that action, what we do, is not imponderable, not merely arbitrary naming but is the field in which we can bring arbitrariness to an end, in which we can clarify and actualize meaning, connecting signs with referents and consummating perspectives. Whereas in reaction to Dickens Eliot ends by stressing the problematic nature of identity and action, Dickens begins with this problematic and ends with at least half of it resolved. For Dickens sees his characters as an arbitrary metonymic chain, whose links come to accept—without any Eliotic contradiction or qualification—their purely nominal differences (differences that make no difference) in exchange for the sake of making a clear and definite difference for each other on the level of action. Dickens's responsibility to the real is manifested in his belief that reality is preeminently an urgent and practicable desire for a liberation from arbitrariness and indefiniteness of action, from doing's entanglement with undoing.

Is this object of Dickens's representation less plausible or verisimilar than the indeterminacy that Eliot represents? The rescue is Dickens's version of the romance quest, which once had its basis in experience and which Dickens attempts to return to the same basis.[7] He wants to make it appear probable that what we ordinarily do or what we can do has undeniable and operable creative efficacy. Whether or not we agree that he succeeds in making this plausible, we must remember that if the plots of Dickens's delegated agents, his characters, had no fulfilling or defining issue as action, chaos and despair would reign in their world. The prevailing sense of life in

Bleak House is of a waking nightmare described by Esther during her disfiguring illness: "Strung together somewhere in great black space, there was a flaming necklace, or ring, or starry circle of some kind, of which *I* was one of the beads! . . . It was . . . inexplicable agony to be part of the dreadful thing." The possibility of plot, of creatively willful and purposeful action, is for Dickens and his characters the hope of rescue and release from this circle of pain. The hope of rescue and release is not confined, as we might say it is in Eliot, to making the dreadful thing explicable by means of defining articulations that come and go or remain virtual; the release here is tied to the possibility of an action that will explain the thing—and that will realize the explanation by consummating it as a clear, enacted rescue from what is dreadful.

How one self acts out the rescue from the circle of pain of another self with which it coincides is made possible in part by the fact that the self is situated in time, which for Dickens does not close down opportunity but continually renews it. If a Dickensian character has missed an opportunity to solve a predicament for himself in *his* time, the crucial time returns in the present predicament of a double. Lady Dedlock's earlier maid, Rosa, is a double of her mistress in her youth, especially since Rosa, in loving the industrialist's son, Watt, repeats the dilemma between spontaneous love and class distinctions that victimized Lady Dedlock. Lady Dedlock helps Rosa overcome those distinctions, thereby contributing to her own self-redeeming rescue. Similarly, we can assume that both Richard Carstone and Captain George duplicate the self-dislike and indolence of Hawdon in his last years, when he went by the name of Nemo. But although Richard sinks along with Nemo, we are made to feel that something of both is saved in the rescue of George by Mrs. Bagnet. Doubles of the past selves of unhappy characters suffering from some choice made or not made in an earlier time can thus be rescued from their past choices by the help of those whose present problems duplicate the past's. In George Eliot's "little

world of man or woman"[8] the time of significant opportunity
does not return with the same clearly discernible possibility
of rescuing transformation.

But how can we speak of successful and creative rescue-
acts in the face of the example of Lady Dedlock's loss and
death? In answer we can say that even the apparently unsuccessful rescue attempt shows how the actions of men and
women speak a definitive truth or meaning about themselves
and their inner feelings. Attempting to evade her rescuers,
Lady Dedlock's evasion itself spells out what the rescue can
accomplish: it makes the dynamic structure of social reality
fully and unequivocally visible; it brings some aspect of ultimate truth and interrelation into sight. Hence the rescue-act
is meaningful—it constitutes meaning as well as consummates it; it is not only a saving of persons but a rescue of truth
from illusions and obscurities. For example, Lady Dedlock's
assumed proletariat disguise acts out a truth concerning social relations and morality: worn by an aristocrat, the work-
er's costume has the effect of showing how little sexual "sin"
weighs in contrast to the general human exploitation on
which privileged social order is founded.[9] The rescue and the
sense of plot that imitates the rescue transform life's potential
or secret relationships and values into clarified and openly
enacted and acknowledged ones. This revelation of relations
and their meaning would not come about otherwise: indeed
many of the "worst" characters in *Bleak House* would rather
not share their identities with others, would rather evasively
speculate on or "feel" truth than enact it, but we can see in
Skimpole how little this kind of evasion triumphs or counts!

Unsuccessful in delivering Lady Dedlock from death, the
rescue attempt and action succeeds nevertheless in bringing
into definitive light the complex truth of the characters' relations. And at the same time there is a way in which Lady
Dedlock rescues herself. Dying of terror and remorse, she
also fulfills her life as she wants to fulfill it. She ends by uttering as action, without arbitrariness, her love for Hawdon.
Exactly equating her self with her passion, she uses action to

establish what she wants definitively to mean to herself and the world. Thus her end is not tragic as was the previous internalization of her passion. And personal issues aside, if only because of the challenge to society's repressions made by the release of Lady Dedlock's passion, her act and even her death are creative. They illustrate both the torture of repression by which society partly functions and the ultimate victory, in spite of the torture, of what is repressed.

In contrast, it is interesting to note how George Eliot tends to equate the externalizing of intense passion with destruction: in *Felix Holt the Radical* Mrs. Transome's old passion for Jermyn is a prototype of the novel's riot. In the Dickensian version of enacted passion, all personal intensities of feeling work their way purposefully and creatively into external form; they are also not potential or virtual, not closed within the silent inexpressible nature of self. What one character may be prevented from acting out, another just like him will succeed in acting out; in effect this makes both characters active agents. And Dickens even countenances the creativity of violent deeds for the truth and feeling that violence rescues from repression or inhibition. For example, the hatred for Tulkinghorn that Lady Dedlock suppresses and that Esther would refuse to recognize in herself must issue as a force and an act in their story. Hortense has no right to eliminate Tulkinghorn, yet his murder is—in relation to the characters for whom Hortense doubles—creative by virtue of its translation of their righteous hatred into an event. In the end, Lady Dedlock's death acts out her love for Hawdon, her defeat of her enemy, and the social truth of her life. Can we possibly feel this as a loss, as a defeat of the rescue? Whereas Felix Holt is only nominally rescued, Lady Dedlock rescues her own life from its nominal status, unshakeably differentiating its reality from its appearance.

On the surface, then, a comparison of our summaries seems to show Felix saved and Lady Dedlock lost and Eliot's story less accidental and coincidental than that of Dickens, but in fact the opposite is true because Dickens's plotting does not undermine action. To do so would be for Dickens a humbling of his form. It is not pride, however, that makes Dickens refuse this humbling. Dickens synonymizes rescue, plot, and labor: the rescue of life's meaning from arbitrariness and indeterminacy is the novelist's work, and it is also apparently Dickens's way of seeing all work. We have already noted George Eliot's own attention to a possible identification of rescue, plot, and labor by considering the efficacy of action through Felix's dedication to the work of small garrets and workshops. In Esther Summerson's nightmare vision of the circle of pain, the agony results as much from the way work in the nightmare counts for nothing—rescues no fruit from chaos—as from the way Esther feels herself to be three separate identities:

> While I was very ill, the way in which . . . divisions of time became confused with one another, distressed my mind exceedingly. At once a child, an elder girl, and the little woman I had been so happy as, I was not only oppressed by cares and difficulties adapted to each station, but by the great perplexity of endlessly trying to reconcile them.
>
> In my disorder—it seemed one long night, but I believe there were both nights and days in it— . . . I labored up colossal staircases, ever striving to reach the top, and ever turned, as I have seen a worm in a garden path, by some obstruction, and laboring again. I knew perfectly at intervals, and I think vaguely at most times, that I was in my bed; . . . yet I would find myself complaining "O more of these never-ending stairs, Charley—more and more—piled up to the sky, I think!" and laboring on again.

The rescue action reconciles the apparently differing selves; the rescue is the labor that breaks down factitious differences and overcomes obstructions to the realization of life as unqualifiedly coherent form. Esther's persistence in labor shows a sense of plot like Dickens's own, working on to resolve obstructions and to enact the formative and definite release of what is obstructed. The dignity and necessity of the attempt is to be measured by the intense desire for reconciliation and by the strong resistance that it meets: we note "the great perplexity of endlessly trying to reconcile" the large disparities of experience as well as its minute details. For Dickens, labor is this attempt at reconciliation—and its successful achievement. To point up his characters' urgent dedication to plot as the featuring of act and to feature enacted plot in life as the labor that rescues life's meaning from indeterminacy (and even its minutiae from insignificance), Dickens reproduces Esther's nightmare staircases during Mrs. Bagnet's rescue of George in Chapter 50. Mrs. Bagnet is bringing George's mother to London by coach, and Dickens describes the landscape through which the coach passes:

> Railroads shall soon traverse all this country, and with a rattle and a glare the engine and train shall shoot like a meteor over the wide night-landscape, turning the moon paler. . . . Preparations are afoot, measurements are made, ground is staked out. Bridges are begun, and their not yet united piers desolately look at one another over roads and streams, like brick and mortar couples with an obstacle to their union; fragments of embankments are thrown up, and left as precipices with torrents of carts and barrows tumbling over them; tripods of tall poles appear on hilltops, where there are rumours of tunnels; everything looks chaotic, and abandoned in full hopelessness.

This landscape repeats the landscape of Esther's dream. But the work being done here looks chaotic only because it is interrupted. It urgently needs completion. The rescue is labor that finally does make the staircases lead somewhere. In the six chapters of *Bleak House* that we have summarized, labor is not only the attempt to rescue Lady Dedlock and George; it is also the baronet's willed recovery of his lost speech, the attempt to allay Guster's fears, and Esther's struggle against the return of the dissociated sensations of her disease. For Dickens, each of these struggles is heroic, since each opposes a disease and paralysis that is communal as well as personal. The social and historical community represented in *Bleak House* is founded on deliberate dissociations. It is committed to a collective self-deceiving and self-punishing evasion of the need to reconcile the disparities and details of experience. In the labor of their rescues Dickens's actors bring to birth a new vision and enactment of community. Plot dramatized as a rescue action by Dickens represents the full humanization of work: a purposive and practicable exertion to liberate, renew, and make significant the total life of its agents.

How interesting it is that this rescue work is characteristically commented upon by modern criticism in terms that show Eliot's and not Dickens's sense of plot in the ascendant. J. Hillis Miller says that in *Bleak House* "there is glimpsed the possibility of a voluntary action which constitutes the world as an order." In fact it is not glimpsed; it is fully and emphatically embodied in "the rescue." But with a perspective that is understandable as an emanation of Eliot's sense of plot revising that of Dickens, Miller goes on to say that the crucial "voluntary action" in *Bleak House* is

> not machinery, not the actual doing or making of anything. Esther's creation of a small area of order and significance around her is primarily a spiritual act. The human will must act negatively rather than coercively and positively. . . . Esther's success comes from the fact that she *submits* to the human condition which she so vividly imagines in her delirious dream.[10]

We would certainly agree to this if Miller were writing about Esther Lyon; but such commentary in regard to Esther Summerson and to the sense of plot that creates her is simply not the truth.

Significantly the critic not only denies the truth but denies the moral dimension of the Dickensian sense of plot. Dickens tells us through the rescue that submission to the unspeaka-

ble circle of pain is immoral: Esther's worst self is the submissive, self-tormenting one. We need to consider, at least more
explicitly than we have so far, the bearing of each writer's
sense of plot on the writer's ideas about moral conduct. Narrative intellectual reason merges imperceptibly but undeniably with moral reasoning, with ethical generalizations about
action. Clearly in *Nicholas Nickleby* Dickens uses plot not only
as a rescue of meaning but as an encouragement to the moral
dimension in relational thought. In speaking of the interrelations of plot, labor, and the rescue, we have been treating the
relation of plot to representations of ideal conduct as well as
of meaningfulness. The labor that reconciles contradictory
perspectives in experience is for Dickens a model of the activity that makes us good as well as happy.

The rightness or goodness of conduct that is underwritten
by George Eliot's storytelling is more difficult to formulate.
We see in Esther Lyon and Felix a desire for reconciliations of
the Dickensian kind, and this desire appears as a moral guide
to conduct; but Eliot suggests it is also good that this desire be
checked. For if it is not checked, there is the chance that
Esther Lyon will reconcile her perspectives with Lady Transome's by an uttering and enacting of passion—even if it is
asocial in tendency or intensity—in the way Esther Summerson reconciles her internal conflicts by acting out her vio-
lences of feeling through her mother and Hortense. Perhaps
for Eliot what is most right for conduct, in a way that directly
complements her sense of plot, is a form of passivity or quiescence resulting from a vigilant skepticism towards the self's
plots, towards their motives and ends, towards their possible
manipulations of life and intrusions upon the lives of others.
The scene in the library epitomizes the restraint of conduct as
a good of conduct: the good of conduct is an intense and passionate inward feeling rather than an overt passionate doing.
In its moral dimension the Dickensian rescue plot becomes in
Eliot a rescue-passion, an ideal of conduct understood as a
particular kind of intense but quiescent feeling rather than a
rescue-act.

Nevertheless, at the end of her career George Eliot, in a wonderfully curious artistic reversal, published *Daniel Deronda*, a novel whose "male" half at least—Deronda's story— is pervaded by memories of a Dickensian sense of plot, by the rescue action. Some attention to *Daniel Deronda*'s plot, then, is especially in order in an examination of Eliot's relation to Dickens. It is my belief that what induced Eliot to take up the structure of the plot that she had deliberately subverted was the moral dimension she wanted finally to give to "the rescue." Now for Dickens and Eliot the moral value as well as the truth of "the rescue" has a relation to the "conduct" of passion—especially of sexual passion—and also to their sense of the possibilities of personal development and maturation. If we briefly examine these subjects in each of these novelists, we can more clearly grasp Eliot's *moral* revision of the Dickensian rescue.

In *Bleak House* Dickens is concerned to show that plot is not only synonymous with purposeful, willed labor and action but with passion as well. For Dickens thinks that what is done purposefully, even the rescue itself, will be ineffectual and sterile or at the very least weighted down with melancholy if it is not reconciled with passion. If Esther, for example, were to "submit" to her nightmare, she would marry Jarndyce and not Woodcourt; she would thus divorce passion from her activity. This would be a disaster for her, a masochistic evasion of her desire, a self-punishment of the very kind that her upbringing and the normative way of life in *Bleak House* have imposed on her. Jarndyce's moral heroism is that he refuses to allow her to submit to his desire rather than to her own, for he rescues Esther from the self-deprecating and inhibiting evasion of her passion for Woodcourt. Yet for poor Jarndyce this rescue demands that he plot against his own passion. And Dickens is unhappy with this, for he would like to show that the rescue action is compatible with passion, that the passion *for* creative action generally is as strong as, indeed even stronger than, sexual passion and yet can be a perfect ally of it. Paradoxical as it is to speak of passion as action, Dickens allies Bucket, Esther, and Wood-court in the quest for Lady Dedlock in order to emblematize in their conduct a reconciliation of passion with purposive moral will and plotting work. Bucket himself is an emblem of work, of rescuing action, married to passion: Dickens goes out of his way to imagine him in bed with his spouse;[11] indeed it is Mrs. Bucket who captures Hortense for the police. Connected with Bucket, Esther stands for the need of child for parent, a no less importunate passion than the sexual one. And of course Woodcourt, who rescues others from disease and even shipwreck, whose work is a vocation of passion and whose love for Esther is also a sexual passion, is the type of actor whose conduct Dickens values as most moral.

The featuring of the rescue action in Dickens expresses the author's desire to wed external purposive deeds and work with passionate feeling, because in fact he fears such a wedding may be impossible. Dickens is finally not overcome by his fear, but if we look back to *David Copperfield*, the novel just preceding *Bleak House*, we can see him debating the possibility or impossibility of this wedding, of this consummation of passion in a conduct that can be called moral. Any intensity of desire, sexual desire's intensity especially, has—as David says of one of Rosa Dartle's expressions of passion—"something fearful in the reality of it." Its intensity is fearful, but even more fearful is its power both to immobilize the man or woman who feels it and to "put all the action inside," that is, to separate feeling from fulfilling utterance and conduct. This immobilization is the very opposite of what the rescue stands for. David's friend Steerforth, whose name promises a creative, active, outward venturing, is undone by his relations with Rosa and Emily; David similarly is immobilized first by his love for his mother and then by a transfer of that love to Dora. David's passion for Dora parallels Steerforth's for Emily; like Steerforth's it is not creatively wedded with active labor. Because it cannot bear fruit in the world, it can rescue nothing positive from meaninglessness and sterility; it has no value for conduct.

For the hero of *David Copperfield* the active labor that is a moral rescue of passion from its immobilizing potential is finally synonymous with storytelling. Released from both his mother and Dora, David begins to be a novelist, and he marries Agnes; but we must not assume that his success as a writer and husband represents his frequently sought "disciplining" of his heart's passion—instead the marriage and the novel-writing represent the unrestrained union of passion with creative externalization, with work that is an ideal of conduct. And it is not only a matter of creative work but also of personal development or maturation; for Dickens the advent of maturity and the achievement of fruitful work go hand in hand. In *David Copperfield* to be trapped in the stasis of passion is to be trapped in childhood—or in a purely subjective world—and to be cut off from growth; Dickens makes his hero a storyteller in the end to show how the plotting motion of consciousness and the featuring of act are the release from the trap. We see this rescuing agency of story in David's first attempt to move beyond his attachment to his mother, when he loses her to Murdstone. Alone at school, "shut out and alienated" from home, David turns to the novels and storybooks left him by his father, and finds relief from his passionate obsession with his mother. This happens when, shut out again, David wins a place among Steerforth and the boys at school by retelling them the stories of his favorite novels. By meditating on the action of the seventeenth- and eighteenth-century plots, David keeps alive his "hope of something beyond that place and time." The hope of action stimulates action itself, so that David rescues himself from the state of being only a spectator of the heroisms and deeds of others and becomes the hero and enactor of his own life. Thus by the agency of what, for Dickens, story inevitably features or ought to feature—purposive action in alliance with intensity of passion—David is rescued from static fixation and the passivity of passion into willed development and active adulthood. We may assume that the stories he writes have similar effects on those who read them, transforming their conduct by rousing them to further growth and relationship.

George Eliot knows as well as Dickens the fearful nature of passion; Mrs. Transome's desire for Jermyn usurped all other realities, blinded her to consequences, to life's inevitable developments and transformations. Even Esther's fosterfather, the sober minister Rufus, has been blinded by passion—indeed has been driven by it to a kind of insanity. In the first stage of his love for Esther's mother, Rufus enters "a spiritual convulsion. . . . These mad wishes [to become Annette's lover and husband] were irreconcilable with that conception of the world which made his faith." But irreconcilable or not, for four years Lyon gives up his vocation for this woman. Eliot admits that the passion satisfies him the way his purposeful moral work in the world should have satisfied him. Suspended in obsessed passivity, turned in upon himself and Annette, Lyon cannot recover the goal of his work, cannot rescue himself from immobility, until the woman dies. What then, is the possibility for conduct, Eliot wonders, of wedding passion to personal development or to creative and active labor? In *Felix Holt the Radical* the union of Esther and Felix represents the tenuous hope that passion will find for itself a plot and an action that transcend stasis and an exclusively sexual goal. But it is as if by the time of *Daniel Deronda* Eliot's hope for something far more than a tenuous wedding of passion and act has grown beyond the possibility of constraint. Apparently it has also grown beyond the need to oppose Dickens by emphasizing internality and by making the rescue a matter of minimal effects and of nominal or imponderable meanings. In no other novel, except perhaps *The Mill on the Floss*, does George Eliot, on the surface at least, allow the rescue plot a fuller reign or a more optimistic bearing than in *Daniel Deronda*.

The results of this return to the rescue plot have always caused justifiable complaints by readers who are used to George Eliot's more characteristic sense of probability and story. At the same time, readers who share Dickens's sense of plot may also justifiably object to the plot of *Daniel Deronda*. For, after all, George Eliot cannot essentially reverse her way of seeing the world or story. Whatever needs propel her back to Dickens, she uses the rescue action intended by Dickens to show the possible reconciliation of action, work, or vocation with passion in a way that ultimately underlines passivity. The rescue action *happens* in *Daniel Deronda*, but it happens always at the instigation of some external, outside agency; it is as if no one of the actors *in* the novel can significantly initiate rescue, but can only be rescued.

We see how this is with Gwendolen Harleth, who when her self-assurance is shattered and when the narrowness of her life is exposed cannot initiate or enact anything for herself or for others. Like Lady Transome and Felix, she faces a constraint whose hope lies in an "habitual feeling of rescue," a feeling rather than an act; the rescue itself is moral sympathy, not a moral deed:

> She was experiencing some of that peaceful melancholy which comes from the renunciation of demands for self, and from taking the ordinary good of existence, and especially kindness, even from a dog, as a gift above expectation. Does one who has been all but lost in a pit of darkness complain of the sweet air and the daylight? There is a way of looking at our life daily as an escape, and taking the quiet return of morn and evening—still more the star-like outglowing of some pure fellow-feeling, some generous impulse breaking our inward darkness—as a salvation that reconciles us to hardship. Those who have self-knowledge prompting such self-accusation as Hamlet's can understand this habitual feeling of rescue.

Gwendolen owes this feeling to Deronda. As for Deronda, actively rescuing others is such a moral habit to him early in the novel that the reader feels Eliot has given herself to a thoughtless, mechanical employment of Dickensian event. But Deronda's story significantly becomes most powerful and convincing when he discovers he is a Jew—a moment in which he finally surrenders the initiatory and willed conduct of action, in which he himself is passive and is passively rescued. In an almost credible way the combined force of English society and the willpower of his extraordinary mother (in her rebelliousness and temper she bears a resemblance to Gwendolen) cannot stand in the way of Daniel's being called to his heritage. Deronda has been traveling unaware and without conscious direction since the dawn of his reflective thought straight towards the fulfillment of his Zionist grandfather's plans for him.

But this is a way of saying that the purposefully plotting Daniel is not plotting or enacting his own rescue or that of others at all: the knight-errant, perpetually rescuing others in distress, finds his activity only the mask of an essential passivity, indeed of a suffering passion. And although his family, his history, his people, and his vocation come to meet Daniel without his stirring, George Eliot presents this passivity as valuably moral. Daniel's conscience, certainly, is intensely active, and his spiritual activity makes him ready to accept the heritage he discovers. But the externalization of this activity comes to George Eliot's hero easily—relatively easily, at least, in comparison with the more plausible difficulty that Gwendolen's conscience meets in attempting to find an appropriate outward and practicable form of expression. And we need not refer only to Gwendolen to suggest that Deronda's rescue is a dramatizing of passivity: the facts of the hero's vocation also feature the conduct of passivity when compared with the facts of the vocation of Klesmer, the German musician. From what Klesmer tells Gwendolen about the extraordinary labor of his work, we can believe George Eliot when she says he embodies "that fervour of creative work and theoretic belief which pierces the whole future of a life with the light of congruous, devoted purpose." In Klesmer's vocation there *is* a union of creative, willed action with passion. But it is the relatively passive Daniel who is the novel's hero and moral center, not Klesmer.

In *Daniel Deronda*, the habitual feeling of rescue is a matrix of conduct that is finally identical with passionate family feeling. Although Mordecai Cohen insists that "the sons of Judah have to choose that God may again choose them [and that the] divine principle of our race is action, choice, resolved memory," familial passion seems to obviate choice or action. When Deronda is rescued by his heritage, he seems released from the needs to choose or to act. The feeling of kinship, a familial state of being, takes precedence over "the rescue" understood as an action determining personal and collective development. The wedding of Deronda and Mordecai's sister is also a wedding of Deronda and Mordecai, a union intended by Eliot to feature passion's alliance with action, but which in effect emphasizes a warmth of emotion, a feeling of always *being* rescued that makes action unnecessary. In contrast, in Dickens no character can be rescued without assertively and actively *doing* something for "the others," without laboring for the "other" no less than feeling for him.

Having "put all the action inside," in *Daniel Deronda* George Eliot could not really go back on herself. Since initially she had been able to communicate her understanding of life only by revising and "naturalizing" Dickensian story, her use of rescuing action in *Daniel Deronda* does not achieve the same wedding of forces that Dickens had used it to represent. Gwendolen has the feeling of rescue *when she submits to passivity*; Deronda does not develop or mature through a rescue he enacts for himself and others—his development comes as a gift in the chest willed to him by his grandfather, who is an active agent virtually *outside* the story. And although David Copperfield's nourishing stories also come to him from a source outside the novel, his way of conducting the rescue of others through the willed narrative motions of consciousness is not reproduced in the ending of Deronda's history. Thus, as an ideal of moral conduct, the outcome of the attempt to wed passion and action by means of the rescue plot is, in Eliot, an ultimate featuring of quiescence. A morality of passivity emerges out of both Gwendolen's and Daniel's story: it

is an ethic derived from a kind of chastening of sexual passion, and it takes for its model more the patient suffering of
eros than the union of that passion with active will. Along
this line, the family passion itself is a passion of quiet receptivity.

As a way of conduct this quiet receptivity in the face of the
complex virtualities of life has one other significant dimension. Given Eliot's natural sense of plot, why did she bother
to return at all, even if only in appearance, to a sense of plot
anterior to her own? D. H. Lawrence again gives us a possible
clue by reminding us in *Fantasia of the Unconscious* that "the
great sex goal . . . always cries for the something beyond:
for . . . the man disappearing ahead into the distance of futu-
rity, that which his purpose stands for, the future."[12] I have
already said that the rescue plot in *Daniel Deronda* belongs to
the "male" half of the novel; and this fact, coupled with
Lawrence's remark, is perhaps most significant. The Dickensian rescuing action may have seemed to Eliot a peculiarly
male production or fantasy of "the beyond"; she turns to this
male structure of story both to honor it and to place it
critically within a female narrative perspective and moral
sense. Indeed if we reflect on the contrasting status of action
in Austen and Scott and on the way the present study implicitly shows that an impulse against plot and story is the
province of great female writers (Stein and Woolf along with
Eliot)—or of a male imagination attempting to represent a
specifically female consciousness, as with Joyce's Molly—we
see that Eliot is reviving the Dickensian rescue story for the
sake of advancing a female narrative sense and of rebuking
the male's identification of "beyond" or of personal development with action. For the truth and for its bearing on
conduct, the female sense of plot values, in the face of the
Dickensian male assurances about action and its significance,
the indeterminacy of allegedly liberating deeds, the unresolved problematic of self and other and of meaning; and although the female sense in *Daniel Deronda*, like the male
sense in Dickens, is concerned that sexual and cultural goals

not be at odds and not stultify maturity, it sees reconciliation of the cultural-sexual conflict emblematized in the familial *passion*. As Eliot sees this passion, it is a quiescent, submissive yielding to experience, to a beyond out of which "the rescue" can come from an agency that transcends will. Thus in the end it may be a female sense of plot in Eliot that sees the necessary redemption of men like Deronda and of plots like Dickens's in the intellectual and moral value of indeterminate meaning, of passive and nonexternalized states of feeling, and of inhibited action.*

* I cannot claim without qualification that George Eliot's assertion of the value of the inhibition of action originates in a specifically female sense of plot. For we have seen Poe challenge Dickensian story in a way that complements Eliot's address to action. In fact if we forget Cooper's place in American literature, or if we declare Cooper's sense of plot to be merely parasitic in relation to Scott's, then we can say that Poe's assertion of the inhibition of action as a value for truth (*pace* conduct) comes from an American sense of plot equivalent to Eliot's female sense. This seems to make nonsense of the possibility of distinguishing sexual differences in senses of plot. Yet it is true that nineteenth-century American novelists and English female novelists write in the shadow of Scott's and Dickens's virtual hegemony of narrative form, in the shadow hence of a representation of action that is the product and possession of males. Any American novelist of the period, male or female, struggling against the influence of Scott and Dickens might well be understood to be rebelling against a limited or narrow, because exclusively male, shaping of experience into form.

❦ FIVE ❧

The Divine Inert: Melville

What [Shelley's] Prometheus does is not a doing but an arrest. . . . The equivalent of faith in Shelley is gnosis which is an act of vision and consciousness, and which is therefore not an act . . . nor a pseudo-act, nor a parody-act, but a withdrawal from action.
—Northrop Frye, *A Study of English Romanticism*

It is human phenomenology which is re-inherited, allowed in, once plot is kissed out.
—Charles Olson, "Introduction to Robert Creeley"

In the American novel of the last century, distrust of narrative reason—and distrust of the Dickensian morality of action—had its greatest exponents in Hawthorne and Melville. Since we will consider Hawthorne in the chapter on James, our interest lies now with Melville. Melville uses narrative reason to check its power (to check it with not only wary distrust but at times with comic exuberance) in the name of a principle and force called the Divine Inert. In so doing he exemplifies the moral dimension always imminent in the sense of plot and in the perspectival functions of story. In writing a narrative whose meaning is bound up with the idea of an inertial divinity, Melville communicates the Divine Inert as a principle governing conduct: it moves those aware of it into a new moral as well as intellectual relation to action. This relation affects conduct in a way that emphasizes the superiority of speculation and intellectual paradox over practical exertions of will and directness of action. The moral effect of this in Melville is a favoring of quiescence and passivity, virtues we have seen in Eliot, and which Melville makes a case for more vigorously and dazzlingly than she. The moral outcome of Melville's sense of plot has a political importance especially worth exploring. His address to narrative reason cannot be understood without considering the prominent and paradoxical place of personal and political revolt in his subject matter and his form of plot. My task, then, is to point out the intertwining of Melville's sense of plot not only with the Divine Inert's formal and intellectual bearing but with its moral and political dimension.

The moral relevance of the Divine Inert appears to be especially political because of the way Melville seems to discover this divinity in the transition from *White Jacket* to *Moby Dick*. In the writing of the former, Melville undergoes a crucial change of heart towards the possibility that democratic political order is founded on each man's capacity to implement his rights by willful and purposefully plotted action, including revolutionary or rebellious action against established unjust authority. This change results from his coming to see action in a new and complex way, one that makes action inextricable from passivity, that seems to highlight what may be called the agency of passivity or the passivity of the agent. By discovering, representing, and embodying this newly perceived passivity in the matter and even in the manner of his writing, Melville shies away from the rebellion he seems to honor for the last time in *White Jacket*. He comes to believe that there is a terrible destructive and self-destructive violence implicit in rebelliousness because it puts a premium on a man's deliberate and willful activism.

At the level of narrative, the paradox of this change of heart shows itself as a revolt against traditional narrative procedures, a revolt in formal terms simultaneous with a derogation of revolt as a practice in the world. This paradox has its own significant logic: although Melville attempts to make his practice of plot revolutionary, the inspiration of his narration is the Divine Inert, an essential quiescence and passiveness he wants to show pervading all intentions and all actions, whether revolution, or the writing and the forming of stories, or whatever. It is my belief that the truths, the way of conduct, and the narrative form the Divine Inert inspires in the narrators of *White Jacket* and *Moby Dick* are Melville's most significant contribution to the characteristic modern sense of plot. But at the same time it must be stressed that Melville is not simply modern; he does not dramatize the Divine Inert, nor does he work out its narrative aesthetic and its political moral without acute internal debate and self-division. His new sense of plot encapsulates this self-division, even as it overcomes it. We need to be aware of this because of the eventual outcome of Melville's use of story to feature the Divine Inert—because of the narrative and moral dimension Melville's modern readers have lost as well as gained as a result of his struggle with story and plot.

That Melville was especially interested in the idea and fact of action and that he invites us to think about acts and to rethink our assumptions about them and about their narrative representation was grasped in the 1950s by the American poet Charles Olson. Olson believed Melville initiated "the business of finding out how all action, and thought, have to be refounded," for according to Olson, Melville "made a push beyond characterization as he inherited it, . . . and beyond fiction. . . . He had to go beyond the familiar causatives of environment, psychology and event." He had to go beyond traditional heroes and antiheroes as well; and in all this he "put himself squarely . . . at the heart of . . . narrative now." Olson emphasizes two significant novelties contributing to Melville's sense of plot. He argues that Melville redefined "the real" by freeing it from "the rigidities of the discrete." "Nothing was now inert fact; all things were there for feeling, to promote it, and be felt; and man, in the midst of it, [knew] well how he was folded in, as well as how suddenly and strikingly he could extend himself, spring or, without even moving, go, to far, the farthest." The first novelty identifies the absence of "inert fact" and of "going" with the absence of movement. According to Olson, in Melville man's extensions, his springing forward into new distances becomes synonymous with absorption in an indefinite inwardness. The second novelty identifies "the actual character and structure of the real itself" not with active motion but with calm. Olson declares: "I pick up on calm, or passivity, Melville's words. . . . *The inertial structure of the world is a real thing which not only exerts effects upon matter but in turn suffers such effects.* I don't know a more relevant single fact to the experience of *Moby Dick* and its writer than this." Thus, Olson is saying that in Melville inertia is active force, passivity is agent, and agency suffers. Olson backs up his contention with a "Riemannian observation"—and an Einsteinian one— "the inertial field itself is flexible" because of "the dependence of the field of inertia on matter." Olson explains how understanding that "the structures of the real are flexible" leads Melville to the idealization of his narrator-hero Ishmael. In the person of Ishmael the novelist "sets up a different sort of a possible man, one of a company that he calls the hustings of the Divine Inert."[1]

Melville also sets up a different sort of a possible plot and a different sort of a possible morality, both of which emanate from the Divine Inert. But in more definite and pragmatic terms, what do I understand this emanation to mean for plot, for the representation of action, and for moral conduct in Melville? Olson seems to be quite right about Melville, but if the influence of the Divine Inert makes Melville's story "flexible," what precisely does this word signify for *Moby Dick*? Melville's plotting is flexible in the most odd and extreme way. The story is more discontinuous or disappearing than flexible; it takes a place among the novel's multiple evanescent and ungraspable "loomings." The story beckons the reader-quester onward, but it can be as elusive as the spiritspout or the whale. When Ishmael speaks of his cetology (Chapter 32), he seems also to congratulate himself on this narrative reticence and inconclusiveness. "Any human thing supposed to be complete, must for that very reason infallibly be faulty." He prays for incompleteness. "God keep me from ever completing anything. This whole book is but a draft— nay, but the draft of a draft."

Can "this whole book" include the tale of Ahab's search? If

so, then the resistance to completion resists Ahab as the active author of an event that can both constitute and complete a narrative. Ahab believes his search must follow a prearranged plan, must have a beginning, middle, and end, must thoroughly enact and externalize—even if ruthlessly—the hidden relations among himself, his men, and the whale. Ahab's realization of his own plot is the acting out of his mastery of the meaning of the world; his pursuit of the whale is an attempt to insist that life speak according to an absolute narrative reason and featuring of act. In contrast, Ishmael's and Melville's prayer for incompleteness resists mastering will and aggressive manipulating enactment; the narrator's own "plot" will be far different from Ahab's. Significantly, the resistance represents not willfulness but a yielding to passivity: Ishmael does not say "I will not finish," but rather "God keep me" from doing so.

Flexibility in Melville means that the plotting author, in so far as he can, yields the authority of articulated finish and fullness to the ambiguous authority of a draft. In *Mardi*, the poet Lombardo is celebrated for his epic the *Koztanza*. When Lombardo "set about his work," Melville says, "he knew not what it would become. He did not build himself in with plans; he wrote right on, and so doing, got deeper and deeper into himself." If we pursue Olson's interpretation here, Lombardo's sense of plot is represented in *Moby Dick*'s method of composition. Now of course, in saying that in *Moby Dick* Melville "did not build himself in with plans" and published "a draft," I am not taking Melville strictly at his word. *Moby Dick* is not an accidental production; and it is a "finished" work. Yet through Ishmael Melville dramatizes his work as unfinished because he wants to communicate an intellectual and moral meaning that might be denied by an emphasis on the novel as an achieved, fully-formed product. As with Eliot, we touch again on an author's humbling or checking of his form—simultaneous with his use of it—as a vehicle of meaning because of the way he sees *life* check or humble form and meaning. Ishmael and Melville pray for flexibility and imitate it because they want to point out experience itself as the "draft of a draft." No doubt too Melville wants us to understand that, however formally his insights may be shaped within the covers of "a novel," they have come to him as surprises, overcoming his predetermined plans while he struggled with his material; consequently he has written right on, getting deeper and deeper into the unplanned and unplotted regions of self and experience. What Melville wants to remind his readers of, even in his work's finished form, is the primacy in life of the depth that forever unsettles deliberate purpose, finish, and achievement.

As an imitation of the flexibility, unstable spontaneity, and resistance to achievement that rules life, Melville's sense of plot can be called an emanation of "the Divine Inert" by adapting and enlarging the reference of his use of the phrase in "The Specksynder," where he designates this inert as a force opposed to hierarchical antidemocratic social forms. The latter are illustrated by the absolute shipboard distinctions between "officer" and "man" by which Ahab incarnates "the sultanism of his brain" in "external arts and entrenchments" that keep "God's true princes ['the choice hidden handful of the Divine Inert'] of the Empire from the world's hustings." By interpreting the Divine Inert as an antagonist to Ahab's inflexible mastering or sultanic intentions—to his unqualified commitment to stiffened will and to action and not just to his political "arts"—it is possible to see this divinity as the inspiration of Ishmael's and Melville's prayer for incompleteness and passivity. And Melville's sense of plot makes it possible to interpret the term by connecting it to other things that he associates with opposition to sultanism and inflexibility.

We can conveniently see how Melville is thinking about quiescence and quietism when he alludes to the Divine Inert if we join Olson's comments on Melville to a discussion of action, will, and purpose in Gregory Bateson's *Steps to an Ecology of Mind*. Bateson argues that purposes and clear differentiations and oppositions of the kind we can say Ahab's sense of plot depends upon—such as human mind and will-ful action against brute nature and inert matter or injured self against injuring other—are purely *fictions*. The conscious, purposive, active self instanced by Ahab is also a fiction, so that Bateson argues for a reduced sense of "the scope of the conscious self." For this reduction Bateson revises evolu-tionary theory, newly identifying its "unit of survival." This unit has been, traditionally, "the breeding organism, or the family line, or the society." But in fact, "if an organism sets to work with a focus on its own survival and thinks that that is the way to select its adaptive moves, its 'progress' ends up with a destroyed environment." This "focus," a selective plotting teleology and a specifically teleological action, in-sures the self-destruction of the agent. The real unit of sur-vival is "a flexible organism-in-its-environment," not an or-ganism inflexibly against its environment.

In *Moby Dick* we may say that this real unit is represented by Ishmael and by the "flexibility" of Melville's plot. What this flexibility means may further be illustrated by Bateson when he says that

> the cybernetic nature of self and the world tends to be imperceptible to consciousness, insofar as the contents of the "screen" of consciousness are determined by consid-erations of purpose. The argument of purpose tends to take the form "*D* is describable; *B* leads to *C*; *C* leads to *D*; so *D* can be achieved by way of *B* and *C*." But, if the total mind and the outer world do not, in general, have this lineal structure, then by forcing this structure upon them, we become blind to the cybernetic circularity of the self and the external world.

Ahab forces this structure upon the world and is blinded. It is "the narrow purposive view which is at fault here."* This view, Bateson adds, is a misleading reinforcement of "the

---

* In contrast, we might recall Lukács's positive remarks on perspectival and teleological functions in plot and life.

myth of self-power." Even when we talk about the self's impulses, it ramifies

> too easily into nonsense about psychic energy, and those
> who talk this kind of nonsense will disregard the infor-
> mation content of *quiescence*. . . . Quiescence and activity
> have equal informational relevance.[2]

When Olson writes of the effects exerted by the world's inertial structure and of Melville's perception of those effects,
he is talking about the informational relevance of quiescence
to which the Divine Inert testifies. And I believe Melville's
appeal to the Divine Inert foreshadows a request by Bateson
that, instead of talking about the "matter of 'control' and the
whole related complex suggested by such words as manipulation, spontaneity, free will and technique," we should
think of experience as not accessible to "control" because it is
an "infinite regress of contexts." The story of *Moby Dick*, or
rather that novel's infinite "draft," represents this continuous
regress. And its human and natural heroes—the narrator and
the whale—stand for both the "informational relevance" of
quiescence and the "organism-in-its-environment" rather
than for the organism attempting to plot or control its environment as Ahab wants to do. The Divine Inert, we assume,
does not plot and acts by suffering, hence is not sultanic; its
divinity rebukes sultanism with the "force" of quiescence. Although the White Whale's last surfacing in the novel has the
look of intended malice, nevertheless in destroying the asser-
tiveness of will and action that Ahab represents the whale
stands for the inertial structure of the world. The monster
exerts his effects upon the human world to correct its activity,
to force it back into nonassertiveness, to make it perceive how
it suffers the action it initiates. The whale makes human action itself appear as "the draft of a draft," hence licensing
Ishmael's and Melville's sense of what plot should be and
should represent. Moreover, the whale's alleged will and
malice are reactions, fatal givens, but not specimens of "control." On the first day of the final chase "the quietude" of

Moby Dick is described as "the vesture of tornadoes." But Melville emphasizes the whale's natural "serenity," its "gentle joyousness" and "mighty mildness of repose," its "calm, enticing calm." Emphatically the whale changes on the second day, becoming "the first assailant himself." But, then, on the third day he is "only intent upon pursuing his own straight path in the sea." "Moby Dick seeks thee not," Starbuck shouts to Ahab. The Captain's plot and quest are not at all the creature's, and are not at all the creator's (considered either as Melville or as the inertial divinity).

The wide latitude or significance that I have given Melville's appeal to this divinity will be justified more concretely if I enlarge Bateson's relevance of quiescence to include the relevance of the nonpurposeful phenomenon of accident and if we compare my understanding of the Inert to the commentary in Daniel Hoffman's *Form and Fable in American Fiction*. Hoffman tells us that Melville was far "from accepting the 'Divine Inert' as his guide to this world," that as a castaway Pip accepts it as such and is accordingly maddened. Like Starbuck's "ineffectual passivity," Pip's "mindless purity"—"the superhuman acceptance of the Divine Inert"—"proves effeminate, passive, deathlike." For Hoffman, Melville invokes this divinity only as one of the fragmentary deities erected by men in partial image of Ishmael's genuine god, "creative power." Hoffman thus uses the same phrase Olson "picks up on" to come to an opposite conclusion. He does so because he is—understandably—bent on reading a definite purposiveness into the finale of *Moby Dick*. This means that he does not understand why Melville emphasizes *Moby Dick* as a draft of a draft rather than as a plot whose mastering perspectival function cannot be questioned. Melville feels that in addition to action in general, it is the purposeful teleological function in plot, in experience, and in action and morality that is challenged by the Divine Inert.

Moby Dick's boldest and most interesting challenge to purposeful motive is Ishmael's survival in the finale. For what purpose—to underwrite what conclusive truth and action—

does Ishmael alone escape the wreck? Hoffman's reading centers on this question. "Freed by his discovery . . . of the organic unity of man with fellow-man, Ishmael wins his right to be the 'sole survivor.' " But this cannot be the way to read a text that is not "built in with plans." Ishmael survives merely by accident: by chance he is thrown clear of the last day's pursuit of the whale. In the final chapter he is described as an anonymous third man thrown from a boat, "helplessly dropping astern, but still afloat and swimming." Since roughly the same accident befalls Pip earlier in the novel, one wonders why the repetition of the similar event does not have a similar outcome. In "The Castaway" Ishmael forecasts a sequel: "it will be seen what like abandonment befell myself." Isolated on the ocean, Pip was "carried down alive to wondrous depths," where his "passive eyes . . . saw God's foot upon the treadle of the loom." This passivity results in his insanity. Hoffman brings in the Divine Inert here to try to differentiate Pip's experience from that of Ishmaels. But Ishmael's "like abandonment" is also a matter of passive eyes. The passivity in his case does not prove ineffectual or deathlike. Far from causing him insanity, the accidental abandonment and his submission to it makes Ishmael survive.[3] I assume that the agent of his survival is the Divine Inert.

The Divine Inert does not aid survival or do any of its work whether maddening or saving by featuring intentions and "control." Its logic is accident, not purpose, so Pip accidentally does not survive his abandonment, and Ishmael accidentally does. Melville is not worried by the inconsistency; unlike George Eliot he does not take pains to make accident meaningful by reclaiming it from appearances, by "naturalizing" it. The "Mat-Maker" tells us that "chance by turn" rules free will and necessity "and has the last featuring blow at events," thus arguing that whatever is being made is best made by passivity—by an absorption that allows intention or plan to lose themselves or by a surrender of intention or plan to contingency or casualty. "The Mat-Maker" ends with

Ishmael's entire boat crew as castaways, lost in squall and fog. *The Pequod* gives them up. Then just by chance, the ship, "a huge vague form," bears down on the lost men and inadvertently rescues them. The outcome of this first lowering is like that of the book's very last, when Ishmael once again is accidentally lost, and when he is unintentionally discovered by the "devious" *Rachel*.

The castaway episodes all testify to the "informational relevance" of quiescence in the face of the truth that chance, not will and plot, "features" events. What is the moral relevance of this phenomenology of a nonlinearly purposeful, accidental world? "Once plot is kissed out," we perceive that the moral agencies of choice and will become uncertain and unreliable. "Queequeg is the agent," Hoffman writes, "both of Tashtego's delivery and of Ishmael's." Hoffman also believes Ishmael "wills himself to live."[4] But nonaccidental moral agency is more radically suspect in Melville than appears in Hoffman's way of fabling the novel. At times Queequeg represents the force of willful moral agency almost as much as Ahab. Perhaps this is only *not* so in his first most active moment in the novel, during the trip from New Bedford to Nantucket. Having spectacularly and magnanimously rescued a man who has insulted him, he shows a remarkable carelessness about his act. "Was there ever such unconsciousness?" Ishmael admiringly wonders. Afterwards Ishmael does assign moralizing purpose to Queequeg's deed. He imagines Queequeg saying to himself, "It's a mutual, joint-stock world. . . . We cannibals must help these Christians." Far more purposefully deliberate is Queequeg's later "running delivery" of Tashtego from a fall into a dead whale's head. And finally the cannibal represents the epitome of deliberate life-mastering plot and choice when he saves *himself* from death. "They asked him whether to live or die was a matter of his own sovereign will and pleasure. He answered, certainly."

But is Melville using Queequeg's rescues of others and of himself from death to satirize the form and morality of

Dickens's rescues? It seems Melville *can* use the Divine Inert's passivities for this purpose. Whatever Queequeg's certainty, it is doubtful that Ishmael—and Melville—can be equally certain of the self's power to activate any plotted form it desires. Melville seems to be asking if there is any willful or moral agency or activity as creative, as formative, as radically dissociated from what it acts upon (and what the Divine Inert says it will suffer from) as Queequeg thinks there is. We can scarcely assert credibly, for example, that Queequeg saves Ishmael by the act or agency of loving friendship. From the moment the two men meet at the Spouter Inn, under the sign of "a coffin," Ishmael's connection with Queequeg remains problematic: Does the friendship tend towards life or death, survival or extinction? Apparently Queequeg cures Ishmael of his hatred of life: "I felt a melting in me. No more my splintered heart and maddened hand were turned against the wolfish world." But it is the melting and the surrender that save here, not the friendship. In fact, friendship as an activity—as a planned or determined effort at moral interrelation, as what the Dickensian rescue would make it—is "a humorously perilous business." We read in the chapter on "The Monkey-Rope," where by virtue of the rope and their work Queequeg becomes Ishmael's "own inseparable twin brother," that their closeness, like their work—caught between the threat of sharks and the threat of misdirected shark-repelling spades—makes Ishmael feel that his "free will had received a mortal wound."

The human will generates the self as a story and as the moral product of story by making the self from one thing into another and by enabling, by means of action, the planned and purposed transformation of potential into realized actuality. We must add will to our understanding of the phenomena represented and stimulated by plot and story as we have defined them from the standpoint of a positive sense. The labor of rescue in Dickens clearly represents the moral efficacy of the will, of a creative, liberating "sultanism" in the will's operation. But the Divine Inert does not present the will to us in this way. In *Moby Dick*, for example, the nature of friendship shows how the will not only becomes vulnerable but is a vulnerability, an agency of doing inextricable from an agency of undoing. By virtue of the agency of willful friendship in "the Monkey-Rope" all mortals become more vulnerable to mortality. Ishmael does not object. "Well, well, . . . what matters it, after all?" If the monkey-rope of human connection is simultaneously a life preserver and a deathtrap, then Ishmael does not will to make it one thing or another. In Chapter 74 he tells how the immense distance between the whale's eyes must amount to "divided and diametrically opposite powers of vision." This "must involve" the whale in "helpless perplexity of volition." In himself Ishmael accepts the perplexing of the will: his story must represent itself as helpless perplexity of volition—hence as something antagonistic not only to political sultanism but to plot, free choice, and action as vehicles of moral effort.

To serve the Divine Inert Melville accepts the perplexing of his moral will, the perplexing of his plot, and the perplexing of the intellectual and moral meaning and status of his action. The saving coffin life buoy of the finale represents this acceptance. In its double character the coffin also stands for the Divine Inert's characteristic mingling of diametrically divided opposites: just as it exerts effects *and* suffers them, it collapses differences between life and death, light and darkness, meaning and insignificance. We would inaccurately simplify the coffin's duplicit meaning by interpreting its last appearance in the novel as a symbol of the ultimate victory of life and meaning over their opposites or by identifying the coffin with Queequeg's deliberate and decisive kind of rescuing agency. Although Queequeg's apparently decisive victory over his own death takes place while he lies ill inside the coffin, the thing itself has a significance that cannot be decided—either by readers or by Queequeg, who decorates the box with symbols not even he can understand. And after Queequeg wills his recovery, the indeterminacy of the coffin's meaning is intensified, when it passes on to the carpenter, who is ordered to turn it into a life buoy. He resents the job because he thinks of it as "cobbling." He feels he is being required to make a cipher more indecipherable. This work, he complains, is "not clean, virgin, fair-and-square mathematical . . . something that regularly begins at the beginning, and is at the middle when midway, and comes to an end at the conclusion" (Chapter 126). The carpenter thinks his work and its objects should have a fashion and form and also a clear meaning that we might assume Aristotelians would prescribe for plot. In contrast it appears that as a storyteller *Melville* does not carpenter his work but cobbles it. To keep the story and its meanings incomplete and paradoxical, not "fair-and-square mathematical" or "regular," is one aspect of the cobbling; to make activity and passivity, will and will's wounding indistinct from each other, hence indecipherable, is another aspect.

The carpenter decides to take refuge from his distaste for cobbling by doing what he must and by not pondering it. This makes him rather more like Melville and Ishmael than his distaste suggests; it certainly makes him more like them than like Ahab. It is part of Ahab's opposition to the Divine Inert that he does not like any collapse of the meaningfulness of differences or oppositions, and he plots, moralizes, and acts accordingly. He asks the carpenter what he means by turning a coffin into a self-contradiction, and he accuses the carpenter of being "as unprincipled as the gods, and as much of a jack-of-all-trades." Ahab is disturbed by this coffin-work because it tempts him—"so far gone in the dark side of earth"—to contemplate "theoretic bright" meanings in the darkness. He does not want finally even to see "that thing"—the cobbled coffin—"here again." The carpenter's defense against Ahab is to say, "I do not mean anything, Sir. I do as I do." What does Melville make of this? Through the coffin, the carpenter, and Ahab, Melville opposes doing without meaning and doing that means only one thing. But by narrating events that argue contradictory meanings, he appears also to oppose doing altogether. Ahab plots against

Melville; the story Ahab wants sultanically to forge by enactment contradicts the variation and unreliability of meaning in
the "cobbled" object that finally saves Ishmael and that is
paradigmatic of the form and the story of Melville's plot.

The shifting and indecipherable character of natural and
human phenomena as clarified by a "cobbling" plot once
again illustrates the influence of the Divine Inert, which represents the tricky, indecipherable nature of nature, the willessness of will, the passivity of actors, the close intertwining
of opposites. We may read the presence of this paradoxical
force in Melville's general representation of labor in the
novel. Melville sees labor as a mixture of doing and undoing,
as a paradoxical offshoot of the Divine Inert that the labor of
his narrative reason takes for its model. The carpenter identifies traditional and valuable work with the traditional shape
of story—with clear beginning, middle, and end, with intelligible form and meaning. In dissociating himself from the
carpenter's favored form of work, Melville looks askance at
any clearly intelligible meaning or finished achievement in
work itself. In contrast Ahab speaks of event as "the living
act, the undoubted deed" (Chapter 36), for a committed plotter trusts in the reality and achieved finish of an "undoubted
deed."

As I have argued in the previous chapter, the plotting of
matter—or matters—into form is one way of considering ordinary labor and its relational and ethical intentions and
achievements. Melville and Ishmael cast suspicion on plot
and any positive relational or moral dimension of labor by
casting suspicion on work as indubitable act and mastering of
matter. "Stowing Down and Clearing Up" (Chapter 98), the
last chapter on whaling as work, "sings the romantic proceeding of decanting off [the whale's] oil into the casks and
striking them down in the hold, where once again Leviathan
returns to his native profundities." One expects that this part
of the labor process will make the "singer" celebrate his
workers' product. Instead the product abruptly evanesces—
and so does the industry. During the making of the sperm

"the entire ship seems great Leviathan himself," strewn with his parts, greased with his oil, heavy with his smell. "A day or two after," the whaleboat is not itself: "You would swear you trod some silent merchant vessel." All the signs of work done or being done have been swept away. "To hint to [the] musked mariners of oil, and bone, and blubber, were little short of audacity. They know not the thing you distantly allude to." Yet just when the ship has been made "a spotless dairy room"

> many is the time the poor fellows, just buttoning the necks of their clean frocks, are startled by the cry "There she blows!" and away they fly to fight another whale, and go through the whole weary thing again. Oh! my friends, but this is man-killing! Yet this is life. For hardly have we mortals by long toilings extracted from this world's vast bulk its small but valuable sperm, and then, with weary patience, cleansed ourselves from its defilements, and learned to live here in clean tabernacles of the soul; hardly is this done, when—*There she blows!*—the ghost is spouted up, and away we sail to fight some other world, and go through young life's old routine again.

By this account man making his living—and making life into valuable form and into a relational and moral form of value—is killing himself. Work is a bewildering cycle of returns from lack to fullness to lack. The fullness is not a matter of fulfillment through a product that is first imagined and then plotted into realization by active will in a kind of moral victory over the unformed chaos of nature; it results from the perpetual frustration of plot and of fixed completion. The workers plot or purpose to live by mastering nature; but their plot or purpose masters them, and they suffer the effects they exert on nature. If Ishmael has a particular survival power, it has to do with his ability to apprehend the passivity and willessness or purposelessness of his own agency and conduct, of his agency's and his conduct's saturation by what we take to be the Divine Inert. Naturally, Ishmael does not *choose* or *act* to learn this. He only sees more clearly than the others; and at the finale, he sees by virtue of being thrown free of the *Pequod*'s last work.

As the "different sort of a possible man," then, Ishmael does equivocal work; indeed, all his doing is doubtful and so is the narrative "doing" of his author, Melville, who insists that life humbles all authorial will. Certainly in regard to will, Ishmael, Melville's delegate, cannot do anything as definite and as definitely independent of his environment as "will himself to live." And although Hoffman argues that Ishmael's "balanced double vision encompasses all extremes and thereby asserts its absolute stability,"[5] the critic's invocation of assertion and stability undermines his point. Neither willed nor asserted, the double vision is suffered, and it is not stable. In terms of plot, Melville dramatizes himself through Ishmael as not actively telling or willfully writing his story and its ending. As an author and agent he, like his hero, wants to be seen as thrown clear of his work, as passive, himself at the mercy of the instability that "features" event. This is his way of proving he is not the story's dictator, an Ahab-like sultanist of the brain. Of course, his acceptance of a limit upon his will to plan advances him as one of God's candidates for the world's hustings. Along with Ishmael and the whale, Melville's storytelling represents the victorious ascendancy of the Divine Inert. And once the operation of this divinity is grasped, the man who sees its inevitable checking of purpose and will has found a guide not only to an adequately phenomenological form of narrative reason but to a genuine principle of conduct. In response to this divinity, he refrains from exerting will on behalf of any morality that assumes as its grounds the efficacy of will, the freedom from accident of deliberate choice and plan, the primacy of activism over quietism and submissiveness.

But in spite of his discovery of the Divine Inert, Melville has left us a remarkable trace of an *alternative* to the informational and moral relevance of both Ahab's sense of plot and the Divine Inert's. His imagination seems to have ventured forward to another possibility, even though at last it drew back, either in distaste or fear. The artifact and proof of this venture lies imbedded in Chapter 54 of *Moby Dick*, the interpolated tale called "The *Town-Ho*'s Story." We shall see that the venture itself has begun in *White Jacket*, and that "The *Town-Ho*'s Story" is the finish; but we ought not to underestimate how both texts show us just what Melville's ultimate sense of plot defines itself against: it not only defines itself against Ahab but also against Steelkilt, the hero of "The *Town-Ho*'s Story," who is a different sort of a possible man from either Ahab or Ishmael. Steelkilt is therefore an exponent of a different sort of a possible sense of plot and of conduct, neither Ahabian nor Inertial. It is in Steelkilt that Melville's change of heart about the value for truth and conduct of action and of democratic antiauthoritarian rebellion is centered. Prior to imagining Steelkilt (in at least half of *White Jacket*) Melville features the creativity of purposeful act and of a willed, assertive, even violent democratic rebelliousness. For a time it is as if Melville thinks of violent rebellion as the archetypal act, the equivalent in his work of Genesis' act of creation as it is described in Kenneth Burke's *Grammar of Motives*. After Steelkilt Melville no longer depicts rebellion as a positive force, and he gives his primary attention and allegiance to Ishmael, the Divine Inert, and a democratic kind of quietism, difficult to call action-centered—or even political. We can now consider the meanings and values that are inscribed in this change.

In the *Town-Ho* story Steelkilt is an alternate version of Ahab: one who is beautiful, sane, and lucky, whose revenge of a personal insult unqualifiedly *succeeds*, and who can manipulate nature to avenge him. He emerges as a figure of deliberate assertive will and inflexible activism; and his absence of calm, quiescence, or passivity must have struck Melville for a while as more powerful even than Ishmael's flexibility. I suggest this partly because of the way Melville seems compelled to dramatize the difficulty Ishmael feels in telling the story that he elaborately swears is true. The difficulty is surely the result of the tale's content: on the one hand, unlike the rest of the novel, the *Town-Ho* episode represents the whale as "the most deadly monster," as willfully malicious and as metaphysically evil as Ahab and the chapter on "The White-ness of the Whale" argue him to be; on the other hand, the episode shows tacit but remarkable respect for Steelkilt and the White Whale, admiring them as immoral or destructively amoral—and glorious. Most remarkable of all is that in this interpolation Melville represents the events Ishmael swears to in such a way as to seriously challenge—if not to utterly overturn—Ishmael's cherished and agnostic perplexities of vision.

The *Town-Ho* story disturbs Ishmael because its content shakes both his characteristic way of "telling" and his idea of the Divine Inert. The plotting of the entire novel, delegated by Melville to Ishmael, is as I have said a "cobbling" busi-ness, a transgression against traditional narrative reasoning and action for the sake of cultivating indefinite outlines, paradoxical unions, resigned and agnostic perplexities of thought and moral judgment. At its most congenial, this cob-bling procedure is rhapsodic play: a feast of nominations and a diversity of styles miming the range of contingencies in the Divine Inert's response to any detail, gesture, or occasion provided by whaling or Ahab. But in the *Town-Ho* tale, action breaks the play of words and styles, speaks peremptorily, routs quiescence and ambiguity as phenomena and as intel-lectual and moral guides. Characteristic Ishmaelite touches of style survive, of course, especially in the narrator's descrip-tion of Lake Erie and the Erie Canal as romantic waters. But the limitation of this style is more striking: Melville may want us to notice this difference by making Ishmael remark that "for my humor's sake, I shall preserve the style in which I once narrated it at Lima." The style is unusually chastened, for what happens in the narration, unlike anything else in the novel, has an unmeditated vividness. Melville's writing for Ishmael's voice becomes all reflectionless presentation, all concentrated featuring of act. Even words entirely fail the teller—they do not begin to be available to him when, at crucial parts of his narrative, Ishmael cannot convey what the story's actors have said. Action speaks instead—an action apparently not mingled with or qualified by passivity, inertia, or imponderable effects.

In itself the action in this story is remarkably highlighted by Melville's stress upon its intensity of violence. This does not mean, however, that doing is undoing here; for the violent deeds accomplish what they intend, and do not show their own passivity. Only the suppression of Ishmael's and Melville's characteristic prose, of the cobbling sense of plot, and of the presence of the Divine Inert can convey the savage content of the *Town-Ho* narrative and its accomplished fullness of event and willful agency. The Golden Inn, the context of the storytelling, represents civil leisure and peaceful indolence, but the story itself is full of human bloodletting. In the rest of the novel the humans are banded tight against the foe, nature. Here the men hate each other and carry on ceaseless internal war. The first mate, Radney, threatens to smash the face of Steelkilt with a hammer. Steelkilt, an ordinary seaman, responds by breaking the jaw of his superior, who falls on the deck "spouting blood like a whale." A mutiny to support Steelkilt's insubordination follows. Its strength is abetted by two Erie Canallers, who "with their keen mincing knives" plan with Steelkilt to "run a muck from the bowsprit to the taffrail." When the Captain of the ship regains control he ties the three rebels to the mizzen rigging "like three quarters of meat," and flogs two of them senseless. The Captain does not flog Steelkilt, but Radney does—his violence now making up for the fact that "such was the state of his mouth that he could hardly speak." Later, Steelkilt, back at his job, plans to kill Radney by opening his head with an iron ball and then throwing him overboard. But there is a lowering for a whale, and Radney becomes Moby Dick's victim. The action does not end there, but continues with Steelkilt's further aggressions against the Captain, whom he had promised to murder.

In this summary of what happens in the *Town-Ho*'s story we can scarcely see Steelkilt as attractive or glorious or of any moral interest whatsoever. And before we can see him as any of these things, we must pay more attention to Ishmael's manner of telling the story and to his difficulties in telling it, since we may suppose that these have to do with defensiveness against Steelkilt's attraction and power. Such is the state of *Ishmael*'s mouth in narrating the tale that *he* can hardly speak. There is apparently no way, verbal or otherwise, to stand aside from—or to soften—the onrush of violent human action. Even Steelkilt wants, momentarily, to stand aside, not to stir up Radney further. But in this situation forbearance has no final power. Feeling must give way to acts, and so must Ishmael's characteristic verbal play—his brilliant powers of nomination. Nevertheless, perhaps so as not to give way to the telling nature of acts, Ishmael sacrifices verbal play at Lima in exchange for frequent lapses into silence. At many points he will not say what is happening or why. And of course this silence very well suits devotion to the Divine Inert: by his reticence Ishmael maintains even this story as the draft of a draft. Moreover, by not articulating causes and effects in any clear way, Ishmael can mute the presence in the tale of will and agency, of organism-against-environment; he can attempt to make out a case for the passivity and essential nonpurposiveness of even this action.

It is not a convincing attempt. The cause of the events is pragmatically identifiable: a leak in the hold, resulting in extra work and extra tensions. Ishmael evades pragmatic cause and effect, pragmatic agency and event. He insists that everything here is fatal and fated—which is a way of appealing to chance or hap as the "featurer" of what happens. Radney is "pre-destinated, . . . a fool branded for the slaughter by the gods." "A strange fatality pervades the whole career of these events, as if verily mapped out before the world was charted." Now in saying this Ishmael may be influenced by the final fatalism of Ahab, who insists in Chapter 134 that "this whole act's immutably decreed." But Ahab's declaration is itself uncharacteristic; it seems to mark his surrender of

his own determined shaping will. Even for Ishmael the remark seems out of character, insofar as it emphasizes not a
double vision but a single way of seeing events. But at the
same time Ishmael's tactic *is* in character. If fate "mapped"
this event, then accident is fate here. The origin or motive of
the event is not human purpose or will. And if the origin is
divine, it is not a willful or purposefully plotting divinity.
Ishmael means that in its first unfolding as action the story's
author is an all-pervasive, immutable given, not a conscious
active making: the Divine Inert, then, not any possible form
of sultanism in Steelkilt or the whale, must be in charge of
both the events and of Ishmael's way of telling.

But is Ishmael's implicit, insistent invocation of the Divine
Inert not merely whistling in the dark? Or is it obscurantist
whistling in the light of what Steelkilt and the whale make
obvious—that quiescence in these events does not have informational relevance equal with purposefully focused activity? Ishmael does not relate what Steelkilt says warningly to
the Captain and to Radney when they come to whip him. But
from the story's outcome we can surmise that he has told his
enemies that injury to himself will be avenged by Moby Dick.
At Steelkilt's warning the Captain lays down the whip; but
Radney does not, and is later carried off in the whale's
mouth. Ishmael does not want to speak of or admit the victory of Steelkilt's purposeful manipulation of nature and of
his assertive act of collaboration with the whale. The challenge to passive quiescence in Steelkilt's democratic, self-
honoring act makes Ishmael especially defensive and confused. For example, in spite of the Captain's and Radney's
nominal charge of the vessel, Steelkilt thoroughly commands
her. He has persuaded the men to stop sighting whales.
Ishmael refers to this as a calling of the crew to passivity.
"The Lakeman had induced the seamen to adopt this sort of
passiveness." This willed passivity is confounded by a man
whom Ishmael calls a "fool." "A stupid Teneriffe man" yells
out, "There she rolls"; the man "had instinctively and in-
voluntarily lifted his voice for the monster." The boats are

lowered, and Radney is carried off, punished by nature and death for commanding, subordinating, and flogging Steelkilt. But why does Ishmael call the Teneriffer and Radney fools? For a moment he seems to be taking Steelkilt's side, since he registers contempt for the men Steelkilt would scorn. The Teneriffer may be a fool because his involuntary voice brings Moby Dick actively into the story—in such a way as to complete the plan or the plot against Radney that Steelkilt has initiated. Ishmael may name-call here because his liking for quiescence is confounded by the "fool." However, quiescence does not check Steelkilt's agency, but instinctively complies with it, thus carrying forward Steelkilt's ruthless act. Not wanting to face this squarely, Ishmael interjects just when the "fool's" voice is "lifted" for the monster: "Gentlemen, a strange fatality pervades the whole career of these events."

It is not a strange fatality, however, but an indomitable strength of deliberately chosen, willfully shaped human action that pervades these events. The whale appears as if to add nature's endorsement to Steelkilt's plot, to make his story tell the supremacy of his will and act and of their distance from passivity and quietism. And what impels Steelkilt's will and conduct is his democratic assurance: no other being has a right to demand his passivity; no one has a right to flog his will into submission; he has a right to utter and assert himself even by violence. His democratic value (a moral value that to convention *and* to Ishmael look immoral) and his value as willful and even violent actor are bound together.

There is an attraction and power in this that the tale conveys in spite of itself and that Ishmael admits in worshipful awe when he describes Steelkilt as "a tall and noble animal with a head like a Roman, and a flowing golden beard like the tasseled housings of your last [Peruvian] viceroy's snorting charger; and a brain, and a heart, and a soul in him, gentlemen, which had made Steelkilt Charlemagne, had he been born son to Charlemagne's father." Clearly this handsome sailor is royal, one of "God's true princes of the Empire."

Surely he would not be kept from the world's hustings by the antidemocratic sultanisms of his captain and his first mate. But can Steelkilt, who has sultanisms of his own, be one of the choice hidden handful of the Divine Inert? Ishmael, doubtless, is one of "that different sort of a possible man." But Ishmael does not illustrate, as Steelkilt does, a divinity that endorses not only plotting human will and aggressive purpose but also the democratic value and morality of plotting will, aggression, and act. It is doubtful that the heaven Ishmael names as the endorser of Steelkilt's will is the Divine Inert. Insofar as Steelkilt stands for a nonaccidental, deliberately planned kind of event—for a force that manipulates nature to its ends and features acts to an extent that makes even violent action a prerogative and adornment of democratic man—the heaven that may step in for Steelkilt is not Ishmael's favored divinity.

Steelkilt thus embodies a general human possibility of plot and conduct, an alternative to Ishmael's and Ahab's possibilities that Melville imagines and draws back from. He stands too for the truth of an active violent democracy in nature that Melville also fears. Steelkilt is thus a unique character in the novel, and what "heaven" endorses in him in Chapter 54 is almost utterly outside *Moby Dick*. *Radney* exhibits similarities to *Ahab* more than to Steelkilt. And for all Ishmael's admiration, Steelkilt is certainly his opposite. Intriguingly, the interpolated tale tells us that the opposites, Steelkilt and Ishmael, have met. "I have seen and talked with Steelkilt since the death of Radney," Ishmael swears. He cannot have seen and talked with him during the gam with the *Town-Ho*. That ship was then manned "almost wholly by Polynesians," those no doubt recruited by their captain at Tahiti after Steelkilt had jumped ship, taking most of the original crew with him. Steelkilt and Ishmael have met after Ishmael's rescue by the coffin and the *Rachel* and before the telling of the story at the Golden Inn. They have met *outside* the novel. This is so, perhaps, because *Moby Dick must* crowd out such a character. If Melville did not want to tell a clearly definite story about the whale, he would have wanted less to tell such a story about *Steelkilt*'s kind of "possible man."

It must be above all the violence Steelkilt unleashes that turns Melville away from him and towards the princes of the Divine Inert. Suggesting that a featuring of act leads inevitably to such violence, in the rest of the novel Melville assigns to Ahab the willfully plotting activity represented by Steelkilt. And whereas Melville accepts and even admires this activity in Steelkilt, he seems to pass it on to Ahab in order to lament it. He equates the plotting and all-shaping will of Ahab with insanity and with a hatred of nature masquerading as a morality; he insists that this activity is admirable because—and insofar as—it is doomed and tragic. Ishmael's assertion in "The Whiteness of the Whale" that he shares Ahab's plotting personal and moral quest drops out of the novel. In relation to Ahab's consciousness, Ishmael's becomes antithetically comic. Simultaneously it becomes antithetical to Steelkilt's by refusing intently purposeful, manipulative, and nonquiescent plot and by seeing in such refusal the only freedom from violence and insanity and the only intellectual and moral way of admiring, loving, and truthfully representing nature and experience.

Steelkilt uses nature and divinity for his own willful, activist ends. He challenges calm, passivity, the inertial structure of the world. His will is not insanity, his inflexibility is beauty, his pride and even his violence ask to be admired, neither as tragic or comic but as natural and valuably republican. Yet Steelkilt's vengeful purpose and republicanism enjoy a success that Melville and Ishmael reject. They argue or imply that such fixed plot and purpose—even if it is without violence and vengefulness—should not succeed or survive as Ishmael's flexibility and unplotted improvisation should and does. Ishmael—to paraphrase the "Try-Works"—will not give himself up to fire, which in one of its forms is the "inverting," deadening fixity and rigidity of Ahab's plotting. Steelkilt *has* given himself up to this fire, but he is neither inverted nor deadened nor mocked by nature or divinity. Had an imperious Steelkilt been aboard the *Pequod*, he might have carried out the rebellion contemplated by Starbuck; and Ishmael would not have escaped alone. What is perhaps most interesting about Steelkilt is the glimpse of a novel morality he provides us: a morality identified with the honor of a democratic self-utterance having nothing to do with the fear of moral or intellectual meaninglessness of life that seems to impel Ahab and his crew. We have the sense that Ishmael has more than a touch of Steelkilt's novel morality, and that this fact may be symbolically reflected in Ishmael's escape from the wreck. But Steelkilt combines a morality that has no Ahabian metaphysical impulse (his is personal, spontaneous, and has no *systematic* intellectual or ethical ideology) with Ahab's commitment to will and action. And this combination makes Steelkilt most significantly different from Ishmael. Thus, in a very strong sense Steelkilt is a mean between Ahab and Ishmael; and so it is all the more curious that Melville gives him so little prominence in the novel and indeed forces him out of it.

If we compare "The *Town-Ho*'s Story" with *White Jacket*, however, we can see that Melville had already prepared the dismissal of Steelkilt as a possible hero and democrat and that he had already prepared the way for the truth, morality, and sense of plot appropriate to Ishmael and the Divine Inert. As the great result of this preparation we have *Moby Dick*; but we have also lost things that Melville might have given us instead: an imagination and justification of the fertility of willful, purposeful action; a positive evaluation of a person-centered control of environment; a startling moral justification of republican violence. And these would have been accompanied by a sense of plot in Melville not as modern as the one he has left us—but one whose results for the truth of action and the value of revolutionary political conduct might have been no less important or interesting. Although the Melville of *White Jacket* is also self-divided and consciously dramatizes his own self-division, for half of the book the narrator of *White Jacket* is far more like the handsome, murderous sailor Steelkilt than he is like Ishmael. And thus White Jacket's adventures, which include a final veering away from the possibility of becoming a double of Steelkilt, especially spell out the gestation of the Divine Inert and of its various meanings for Melville—especially of its meanings for plot and for politics.

The direct reference to the Divine Inert in *Moby Dick* redacts the essential *political* theme in *White Jacket*. In the latter, the hollow imperial or sultanic hierarchy that structures the society of the man-of-war *Neversink* thwarts God's true princes—"the people," the ship's ordinary seamen—and keeps them from the hustings. Melville protests this thwarting emphatically: the central political line of *White Jacket* does not derive from an Ishmael-like perplexity of volition. Although its author stands unconditionally for pacifism, his egalitarian defiance drives the book with an assertive legislative will. He insists that the reader oppose with him the injustice of flogging and the unconstitutional nature of the American Navy's Articles of War and of its code of martial law.

But at the same time, in contrast to Melville's moral polemic, the sense of plot in *White Jacket* does evidence both an Ishmael-like perplexity of volition and diametrically opposed yet intertwined points of view. Melville is not sure whether or not he can—or should—plot, enact, and finish a story to fulfill his moral and legislative intention. He seems to wonder (as Robert Scholes thinking about plot wonders) if "fiction can exist without . . . hierarchical relationships."[6] In demolishing the social authority of the *Neversink*'s hierarchy, *White Jacket* replaces the fiction of hierarchy with flat, factual reporting. Simultaneously it attempts to find—through the story of the narrator's purely personal predicament—a fictional plot whereby to enact democratic feeling and conduct, a plot not either positively or adversely dependent on hierarchy. But the fanciful story that Melville weaves around and through his journalism is a tale of frustration, and the bafflement that is its content may stand for his inability to find a fulfilling plot for his attempt at a written act of rebellion. He is relieved to be released from his story in the end. The white jacket is left behind, as if—as a fictional plot—it is as trammeling to the author's life and views as the false social hierarchy. Political liberation and a liberation from story would thus seem to occur simultaneously. And yet throughout *White Jacket* Melville muses uncertainly over the double process of this liberation from hierarchy and from story. He appears to weigh whether or not release should come from active purposeful resistance or from a supersession not only of the forms of hierarchy but of the forms of opposition to it. And so it is as if he self-dividedly questions, as he proceeds with his book, both its story and the rebelliousness of its directly polemical chapters.

Of course, Melville could not have made more clear the hollowness of the ship's publicly instituted and sanctioned structures of control and subordination. Its officers have neither practical skill nor human distinction to make good their functions and their titles. In order to offset this hierarchy, which is "a system of cruel cogs and wheels, . . . grinding up . . . all that might minister to the well-being of the crew," White Jacket attempts to structure an alternative hierarchy—in his heart. As Melville's delegated plotter opposing hierarchy in the world, White Jacket makes a story out of a spiritual relation with Jack Chase, his personal captain. But Chase has a flaw that subverts his detachment from the cruel system. He enjoys the violence of combat and the terrors of bloodshed, so that White Jacket laments: "War almost makes blasphemers of the best of men, and brings them all down to the Feejee standard of humanity."[7] In his disappointment he looks for yet another captain and yet another source whereby to turn fact into fictional or storied relation.

Although he has neither the glamor nor the literariness of Chase, Old Ushant, chief of the forecastle, emerges as the final hero of Melville's attempt to plot White Jacket's polemics under the guidance of an alternative, purely spiritual hierarchy and relation. It happens that the *Neversink*'s crew have all grown beards, which they call homeward-bounders; but as their goal is approached, the officers order the beards shaved off. The sailors plan and partly enact a mutiny, but at last they acquiesce to the orders. Only a few, including Ushant, refuse compliance. They are flogged accordingly, but Ushant still will not be shaved. He ends the trip in chains, stripped of his office by Captain Claret. In prison he proudly braids his beard and interweaves it with red bunting. This affair of the "assassinated beards" is related by White Jacket with good humor, but also with great underlying earnestness. He idolizes Ushant, and he is not joking when he says that Ushant's victory "was a glorious conquest over the Conqueror himself, as well worthy to be celebrated as the battle of the Nile." As White Jacket sees it, the old man's resistance has kept intact his very manhood. And manhood is crucially important here, for the antidemocratic order of the ship represents a social state "unmanning to think of." Portraying this state, the writer's soul "sinks" because he has delineated "the head of Medusa." Jack Chase says to the fatal barber, "You are about to sheer off my manhood." White Jacket expresses his anger at flogging "in the name of immortal manhood"—a name also invoked to curse the proponents of flogging. "The political Messiah," Melville declares, "has come in *us*, if we would but give utterance to his promptings"; and this Messiah is emphatically baritone: "At a period when other nations have but lisped, our deep voice is heard afar."[8]

But although the male response to this unmanning state is decidedly Ushant's, when White Jacket is faced with flogging and with the immediate possibility of overt rebellion he *feels* his assertive and rebellious male impulse—and he does *not* act it out. Rather than imitating Ushant, he in effect overturns Ushant in his heart's hierarchy, perhaps freeing himself internally from all hierarchy, but certainly leaving intact the captain's position in the world's hierarchical structure of relations. The search for an action by White Jacket that would complement Melville's own rebellion finds an opportunity for externalization in willful, active revolt—and then avoids it. It may be that Melville wants to suggest, as Shelley does in

Prometheus Unbound, that to actively rebel against hierarchy is yet to participate in it, to be enslaved by what one resists.

But the implications of this scene are deeper and more general: at just this point in *White Jacket*, we can foresee Melville's treatment of Steelkilt and his turn towards the Divine Inert. White Jacket is facing the same kind of insult and punishment Steelkilt will face, and he responds at first just as violently as Steelkilt will. He wants to kill the Captain by pitching him overboard, even though he knows he will have to go overboard too. But he is not ashamed of his desire to kill; indeed he announces that his murderousness derives from "the privilege, inborn and inalienable, that every man has, of dying himself, and inflicting death upon another," as "the last resources of an insulted and unendurable existence." This claim of such a privilege, "inborn and inalienable," is a remarkable contribution by White Jacket and Melville to the rights of man. It is scarcely a pacific or quiescent claim—it is worthy of Steelkilt or of Ahab. Yet simultaneous with the claiming of this right, White Jacket's manhood cannot or does not strike out and enact the right.

It can be argued that there is no need for White Jacket to act out this right; that its enactment would be suicidal, and that, after all, Jack Chase and the marine corporal, Colbrook, save White Jacket from the flogging by speaking up on his behalf. Yet Ushant's rebellion is not suicidal, so we need not assume White Jacket's would be. Nor need we assume that Chase's and Colbrook's intervention are meant to dramatize the superiority of fraternal feeling over rebellion: Melville scarcely gives the intervention sufficient treatment to warrant such an assumption. And when we look ahead to what Melville allows Steelkilt, albeit for only one chapter, we can see it is possible for Melville to imagine the successful accomplishment of a desire to kill the captains of the world. By mutiny Steelkilt figuratively kills his captain for even attempting to flog him; indeed, he has only to hiss a warning to the ship's hierarchy, and—with nature's collaboration—it crumbles. Yet at the brink of embodying Steelkilt's action, his self-assertion, and his violent republican will, White Jacket is halted—not only by others but by something in himself and in Melville.

Melville seems to insist that if White Jacket is to be a hero himself, his moral distinction, even his revolutionary polemics, must come from sources other than action, other than violence, other than the self controlling its context by the realization of a plot. The moral heroism of Ushant belongs, perhaps, to an *old* humanity, one which believes that the self *does* have the force to determine its environment. And Steelkilt's humanity is glamorous but also apparently monstrous in its manipulative action and fearless bloodshed. The Divine Inert does not sanction Ushant or Steelkilt because their forms of action forget the passivity of all agency that is transgressed by both sultanic hierarchy and Steelkilt-like republican selfhood.

In contrast, White Jacket is finally made to live out, as general moral conduct, the paradox of action's inertial structure. And thus Melville withdraws him from the rebellion against the Captain, from an act that would show his intentions and his will purposefully mastering and recreating the meaning and the truth of the world's order. We remember that White Jacket is preeminently a bungler, an inept plotter and enactor of his life and its form. But this is emblematic of his understanding and his embodiment of the principle that all doing is a suffering of its own effects. The acting out of even a just aggression is a blessing inextricable from a curse. As the remarkable coda to "Sink, Burn, and Destroy" (Chapter 75) tells us, all "carnage" is imponderable; we cannot know if it is for good or ill. Indeed "all events are mixed in a fusion indistinguishable." White Jacket and Melville, avatars of the Ishmael of "The *Town-Ho*'s Story," refer the imponderableness of events to "even, heartless, and impartial" Fate, which overwhelms our intentions and acts with "armed neutrality." Certainly we have wills: "I have a voice that helps to shape eternity; and my volitions stir the orbits of the furthest suns"; "ourselves are Fate." But as Melville *dramatizes* what White Jacket *says*, it looks as if he is saying that ourselves are also fatal and that our volitions are our shrouds. The narrative motion or plot of active rebellious consciousness is as doomed to fruitlessness and supersession as that of hierarchical structure. Indeed for Melville, plotting narrative consciousness becomes inevitably Ahab-like, and instigates psychical, intellectual, and moral carnage, if not physical carnage. What needs to replace the plotting motion of consciousness, the purposeful linear enactment (going from *B* to *C* to get to *D*) Bateson speaks of, is the consciousness of the Divine Inert, of the flexibility and calm that knows even revolutionary democratic action is self-reflexive and self-undoing. Of course it is not the Ushants or Steelkilts of the world but the Divine Inert itself that is the universal and metaphysical leveler, the essential democratic force.

In the end, Melville has located his polemic in the consciousness of the man who makes and wears the white jacket because this article of clothing is the clearest emblem of the duplicities of human "volitions" and conduct. Representing the narrator's deliberately made or plotted and enacted self, the jacket nearly causes its maker's death twice, and it is thought of by others as a fatality to them as well as to its owner. This shows, on the one hand, the illusion of plotted self-making, the fruitlessness of attempting to act as an organism-against-its-environment. (The plotting agent, whether author or author's delegate, is indeed an attempt to control contexts or to reassert control against the victories of context.) On the other hand, the jacket emblematizes its wearer as a submissive sufferer whose sense of plot and of life is the continuous double vision of inertial divinity; as a makeshift actor whose actions are fruitful assertions only insofar as they are also quietistic sufferings. Moreover, his creative assertions, when they take the form of rhapsodic Ishmaelite flights of narrative intellectual reason, are flights that dissociate speculation from practice and thematizing and hypothesizing perspectives from verification by action.

When "that unfortunate but indispensable garment" for the second time comes "near proving his shroud," White

Jacket at last rids himself of it. The re-creation of himself, a new violence of making, sounds like suicide:

> I whipped out my knife, that was tucked at my belt, and ripped my jacket straight up and down, as if I were ripping open myself. With a violent struggle I then burst out of it, and was free.

Since the story ends here, the garment itself is plot, the willful, shaping activity of narration that Melville has now freed himself from. But this is also the moment when *White Jacket* becomes free from all emphatic definition, both personal and political. By "ripping open myself" Melville's hero gains an alternative indefiniteness:

> We mortals are all on board a . . . world-frigate. . . . We . . . sail with sealed orders, and our last destination remains a secret. . . . We ourselves are the repositories of the secret packet, whose mysterious contents we long to learn. There are no mysteries out of ourselves.[9]

Melville's arguments against naval life are not founded on indefinite mysteries. But the ending of *White Jacket* exchanges clear pragmatic polemic and plotting movement towards violent revolt for the cultivation of indefinite strangeness and wonder. Perhaps this means that the rights of man and manhood and the plots representing such manhood are—or ought to be—founded in just those qualities. The clumsy, equivocal jacket, then, insofar as it stands for wonder, is *not* left behind. It reappears in Melville as "the draft of a draft," *Moby Dick*—as that book's compounding or cobbling of forms and mysteries.

When the white jacket causes its wearer to fall into the ocean from a height of above one hundred feet, it is cursed and condemned. But the wearer's return to life is marked by a curious detail—one that is an analogy of the jacket itself. "I wondered," says the narrator about his sinking, "whether I was yet dead, or still dying. But of a sudden, some fashionless form brushed my side—some inert, coiled fish of the sea;

the thrill of being alive again tingled in my nerves, and the strong shunning of death shocked me through." In the end *White Jacket* turns out to be almost as much "fashionless form" as the novel that succeeds it—the novel whose center is the "inert, coiled fish," the whale. What Melville finally rips open and sinks in *White Jacket* is an endorsement of assertive will and the idea of realizing democratic manhood through rebellious or violent enactment rather than—at least primarily—through humane *feeling* and marveling wonder. These latter are apparently most in touch with the inertial structure of the world. This means that Melville also rips open and sinks any plotting intention and intention-laden storytelling not approximate with the "fashionless form" of life, with the flexibility of "a draft of a draft."

In *Moby Dick* precipitation into the Divine Inert and the inhibition of decided and decisive purpose will strongly shun and survive, if not death, certainly the representation of action and of purposive and willful plot as vitally and morally valuable. These phenomena are apparently not divinely inertial, therefore not genuinely democratic. But I might close this chapter by pointing out that the one moment the white jacket is not worn by White Jacket is the moment he is called to the mast to face the temptation to rebel. Freed from his "cobbled" apparel, the narrator comes closest to being like Ushant or Steelkilt—to being the unqualifiedly activist hero of the "novel," willfully plotting his own life and death in a way that makes and unequivocally defines his personal meaning and moral dignity. Melville's change of heart at this moment helps make way not only for Ishmael and the Divine Inert but for the modern sense of plot that, since the 1920s, has made *Moby Dick* a classic. But we should remember that the novel's elevation by readers carries with it the elevation of the Divine Inert and the subordination of the possible value—for truth about the world's structure and for political conduct—of White Jacket's righteous and certainly self-revering moment of revolt and of Steelkilt's awesomely self-assertive act, one implicitly avowed even by Ishmael as perhaps as noble as the actor.[10]

SIX

Plot, Purpose, and the Modern Self

Who but a prig would set himself high aims, or make high
resolves at all?   —Samuel Butler, *The Way of All Flesh*

We are about to consider examples of how purpose in
story, like narrative reason, may or may not be grounded in
"facts of life." The need for this consideration is our continuing attempt to evaluate the truthfulness and the practical
meaning of plot, not merely its abstract or literary significance. And whereas in Chapter Three narrative reason impli-
cates us especially in a consideration of the truth of plot's
meaning in relation to life, narrative purposefulness impli-
cates us especially in a consideration of plot's value for life.
Not only meaning and truth reside in the choice and realization of ends but decisions about what ends are more valuable
than others or about whether or not a choice of ends is valuable at all. Thus we shall now examine the status of purpose
and plot as meaningful and valuable facts of life. And we
shall use as the focusing center of the examination the nonfic-
tive self attempting to find adequate narrative expression in
terms of purpose and plot. The self, plotting the form and action of its life, is to be considered here as symbolic of the authorial agent plotting—or considering the need to plot—a
story about experience.

But before focusing on purpose, I must review its use as a
term in the characterizations of plot and story that have been
employed here, in order to show how a focus on purpose is
still a consideration of action. In the last two chapters, when
interpreting the novelists' treatment of action, I have spoken
frequently of *agency* and *will* along with *purpose*. These terms

were introduced in the first chapter as connected with the representation of action through Kenneth Burke's definition of action as, basically, the body in purposive motion. An agent is any motivating force, and purposive motion implies the will as its agent; thus we can call purpose itself an agent. Considered as agents, will and purpose are both actors; even when and if they are considered as representatives or vehicles of action, they are the transformers of one condition into another—and an act always implies a transformation, a new change, and a significant difference. Thus the terms *purpose, agent,* and *will* slide towards synonymity with action— although they seem to exist just prior to the act that occurs as the success of their initiative. Because of the closeness of act and agent in what Burke calls "the act-agent ratio,"[1] in the preceding studies of Dickens, Eliot, and Melville I have compounded the consideration of actions and of their instrumental agents. When those agents have been represented as in themselves passive, inert, accidental, and unsuccessful—as Eliot and Melville represent them—I have argued an indifference to or distrust of action on the ground that distrust of acts in those writers is distrust of agents as well. Now distrust of the self (not in general but considered as a purposeful actor) seems to grow in the writing of literary autobiography as we approach the modern era of the sense of plot. Our examination of the role and value of purposeful plot in the life of the self finds in the era of the *fin de siècle* few positive testimonies to the meaning and value of either action or purpose.

In disengaging purpose from the other agents of action, we recall Lukács's claim that the *terminus ad quem* mediates all life and writing, determining their meaning and shape. In fact, Lukács shows an unconscious Dickensian sense of purpose, declaring in effect that purpose rescues life from chaos, meaning from indeterminacy, and value from an absence of selective discrimination. Without purpose life and art are neither telling nor actual; any representation of life that neglects ends untruthfully emphasizes absences of relation, static states of mind or feeling, a false indifference to evaluations. It might be well to recall here that the plot of a Dickens novel is rigidly and even obsessively teleological in pursuit of meaning and value. However much Dickensian plot cultivates diverse meanings and multiple directions, however much it expands and playfully opens undirected possibilities of significance or value, this expansion is resolved and brought to closure by the story's finish and by the acts that execute its ending. The end, considered not as finale but as *telos*, organizes all that precedes, explains all suspenseful mysteries and indeterminacies, marshalls every earlier detail and contingency, every event and character, into a structure revealed—at the last—as purposeful. And the final disclosure fully discriminates the value as well as the meaning of what comes before.

It is precisely such an all-telling end for which the selves in a Dickensian plot are searching. The purposeful ending of the story answers to and fulfills the personal purposes, meanings, and values the characters want fixedly to realize for themselves. Now Dickens believes such teleological desire, direction, and fulfillment are facts of life underlying the form of his fictional (yet truthful) sense of plot. We can keep Dickens's example in mind as we consider in this chapter implicit and explicit questionings of the fact and fictional form of purpose. For just how true is Dickens? How true is Lukács's claim about the *terminus ad quem*? Has life no intelligibility or meaning or value if it is not understood, like plot, as a perspectival function? Is the self essentially characterized or mediated by purposeful motive?

Our modern sense of plot has conditioned us to answer these questions negatively. Towards the end of the last century, influential writers thought of their lives as modern because they were ventures in the negation of purpose. In their memoirs these writers present their selves as free from definition by particular fixed ends and indeed free from definitions by ends in general. Consequently the memoirs attempt to use narrative forms disengaged from plotted purpose. If the freedom from ends and the corresponding freedom of autobio-

graphical forms means an erosion of meaning and of narrative reason in life, then the autobiographies welcome this
erosion as a liberation, a renewal of humanity. The new
forms of life-story are various: autobiography becomes a pur-
pose-suspending juxtaposition of portraits, or an epistle
emphasizing the self as a flexible, omnidirectional player of
momentary roles, or an attempt at imitating a meaningless
and purposeless biological rhythm. These innovations in the
sense of life's plots frequently accompany subversion of purposeful perspectives with a breaking down of the experience
and structure of reversal—an experience in narrative to which
crisis and conversion in life are analogous. Where purposefulness and meaningful narrative reason is eroded, so is the
experience of the turning point. Nevertheless a purposefulness can creep back into these memoirs in the form of moral
claims; the modern self can see purposeful plot as the ally of
moral constraint or of factitious meaning, but at the same
time the modern self avows its own superior value and meaning in being without fixed or defining ends.

In responding to Lukács's kind of claim about ends, this
present investigation into the purposive element of plot in relation to life and life-story is no more meant to establish truth
or falsity on this matter than Chapter Two is meant to establish the truth or falsity of narrative reason. What follows is a
collection of cases, enabling us to consider the relevance and
value of plotted purpose and purposeful plot to the being or
making and the intellectual and moral meaning of the self
and of its life. The cases are various and mostly negative
about purpose, although we will find a striking contrast to
this negativity in Yeats's autobiography. Yeats's position here
goes along with the fact that not all of our writers are
novelists; but all have great importance for the culture of
novelists and for the sense of plot that has affected the modern novel.

Our first case, exemplified by Edmund Gosse's *Father and
Son*, argues that a life organized and plotted towards one
purposefully chosen and valued end is nothing like a Dicken-

sian rescue. It is an inhumane and absurd coercion of experience, and for the plotter it results in a rigid inhibition of the self. But Gosse does not press his opposition to purposefulness, since he does not want to be coercive himself or even to stress purpose in the narrative form of his memoir. *Father and Son* is described by its author as a study of two temperaments, his parents' and his own. The temperament the elder Gosses represent is one that plots all present life and endeavor towards an absent spiritual goal and meaning that it yearns for, holds onto willfully, and pursues in order to realize. Edmund Gosse does not have this temperament. His book creates and compares pictures of its subjects in such a way as to replace narrative movement (and to inhibit if not to escape purpose completely) with comparative still portraiture. It is the nature of this portraitist to observe with sympathetic dispassion and objectivity the persons and experiences of his life. He does not so much want to selectively shape his material toward a goal or to represent a polemical stance as to be generously analytic and appreciative of what he portrays. His parents, he believes, did not appreciate life; his book about his parents is a "study" that draws back from the driving narrative movements characteristic of their consciousness and of their *kind* of self.

The Gosses' virtual obsession with dedication is specifically Christian. According to Edmund Gosse's viewpoint his appreciative and open nature seems to have been coerced by the religion of his parents from the time he was six weeks old. They make him a ritual offering to their God and to their God's service in "the opening act of that 'dedication' which was never forgotten. . . . What a weight, intolerable as the burden of Atlas, to lay on the shoulders of a little fragile child!" Throughout childhood Gosse experiences nothing without being made to feel that religious and ethical purpose and meaning inform the most petty incidents and contacts of his life. One Christmas, against the father's orders, the house servants secretly make a plum pudding for themselves, and offer Edmund a slice of it in the kitchen. The boy accepts, but then—sick with guilt—confesses to his father: "Oh! Papa, Papa, I have eaten of flesh offered to idols." The father runs to the kitchen "into the midst of the startled servants," and hurls the pudding, which he calls "the accursed thing," into the fire.

In the end Gosse judges this inflexible plotting of the merest details of existence towards a distant, difficult, spiritual and ethical goal not only as meaningless and value-less but as nothing less than insane and inhuman. He insists especially on its inhumanity. Although his mother's death "awakened his heart," his parents' obsession with purpose left him with "still no idea of the relations of human beings to each other. . . . I had no humanity." His father "contrived to stifle with a deplorable success alike the function of imagina-tion, the sense of moral justice, and his own deep and instinc-tive tenderness"; and Gosse found similar qualities in his maternal grandfather: "narrowness, isolation, an absence of perspective, let it be boldly admitted, an absence of humani-ty." He identifies even the activity of conscience with inhu-manity, for this seems the tendency of his remark that only in seaside research on marine biology did his father become "most easy, most happy, most human. That hard look upon his brows, the look that came from sleepless anxiety of con-science, faded away." Conscience, by favoring some values rather than others, is apparently an anxious teleological or-gan, driven always by one purpose rather than another. Gosse implies that in his father's best scientific work—the work not distorted by religious and ethical purposes—he re-vealed a temperament coinciding with his son's: curious, in-terested, impartial, objective yet tender, even sensuous, re-laxedly open to life, not shaping it anxiously for the sake of some one—or of any—end. This relaxed and curious open-ness is characteristic of what Gosse calls the "most human" self. Not that Gosse believes, we might add, that humanity is *significant* or meaningful because of its flexibility and open-ness: indeed he believes that we live "a pathetic and fugitive existence." But it appears more valuable to Gosse to make the best of life's fugitive pathos by recognizing it rather than by evading it as his parents did with the erection of a spurious structure and morality of purpose.[2]

It is possible to admire the elder Gosses nevertheless—even without the sort of melancholy and at times condescending pity their son feels. Working hard and ceaselessly in the face of penury and sickness, revering and serving without complaints an exacting God, showing remarkable tenderness for each other and for their son (even though the son denies such feeling in them), the parents' temperament perhaps amounts to something more impressive and of more worth than Edmund Gosse's. He argues that his parents lived in the service of illusions; and this may be true. Yet although the son claims superior vitality for his kind of self, are not the parents more vivid? The elder Gosses strike one at times as much more forcefully alive than their son. Gosse accuses his parents of being too much out of this world as a result of their purposefulness. But their greater vitality seems to result from their insistently teleological plotting of life; their dedication to another world imbeds them deeply in the one they want to escape. Commitment to an absent end is a plot or project directed out of this world, at least relatively: yet such commitment, as Lukács points out, seems to give daily experience more meaning than experience that is not pervaded by it.[3] The *terminus ad quem* may not be justifiable metaphysically, but it may have a value for life because its effects are more creative than any alternative. (Analogously, the perspectival function of plot and story may help create vivid differences, hence meanings, within the experience they represent.)

Even men who directly dedicate themselves to the humanity that is Gosse's ultimate appeal have found meaning and value in pursuing an absent end—an end not much less beyond present and immediate actualities than the heaven Gosse's parents believed in. Since Gosse seems to believe that the self and its life are not fruitfully identified with either Christian dedication per se or with any purpose similar to the structure of such dedication, it might be useful to contrast

him with Ruskin and Mill, who define their selves and tell
their lives as a plot towards distant goals—even though both
men served immediate and humanitarian ends. Their personal histories testify to the drama of committed purpose as
inescapably life's essential meaning and *story*.

Ruskin in *Praeterita* believes that he can precisely delineate
the purposefully consecrating moments of his experience.
While in the Alps in 1833 he discovered "not only the revelation of the beauty of the earth, but the opening of the first
page of its volume. . . . I went down . . . fixed in all . . . that
was to be sacred and useful." One of the fixed dedications is
to a broad humanitarianism. "Men had been curiously judging themselves," he decides at a later point, "by always calling the day they expected *Dies Irae*, instead of *Dies Amoris*";
thereafter he plots his life as a pilgrim's progress towards *Dies
Amoris*. This final end is not abstract or theological since it is
embodied in the persons of Charles Eliot Norton and Rose
LaTouche, but neither of them are actually present in his life.
They become images of the absent good he chooses to hold
onto and to pursue.

> Another "new life" or "new epoch of life" began for me
> in this wise, that my father and mother could travel with
> me no more, but Rose, in heart, was with me always,
> and all I did was for her sake. . . . As much for her sake,
> . . . as of old, for theirs, and more distinctly also in the
> choice and tenor of it beginning with *Unto This Last*.[4]

Clearly in *Praeterita* Ruskin delineates his personal dedications and pursuits with a trust in purpose very unlike his
doubts about the reliability of the key of Destiny.

John Stuart Mill first experienced life as a valuable form of
plotted, meaningful dedication through his early studies with
his father. When Mill felt compelled to rebel against the absence of feeling in his father's rigidly analytic utilitarianism
he did not rebel against the strenuous purpose and dedication that he had been schooled under. For he himself worked
to realize ideal and absent values in contemporary life such as

the "heroic virtue" he found described in Condorcet's *Life of Turgot*, or the "ideal conception of a Perfect Being, to which [all religions] habitually refer as the guide of their conscience," or the "ideal nobleness" which he found more in France than in England and which he found most in the woman he waited long years to marry. When Harriet Taylor died, Mill transformed her into a kind of church. "Her memory is to me a religion, and her approbation the standard by which, summing up as it does all worthiness, I endeavor to regulate my life." "Those only are happy," Mill concludes, "who have their minds fixed on some object other than their own happiness; on the happiness of others, on the improvement of mankind, even on some art of pursuit, followed not as a means, but as itself an ideal end."[5] Ruskin's and Mill's accounts of their lives demonstrate how even the most careful and pragmatic attention to the present, to the immediate human and social aspects of life, cannot escape transcendent and ideal plots and fixed purposes. And the self that this kind of pursuit engenders, though it may look narrow, dry, and meaningless or worthless to a man like Edmund Gosse, seems to be the creative agent of remarkable effects.

For Gosse, however, the effects of the purposeful self may be remarkable, but they are also tragic. Certainly, commitment and dedication to a single end seem to the son to destroy Philip Gosse. When the latter begins to see that his religious and scientific ends are at odds with each other, he decides that his life is at a turning point he cannot evade. He must commit himself to one purpose exclusively—to the religious telos; and he therefore undertakes the writing of *Omphalos*. With this choice Edmund Gosse believes his father "closed the door upon himself forever." The son repeats how sad it is that "circumstance after circumstance combined to drive [my father] further from humanity." But it is not so much circumstance as much as rigid dedicated purpose that is the commitment-provoking, hence crisis-provoking and dehumanizing agent here. Edmund Gosse believes that a genuine and genuinely valuable self—the kind his father closed the door upon—is born in freedom from teleological commitments and from any need to make choices about the crises those commitments engender.

The self, free of purpose and its deformations, is imaged for Gosse in literature and art, which never ask that we confine ourselves to developing one human or personal purpose rather than another. Indeed for Gosse literature and art give the self whatever meaning and value fugitive existence can have by suspending the self's purposes, commitments, and crises. Inspired by art, Edmund, at age twenty-one, "threw off once and for all the yoke of his 'dedication' [and] took a human being's privilege to fashion his inner life for himself." This privilege—and the form of its fashioning—need never be limited to the service of a single purpose or to a choice between two restricting alternatives. The genuinely human self reconciles alternatives and cultivates contradictory possibilities. "In my hot and silly brain, Jesus and Pan held sway together," Gosse says. The heat and the silliness belong to his adolescence, but the desire to reconcile incompatibilities without selective exclusiveness does not.

We can see how this desire for reconciliations carries over into the "plot" of *Father and Son*, for even though Gosse opposes his parents' obsessions with purpose, he wants a form that will enable the two temperaments in his book to coexist without one driving out the other. Although we feel there is an inevitable battle under way between the two temperaments, Gosse is sincere in his attempt to appreciate both; and this appreciativeness is one of the hallmarks of the genuine self and value that Gosse's wary sense of plot develops. For Gosse the self's expression of some of its potential in one direction is less important than the expression of the self as a continual unselective presence of being. In all its powers and possibilities, this kind of present self is God for Gosse; on the other hand, traditional purposive dedication or narration of one's life, a story featuring *one* temperament, would distort and betray this presence. "What came to me," at the age of five, "was the consciousness of self, as a force and as a companion." Apparently innate and unconditioned, Gosse's self appears to him as a persistent, speculating double who watches in imperturbable aesthetic detachment—even when young Edmund has hysterical nightmares or when, in rages at himself and his parents, he sticks his body with pins and beats his joints with books. By finding suddenly the source of all power, meaning, and value in himself, young Gosse seems to have begun to think he need not look beyond his sustaining double—to God, or to an ideal way of conduct, or to any demanding distant and external reality—as an end towards which he might plot his life. His end or purpose, like his meaning and value, is present in him from his earliest memories in the sustaining sense of his own distinctive and persistent being. The humanity of the writers Gosse turns to in reaction to his parents lies for him in their ability to stimulate a directionless (or perhaps omnidirectional) intense appreciativeness, which the detached "study" of the narrative form of *Father and Son* attempts as much as possible to represent.[6]

There is a more complex and subtle approach to purpose and to the plotting of personal life or "temperament" in Oscar Wilde. In his epistolary memoir, *De Profundis*, Wilde says of the self: "Every human being should be the realization of some ideal." But what does Wilde mean by "realization" and "ideal"? He is not repeating the older Gosses' purposive and teleological address to life, but at the same time he is not altogether eschewing ends as much as Gosse does. In Wilde's sense of the self and its life there is an implicit notion of a developing purpose, meaning, or value—an end that shows itself, recedes, is revised, comes newly forward, recedes again, but is perhaps always emergent. What Wilde seems to be saying is that a purpose is, after all, a hypothetical end or value; if any form of life invokes purpose as its ground, it must be willing to shift the ground if the hypothetical end or value appears unreliable or distasteful. Moreover, for Wilde, once an "ideal" end is "realized" another should take its place.

What Wilde is saying about purposes is no more "aesthetic" than pragmatic; the logic of "ideals" and "realizations" in such plays as *An Ideal Husband* and *The Importance of Being Earnest* as well as in the memoir can be illustrated, perhaps surprisingly, by John Dewey. "All tenets and creeds about good and goods," Dewey writes in *The Quest for Certainty*,

> [should] be recognized as hypotheses. Instead of being rigidly fixed, they [should] be treated as intellectual instruments to be tested and confirmed. They [should] lose all pretence of finality. . . . Any belief as such is tentative, hypothetical; it is not just to be acted upon, but is to be *framed* with reference to its office as a guide to action. Consequently, it should be the last thing in the world to be picked up casually and then clung to rigidly.[7]

This seems remarkably like Wilde in terms of purposes and meanings as well as of "tenets about good." Wilde insists that, like such tenets, no end, purpose, or meaning be clung to rigidly. And this is so even if it concerns an end *not* picked up casually. Such ends include those set for themselves by rigidly obsessive human appetites. In his plays Wilde frequently dramatizes appetitive obsessions (from hunger for the ideal to hunger for Bunburying) as if they were models of the old form of the inflexibly purposeful self epitomized by the elder Gosses. At the same time he tries to show that these obsessions change their objects and enjoy doing so, that their purpose is to consume one purpose after another.

The "realization" of the "ideal" self in Wilde turns out to be a continuous play with ends, values, and purposes; earnest purpose and meaningfulness in fact emerge as play, as the object of constant experiment by the self, which is a plotting agent insofar as it is a playful agent. Like purpose, plot or value is play for Wilde, a provisional and temporary hypothesis to be "realized"—and then to be left behind for others. The truth—the narrative reason, meaning, or value of any plot or the truth, meaning, or value of any self—is thus always momentary. This is very different from the selective movement of the self or of plot towards an absolute goal or a fixed achievement in Dickens's stories or in the generation represented by Gosse's parents. The older characters do not plot ends for themselves just because they like to, just because the realization of an ideal is the pleasure of play in the present moment.

In *De Profundis* the purpose that plots and maintains the self is continuously self-revising and self-suspending. Here, the motive for Wilde's sense of plot and purpose is, of course, the attempt to recover from the disasters of his prison sentence and of his affair with Lord Alfred Douglas. Wilde insists that the crisis in his life has not destroyed any one cherished purpose or any essential identity. His purposes and his self are always in a metamorphic state; playful change of direction is all they are dedicated to, and the prison sentence is a link in the continuous metamorphosis. Whereas earlier life-writers (such as Mill and Ruskin) take the determination and fixing of their selfhood from a conversion experience in which they shift allegiance from one crucial purpose or hierarchy of values to another, Wilde's innovation in *De Profundis* is to write in the very moment of conversion, to make writing itself the process and moment of converting his experience into whatever reality, meaning, and estimate of worth his desire and imagination assign it. This is playing with the structure of reversal, as well as with purpose. The use of both conversion and of purposeful plot are not intended by Wilde to fix the self in any one direction, but rather to unfix it. Wilde emphasizes his desire to unfix all limits and conditions: "I have got to make everything that has happened to me good for me." These transformations or re-creations of the self are what Wilde calls "spiritual": "There is not a single degradation of the body which I must not try and make into a spiritualizing of the soul." Degradation, sin, or failure are in fact "a mode of perfection," to be atoned for only for the sake of comprehension, not of repentance. Even the past, especially if it includes a degradation, can be re-created and is no more fixed than the self: "Do not be afraid of the past," Wilde counsels Douglas; "if people tell you that it is irrevocable, do not believe them."[8]

If this emphasis on the re-creative power of the self and on its "spiritualizing" capacity seems to highlight the self as active agent, we must remember that in fact both the Wildean agent and action—and Wildean values, too—are of such fluidity and flexibility that they are difficult to identify. Because Wilde's "purpose" is to unfix the definitions of his self and his life as the past has apparently dictated them, in *De Profundis* he puts us in the presence of what we feel as the immediacy of growth rather than as a clearly explicit self, action, or end of growth. This immediacy of growth *is* meaning and value for Wilde. The casting of *De Profundis* in the form of a *letter* to Douglas may emphasize for Wilde this feeling of the immediate presence of growth. For this form keeps Wilde free from the temptation—the *narrative* or *plotting* temptation—of abstracting or selecting from his past life one exclusively defining shape and narrative reasoning for it. It is for the sake of projecting his self's purpose and the plot of his life as constant reformation that Wilde suggests to us the possibility of a purpose, an identity or agency of self, and a scheme of values always emerging and always receding, in a forever open indeterminacy of development. What Wilde is attempting in *De Profundis* has another appropriate gloss in Dewey, who declares the modern sense of end-purpose as

> no longer a terminus or limit to be reached. It is the active process of transforming the existent situation. Not perfection as a final goal, but the ever-enduring process of perfecting, maturing, refining is the aim of living. . . . Growth itself is the only moral "end."[9]

And we might also say that growth in Wilde and in the self, too, are states of mind or feeling rather than active agents— that they are "noble attitudes" with which Wilde watches and even resists the natural necessities and acts of his life as well as any fixed identity and perhaps any obstacles to growth that they carry with them.[10]

Wilde's sense of plot and purpose as play (we have already seen a version of this in Poe) revises and reverses Lukács's treatment of purpose as the essential fact of life and story. For Wilde, self and life do not depend upon a chosen end for their representation and meaning. Ends are only among numerous expressions of the self or of life, and no end is a single defining agent. But at the same time that *De Profundis* asserts its author's self and life as a free and unconditioned process of making and creating—a growing first towards one kind of good, then towards another—the memoir continuously stirs up contradictions of this assertion. Whatever noble attitude, whatever playfulness, whatever resistance to determination and fixation Wilde marshals for the sake of self-utterance and his version of meaning, it is as if life itself were inflexibly plotting, purposefully realizing Wilde's destruction through an unalterable finality in Alfred Douglas—a figure instigated by a doom that seems to take the creative replotting and meaning of experience quite out of Wilde's control. Wilde sadly all but admits as much. He tells "Bosie" that he discerns "in all our relations, not Destiny merely, but Doom . . . the strange Doom you seem to have brought on me in all things big or little." There is in such a sentence the suggestion that Wilde realizes he has himself intended this doom, fixed his life after all in the pursuit of one tragic and unredeemably destructive selective purpose.

There is also testimony to this in Wilde's retrenchment of his thinking about the essential playfulness and satisfaction of obsessive appetite: he condemns Douglas for having "appetites merely," and now in *De Profundis*, "the secret of life is suffering. It is what is hidden behind everything." Hidden behind the "spiritualizings" of growth, this invocation of suffering also intensifies our sense that Wilde's idea of self-reformation is more to be "realized" as an attitude, as a detached state of mind dissociated from events and from the enactments of actual practice. Wilde himself acknowledges the memoir's "changing, uncertain moods, its scorn and bitterness, its aspirations and its failure to realize those aspirations.''[11] Are the contradictions the result of his trying to plot the form of personal life this new way: as continuous play and constant conversion, approximating growth and achievement by the re-creative realization, in fancy at least, of whatever experiences cross his attention? Insisting that reality can be changed by his way of looking at it, by the depth of his vision, or by the force of his desire, Wilde fails to convince the reader—and himself—that there is not a gap between the reality of his life and the attitudes he adopts towards it. One is left with the impression that Wilde's "goal" of the "ideal realization" of the self is less effective in coming to grips with life than is the fixedly plotting dedication and struggle found in the lives of the older generation.

It is arguable that Gosse's appreciation of nonpurposeful life and that Wilde's play with purposes inevitably tends to separate *what* happens from *how* the self thinks or feels about what happens. Appreciativeness or "ideal realizations" may dissociate a way of seeing or feeling from practice, and subordinate the latter. This dissociation and subordination might be all to the good; but "making whatever happens to me good for me," pursued to its limits, may also yield the recreation of self and event less than it produces the sense that life as action or event is indeed pathetic and fugitive, a doom redeemed only by illusions, by those imaginative appreciations that throw a veil, purposeful or otherwise, over the essential purposelessness and valuelessness of experience. Here we must add to our first two cases of the modern self's relation to purpose and plot the case of George Moore, whose understanding of life brings out far more clearly than Gosse's sense of human pathos or Wilde's sense of Doom the idea of experience as a kind of purposeless, raw happening. For Moore life is valueless and without qualities, unredeemable by creative intentions, acts, or ends which Moore feels are merely names for biological impulses, themselves part of a meaningless physical flux of experience.

The self Moore creates and the sense of plot he pursues are attempts both to live in this flux without illusions and to express this without distortion in writing. The first step of this attempt is, like Gosse's, a flight to art. Accordingly Moore, who in the early 1870s patterned a way of life to which Joyce, Stein, Hemingway, and Miller added nothing original, vowed *non serviam* to the church and was expelled from his Irish Catholic college for refusing to confess; he then exiled himself to Paris, lived in a circle of brillant bohemians, and tried his hand at painting and writing. In 1888 he published *The Confessions of a Young Man*, the prototype of *A Portrait of the Artist as a Young Man*. In these confessions Moore pays at least lip service to the pursuit of consecrating purpose. He tells his readers that his soul is "art-tortured," and that he serves two ideals: the ideal of the young man and the ideal of perfection of form in art. He also has an experience of crisis and conversion, the result of accidentally reading an article by Zola in the *Voltaire:*

> *Naturalisme, la verité, la science.* . . . Hardly able to believe my eyes, I read that one should write with as little imagination as possible, that plot in a novel or in a play was illiterate and puerile, and that the art of M. Scribe was an art of strings and wires. . . . Words heard in an unexpected quarter, but applying marvelously well to the besetting difficulty of the moment. The reader . . . will remember the instant effect the word "Shelley" had upon me in childhood, and how it called into existence feeling that illuminated the vicissitudes and passions of many years, until it . . . became part of my being; the reader will also remember how the mere mention, at a certain moment, of the word "France" awoke a vital impulse, even a sense of final ordination, and how it led to the creation of a mental existence.
>
> And now for the third time I experienced the pain and joy of a sudden and inward light. Naturalism, truth, the new art. . . .

At this point he throws away his attempts to write symbolist poetry in order to fulfill a new creative mission. But in the

end Moore seems rather indifferent to—and even bored
with—exaltations and "ordinations." The first mission of his
life had seemed to be a creation of what he called his self. He
had been almost ecstatic at his father's death because "before
me . . . was self; not the self that was then mine, but the self
on whose creation I was enthusiastically determined."[12] At
the end of the confessions he inserts a dialogue between his
ego and his conscience, during which his conscience asks just
what he has achieved in the way of that self-realization. The
answer is negative.

Moore's way of closing his book suggests that he has
achieved nothing: neither a self nor any actual artistic accomplishment (on the last page he is just *about* to begin writing a first novel); moreover, he no longer has the youth he
idealizes. Surprisingly, this lack of achievement and this absence of the ideal seem very satisfactory to him. He appears
to be re-creating his life deliberately as a sort of existential
middle ground that rejects origins, ends, and any plotted or
structured purpose and movement and any achievement that
might fall between them. The achieved and fully-formed self
does not matter—"I came into the world apparently with a
nature like a smooth sheet of wax, bearing no impress, but
capable of receiving many." He continues comfortably in this
waxen state, too malleable for the formation of a definite self.
But in such a self there is far more superior truth to life, for
Moore believes life in itself is a formless and blind physical
state. Moore may have suspected the very idea of the self as
inauthentically purposeful and spiritual, the ally of ideals and
values that spuriously form the wax and that break what he
calls "the peace of unconsciousness." Now as he pays lip
service to ideals, he pays his respects to spirit and spiritual
values; he even pays them ostentatiously. Balzac, he says,
saved him from all the false elements of aestheticism, natu-
ralism, and symbolism: "Thinking of him I could not forget
that it is the spirit and not the flesh that is eternal." He likes
Pater too for valuing spirit and intellect more than flesh.

But at the same time Moore cannot speak convincingly

about anything but the flesh and its resistance to purpose, spirit, meaning, and value. "My poor conscience," he says to that faculty when it upbraids him for a recent seduction, "are you still struggling in the fallacy of free will? . . . Life is merely the breaking of the peace of unconsciousness." In the last third of the confessions he curses those men whose persistent love of conscience he identifies with stupidity. He is himself a barbaric pagan: "I cried 'Ave' to it all: lust, cruelty, slavery." He hates pity and goodness; he symbolically identifies his self and the truth of life with the person of the maid in his shabby boarding house in the Strand. She is a mule, without sense, "a drudge too horrible for anything but work; and I suppose, all things considered, that the fat landlady with a dozen children did well to work you seventeen hours a day, and cheat you out of your miserable wages." In his callousness Moore is addressing himself as well as the maid. He thinks of himself as the same kind of drudge—his character and his industry for art being as physical, blindly driven, and even stupid as the maid's work. "The morality of the world will always be the same," and books will not change that: "Art . . . is now—a mere emotion, right or wrong in proportion to its intensity." Moore's likings and dislikings in literary matters are "analogous to sexual affinities—the same unreasoned attractions, the same pleasures, the same lassitudes."[13] His "making" of a self and of books turns out to be no purposeful plotted dedication but an adventure in sensation amidst the flux of material sensations that is life understood without illusions.

In the self that is forever malleable in response to the drift of sensation, Moore finds not depression or doom but a kind of happy carelessness, an irresponsible freedom. One of the first modern men "inside the whale," Moore discovers that turning one's back on the narrative motions of life and consciousness (as one keeps writing!) creates a blessed indifference to what happens to him for better or worse. His closeness to life as random flux of sensation makes him feel careless even about death. This feeling also diminishes his

sense of self or life as a matter of purposeful commitment. For
no doubt men have lived out plotted dedications to fixed
purposes because in the face of death and insignificance they
have felt that their choices and activities take on an awesome
urgency.

But in his second autobiographical book, *Memoirs of My
Dead Life* (1906), Moore makes death itself an event that, in a
kind of Wildean exercise of playful re-creation, he can both
accept and snap his fingers at. Wondering what sort of attitude he should take towards death (especially since "all
modern literature [is] but a reek of regret that we are all but
bubbles on a stream"), in his second memoir he decides to
plan his funeral. It will be a pagan feast, and his ashes will be
deposited in a Greek vase, decorated with bacchants. He
thinks that "neither in my prose nor verse have I ever traced
out my thoughts as completely or perfectly as I have done in
this order for my tomb." His final direction is that the urn be
dropped into the sea, where it will remain until, at some future natural apocalypse, the earth will consume itself and be
reborn. Thereupon his ashes will engender new life, and will
eventually engender again his very own life. At a distant
moment he will be in the same room, at the same desk, once
more writing memoirs of his dead life. These thoughts are all
the while taking place in him during his mother's funeral.
While the past of his childhood is nostalgically present to
him, he is also foreseeing the future; and suddenly he feels
convinced that his present moment is eternal.[14] For Moore
this is a triumph of both the present physical moment and of
"making whatever happens to me good for me." It is also a
moment in which he is convinced that life is an enduring
egocentric pleasure, free of demanding purpose. And like
both Gosse and Wilde, Moore here manages to present the
self as a metamorphic, protean presence, a cool spectator
playing with what happens to it.

But for Moore, unlike Wilde and in spite of the momentary
triumph of self-expression in the fantasy of his funeral, what
happens is accepted for what it is, without an attempt to con-

vert it into anything remotely spiritual or conventionally successful or "good." Moore seeks intense moments to impress
upon his waxen state, but they are generally not planned—
for planning would be factitious and would presuppose
values that would not say " 'Ave' to it all." For Moore there is
no more plan in general or individual life than there is a linear
plot in his own narrative. In the memoirs—as in the confessions—rhythm replaces narrative and takes a biological
model for itself. Now there is a heartbeat, now there is the
heartbeat's negation. Purposeful plot is replaced, as the purposeful self is replaced, by the pathos and pleasure of the
body's sensations at random directionless moments. At one
point Moore describes himself as about to write a story, going
over the possibilities of a plot and then rejecting the whole
business because he wants to express the rhythm of

> death and life always overlapping, mixed inextricably,
> and no meaning in anything, merely a stream of change
> in which things happen. Sometimes the happenings are
> pleasant, sometimes unpleasant, and in neither the
> pleasant nor the unpleasant can we detect any pur-
> pose.[15]

In Moore story becomes the arbitrary and sometimes happy
expression of a careless, spontaneous life that he himself calls
interesting and nevertheless, since it is without purpose,
meaningless.

So far, the kind of self we have seen develop without plot
and purpose or with an innovatively revised playfulness of
purpose verges on being incommunicable. Its resistance to
purpose or to any fixity of purpose cultivates a form—or
formlessness—of being that the self resists sharing with
others. For example, Gosse jealously guards the difference of
his temperament from that of his parents; Wilde and Moore
condemn their historical communities as fatal constraints;
Wilde writes not to the public but to Douglas, and Moore asserts himself out of love for his sensations but not to have
them "accepted" by his readers. Of course Moore's formless

waxen state may be "incommunicable" because we can assume that everyone shares it and that there is no need to plot
or objectify the body as narrative form for the purpose of exchanging intelligence about it. Yet what a different picture of
the essential community of selves and what a different picture of Moore the waxen self we find in Yeats's autobiography, a text which is a remarkable and anomalous testimony
to the persistence of fixed purposes in the modern self's plotting of life. In Yeats' *Dramatis Personae 1896-1902*, we find
Moore the novelist living and writing in the service of a rigid,
obsessive, and even genuinely spiritual *terminus ad quem*:

> England had turned from style, as it has been under-
> stood from the translators of the Bible to Walter Pater,
> sought mere clarity in statement and debate, a journalis-
> tic effectiveness, at the moment when Irish men of letters
> began to quote the saying of Sainte-Beauve: "There is
> nothing immortal in literature except style." Style was
> [Moore's] growing obsession, he would point out all the
> errors of some silly experiment of mine, then copy it. It
> was from some such experiment that he learnt those
> long, flaccid, structureless sentences, "and, and, and";
> there is one of twenty-eight lines in *Muslin*. Sometimes
> he rebelled: "Yeats, I have a deep distrust of any man
> who has a style," but it was generally I who tried to stop
> the obsession. "Moore, if you ever get a style," I would
> say, "it will ruin you. It is coloured glass and you need a
> plate-glass window." When he formed his own circle he
> found no escape; the difficulties of modern Irish litera-
> ture, from the loose, romantic, legendary stories of Stan-
> dish O'Grady to James Joyce and Synge, had been the
> formation of a style. He heard those difficulties dis-
> cussed. All his life he had learnt from conversation, not
> from books. His nature, bitter, violent, discordant, did
> not fit him to write the sentences men murmur again and
> again for years. Charm and rhythm had been denied
> him. Improvement makes straight roads; he pumice-

stoned every surface because will had to do the work for nature. I said once: "You work so hard that, like the Lancelot of Tennyson, you will almost see the Grail." But now, his finished work before me, I am convinced he was denied even that "almost."[16]

Moore's life is revealed here as a tragically shaped drama. From Yeats's point of view the written work amounts to a mask insofar as it represents a rebellious and bohemian loafer. But underneath the mask is a man committed to a pursuit of the sort that his writing usually asserts to be pointless and outmoded.

For Yeats there are no mere happenings in life. The principal figures of his autobiography—himself, Moore, Lady Gregory, Edward Martyn, Synge—are each forging their lives as earnest and meaningful dramas because they pursue abstract, absent images of selves that they want to make real and historical.

> A writer must die every day he lives, be reborn, as it is said in the Burial Service, an incorruptible self, that self opposite of all that he has named "himself." George Moore, dreading the annihilation of an impersonal bleak realism, used life like a medieval ghost making a body for itself out of drifting dust and vapour; and have I not sung in describing guests at Coole—"There one that ruffled in a manly pose, For all his timid heart"—that one myself? Synge was a sick man picturing energy, a doomed man picturing gaiety; Lady Gregory, in her life much artifice, in her nature much pride, was born to see the glory of the world in a peasant mirror.[17]

Yeats's way of seeing plot in life is obviously synonymous with his familiar doctrine of the antithetical self and the mask. This doctrine needs to be understood as an attempt—in the face of prestigious opposition in literary culture—to salvage the idea, meaning, and value of inflexibly purposeful human activity and of a corresponding sense of plot in art.

In this light the fact that Yeats writes *Dramatis Personae 1896-1902* as the history of a man who is a dramatist first, and a lyric poet second, becomes clearer. His doing so underscores the reality of plot and drama in daily life—indeed, he says at one point that he became a dramatist in order simply to be "that forgotten thing, the normal active man." *The Bounty of Sweden* does not end the collection of Yeats's various memoirs in any ironic way. The Nobel prize was given Yeats primarily for his plays and for the public activity that created, along with them, the Irish Theatre, and he considers this reasoning to have been just. The success of his life has been essentially a matter of theater—of theater considered as permanent and real rather than as temporary and factitious: "Active virtue as distinguished from the passive acceptance of a current code is . . . consciously dramatic, the wearing of a mask. It is the condition of arduous full life."[18]

Gosse, Wilde, and Moore forget the normal, active man and *his* storytelling, dramatizing forms of life. Of course Yeats derives his thinking about masks from Wilde; but whereas Wilde arguably opens a gap between a man's activity and his imagination's attitude towards it, Yeats uses plot to narrow the distance between the real and the imaginative, between natural necessity and the creative shaping of it. The dramas plotted by individual imaginations in Yeats's autobiography are at one with both a public and a cosmic drama, which Yeats argues again and again—with considerable attempts to be prudently scientific in his demonstration—are historical, not merely symbolic and momentary or imitative of art. The association of Yeats with symbolism has obscured how urgently actual, how unlike playfulness, he took the dramatic plotting of his generation to be.

Here Yeats's earnestness is directed towards establishing the common structure shared by individual lives. His emphasis on the purposeful plotting of these lives seems to intensify the fact of their interrelations with each other. It is as if the Yeatsian kind of self creates a community of relations by its persistent teleological commitment. Unlike Gosse, Wilde, and Moore, Yeats sets out to trace the plotted form of his life and other lives in the hope of revealing what they have in common. In his Nobel prize lecture to the Swedish Royal Academy, Yeats speaks of "how deep down we have gone, below all that is individual, modern and restless, seeking foundations for . . . Ireland"—and for Europe.[19] Yet Yeats the poet and dramatist is in the anomalous position of articulating personal and social life by a commitment to plot and story that is worthy of a novelist—at a time when novelists proper seem to have been tired of both plot and story in fiction and autobiography. And we can see that Yeats's autobiographical form is also not unaffected by the suspension of purposes happening around him. Yeats describes lives that are, as a result of their fixed ends, all of a piece. But the form of Yeats's personal story is rather fragmentary, a gradual piecing together of bits of life, as if Yeats trusted all-shaping purposefulness in literary form *less* than in life.

Since Yeats's way of seeing the self dramatically identifies the self with the power to transform an intention into objectified activity, it does not identify the self and its meaning or value with a state of mind or feeling, with a purely internal dimension. This aspect of Yeats seems deeply conservative, opposed to "the modern." But the internalized self, which we can identify with Wilde and Gosse especially, is perhaps no more modern than Yeats's or the elder Gosses' pursuit of dramatic dedications and ideal projections. In the *fin de siècle* life-writing, the more radical modernity challenges the notion of "self" altogether, and hence includes a more radical elision of purposefulness, meaning, and value than we have yet met. In two of the best known American autobiographies, *The Education of Henry Adams* and *The Autobiography of Alice B. Toklas*, the self and its purposes are, in the first case, fragile and indeed negligible in the face of the physical and social forces they confront; in the second case, they can scarcely be identified as a reality other than a purely "written" one. And in its reality outside writing (if it has one) the self is of course very happily without either marked individuation or purposefulness.

At the end of Adams's book, social and physical "force" and "acceleration" become understandable to Adams, but they disclose themselves as energies robbing individual will and purpose of creative possibility. The individual cannot "count" by making or remaking himself according to a desired purpose, nor can he realize personal purpose in the form of social effects that genuinely matter. Adams admits that his conclusions are "profoundly unmoral, and tend to discourage effort." He finds compensation for this in the way his thinking "tend[s] to encourage foresight and to economize waste of mind." But the encouragement is feeble in the face of the powerlessness of any of the self's plottings. Whether defined in terms of fixed purpose, or of Wilde's manifold intentions of desire, or of Moore's rebellious scoffing and loafing, the modern self in Adams is a negligible unit in a multiverse of supersensual chaos. To attempt to cultivate the self or to plot a form of life for it as an ordered refuge from the chaos would be to evade the fact that the self is only an isolated spidery presence in the multiverse.[20]

What of other selves in Adams's book? One might expect an individual's connections with others either to establish or to reinforce purposeful motions of consciousness, as seems to be the case in Yeats's dramatic communities. Adams the historian and novelist must have understood other persons as forces not supersensual, not necessarily chaotic, inspiring the individual self to purposeful plot. But Adams the autobiographer clears away the inspiring effect of other personal purposes upon his own—with only one exception. While most figures in Adams's book are ghostlike, when the geographer Clarence King bursts in upon Adams's awareness (in a chapter called "Failure") the reader has a sense of encountering a force as great as the Dynamo's and The Virgin's, but one specifically and measurably purposeful. King "had everything to interest and delight Adams. . . . King had molded and directed his life logically, scientifically, as Adams thought American life should be directed." The effect of this encounter for both men, Adams says, was that suddenly "history and science spread out in personal horizons towards goals no longer far away." Adams went from here to twenty years of life and work. Yet he remains silent about these twenty years. The achievements of the personal goals as a significant contribution to the making of self are dropped. And King too is dropped: he is a type of Dantesque Virgil in the Rockies (Adams, having lost his way in the middle of a rocky wood, met him at the age of thirty-three) who consecrates Adams to the goals achieved in 1872-1892, but his most fruitful direct effects upon Adams are not discussed in the autobiography.

Are we to think, then, that King's purpose-inspiring agency is less powerful than abstract supersensual force? Apparently so, since the purpose-inspiring relations among persons do not become relevant to the dynamic of forces Adams concludes by discovering. In the end, in Adams we see another version—a highly intelligent and intellectualized one—of Moore's idea of a personal life as a passive happening. Of course in his quest for "education," Adams endeavors to resist passivity. But he finally makes us feel that the form of quest on which his narrative is based is very much a frustration of willful action: the searching achieves an end that dehumanizes both the quest and the quester. What the quest reveals mocks the questing form, making it into a kind of fiction that may possibly reveal truth but that is certainly and paradoxically not consonant with truth. Perhaps this paradox causes Adams in 1908 to write William James, *à propos* of the *Education*:

St. Augustine alone has an idea of literary form,—a notion of writing a story with an end and object, not for the sake of the object, but for the form, like a romance. I have worked ten years to satisfy myself that the thing cannot be done today.

In his pursuit of the "object" of education, Adams hardly seems to care what happens to him personally, and he invites the reader to substitute abstract detachment and computation for the relative intensity of concern about personal happiness or sadness that can make us want to go on reading or hearing a story—even when the story is as "purely" an intellectual quest as Adams's. Of course to care about personal happiness or sadness, good or ill, implies a search for a discrimination of *values*, a knowledge and feeling of some kind that this end is more meaningful or better than that end. Such discriminating purpose or plot may be made use of by Adams, but only for the sake of demonstrating its irrelevance to rational "educational" considerations.

And when we turn to an even more "modern" work, *The Autobiography of Alice B. Toklas*, we find a similar dismissal of discriminations of value as the end of a significant purposeful endeavor. "Toklas's" world of course looks much more human than that of Adams; genius in it is remarkably relaxed and neighborly; instead of a supersensual multiverse, we find here a cheerful domestication and a flattening democratization of all experiences: war, needlework, artistic revolution, worries about household objects and menus. But *is* this experience even "real?" The self in Stein is not so much a reality as a *fiction enabling writing*; Stein's "autobiography" can perhaps only represent writing, not a person or a life. In the fourth lecture of *Narration*, Stein explains her reason for writing as if she were Toklas. She believes her own memories will not be sufficiently interesting to keep her at the task of composition. "Remembering is seeing," she explains, "and so anything is an important enough thing for seeing but it is not an important enough thing for writing."[21] Stein claims a writer must believe he is giving a subject an existence and value it has not had—and which he does not recognize—until the moment he writes about it. Are we then recognizing the "real" self of Stein or Toklas in the writing? It is arguable that we are only recognizing the immediate presence of composition, writing's autohistory, whose particular instance at the moment of our reading is Stein's book. The emphasis upon life-writing as *writing* of course reminds us that the author's purpose is not to communicate a life as an urgent and dramatic history of attempts to reach an all-consuming goal. Such a history, Stein implies, is misleading about all arts and artists: the "goal" of writing and of artists is the sort of continuing creativity whereby Stein keeps seeing "herself," in a way more interesting than any way provided by memory, foresight, will, or the discrimination of meanings or values in the service of plot and purpose.

Of course Stein's interest in fidelity to what is actual allows us to consider *The Autobiography of Alice B. Toklas* as equally representative of life as well as of the formal processes and idiosyncratic functions of writing. From this point of consideration, we can see that the book is meant to persuade us that ordinary life is not meaningful or interesting or even healthy if it is tied to selective ends and evaluations. There is no purposeful dedication or crisis in the lives of Stein, Matisse, or Picasso to which their experience or work must refer itself to take on significance. As for the revolutionary aspects of their art, it just so happens that *others* understood them to be radically purposeful. Life in Stein's book is a genial domestic symposium in which commitments and turning points and quests for value make an amusing occasional hubbub. Unlike Yeats, she sees communities of self as the result of a relaxation of purpose and of selective projections. For Stein the genial relaxation of ends is finally the essential form of normalcy. "Toklas" writes that Gertrude Stein "always says" that "she dislikes the abnormal, it is so obvious. She says the normal is so much more simply complicated and interesting."[22] Moreover, because "Toklas" is normal, she is not a sharply defined or individuated self. The autobiography is offered as the chronicle of such normal life—sensitive, feeling, and busy, free of the *abnormalcy* of significant differentiation, and free most of all from the *sickness* of strenuously intent and plotted dedications. There is no intently purposeful plot for the life of Alice Toklas, no selective storylike shaping of her achievement, meaning, and value, for from Stein's point of view this selectivity would cooperate treacherously with a component of psychic disease in the more traditional narrative impulse.

In summary, what can be made of the bearing of our autobiographical cases on the relation of purpose to facts of life, to the sense of plot, and to the plotting of novels? The idea that strenuous purpose and dedication are antihuman or discouraging—and the coincidence of the idea with theories about just "being," about creating or re-creating the self without "ends," or about forces that nullify persons and plots—remains powerful but is perhaps more questionable now than when it first appeared. Paul Goodman sees the idea as a symptom of a

> lifeless future. . . . In our changing world, the young must be trained to be adaptable, to "play various roles." This will "free" people from being "tied down." Young people I have talked to like this idea; they want to be "just human" and not limited to a vocation or profession. They want to be "into" various activities. As, presumably, Shakespeare was heavily "into" writing plays and Niels Bohr was "into" atomic physics. It is a curious view of personality and commitment.[23]

It also looks like a curious view of what is meaningful and valuable and of how meaning and value may be created and achieved. But it is odd for a man of such personal and social radicalism as Goodman to show discontent with ideas about purpose as an unnecessary or doomed fact of life, self, meaning, and value when it was the radical and prestigious literary culture that initiated the ideas at the end of the last century. The young could do worse perhaps than to model themselves on Wilde and Moore, Adams and Stein. If they do so, of course, their sense of plot will not be drawn to the nineteenth-century novelists who, because they desire to discriminate value (what is better and worse) as well as meaning in the relations among their fictional characters, trust to the imitation of plot, purpose, and dedication in order to make the discriminations possible and plausible. The sense of plot that finds itself reflected in memoirs revising or dispensing with purpose as life's essential mediator will look for truthfulness—or the only possible rewarding playfulness—in novels and novelistic stories that represent and formally imitate the defeat of meaningful intentions or ends, the coerciveness of perspectival functions, the irrelevance of the realization of significance or value by action or by other than skeptical or playful means. To such a sense of plot, plot's imitation of purpose will seem a game, a hypothesis, a net that cannot hold the life it seeks to catch. And to such a sense of plot, story's purposeful organization (the more earnest and consolidated is its teleology) will seem fictive, untrue, and even immoral in its attempt to ignore the idea that *all* happenings are "good" or are not amenable to evaluative discrimination.

SEVEN

The Story in It: James

> The adventures of innocence have so often been the
> material of fiction? Yes. . . . That's exactly what the bored
> reader complains of. . . . What is it but . . . a question of
> interest, or, as people say, of the story? What's a situation
> undeveloped but a subject lost? If a relation stops, where's
> the story? If it doesn't stop, where's the innocence? It
> seems to me you must choose.   —James, "The Story in It"

> The pleasure of handling an action (or, otherwise
> expressed, of a "story") is, . . . for a storyteller, immense.
> —James, Preface to *The Tragic Muse*

The modern sense of plot ignores a crucial step in Melville's
development by overlooking and undervaluing the impulse
to plot willful political action in *White Jacket* and by canonizing
Moby Dick without paying attention to the narrative and
moral meaning of Steelkilt. When we come to the case of
Henry James, the modern sense of plot makes us overlook
and undervalue even more; it excludes both an accurate view
of James's work from *The Awkward Age* on and an accurate
understanding of James's career as a revolution in moral and
formal allegiances. It has been the assumption of modern criticism that James's novels, especially the last ones, contain
scarcely any overt or externalized acts, and that they
emblematize what *The Sense of the Past* calls "the force of the
stillness in which nothing happened." According to modern
criticism stillness is informed, of course, by reflection, by intensely speculative consciousness, by narrative reasonings
seeking detachment from concrete practice. Now it is arguable that consciousness is the only "happening" of conse-

quence, that it is the force of the stillness in which everything happens. James certainly gives us reason to claim the relative insignificance of acts in relation to the effective intellectual, imaginative, or moral "picturing" of them; but my contention here is that increasingly with his maturity he gives us powerful reasons to claim otherwise. What happens as sheer act in Jamesian story enlarges in importance as James grows older, and the force of a reflective stillness, of a kind of narrative reason seeking to contain and inhibit action, turns out to be the characteristic mark of James's *earlier work*. Admittedly, the change is obscured not only by the modern sense of plot but by James himself—by the James of the New York Edition, whose prefaces attempt to unify more than thirty years of work, to suppress transitions and discontinuities for the sake of an appearance of consistency. It was perhaps odd of James to make so much of consistency; but it has been more odd for criticism to have followed James's endeavor without raising any questions—until, that is, Laurence Holland began to point out the conflicts underneath the appearance.[1] We need to designate and liberate these conflicts even more. What is at issue is the mature James's evergrowing conviction that the featuring of act in story is of positive importance not just to "the novel" but to any civilization worth the name.

The transformation we can see in James's career is both thematic and formal. He shifts his allegiances from subjects and persons who are valuably innocent by virtue of their freedom from plot, understood as intrigue and action, to those who are valuably experienced by commitment to the intriguing and plotting enactments of story. *The Awkward Age* is a turning point in James's career, for it represents a clear break with values and forms best represented by Christopher Newman and *The American*; by 1899 James is ready to begin attaching supreme value and distinction to the strenuous intriguers, not at all like Newman, who will be the heroes and heroines of *The Wings of the Dove* and *The Golden Bowl*. This change of allegiance and evaluation is the essential moral story in James's stories—the story the prefaces leave us to spell out: the story of a change in James's form complementing the change in his thematics and values.

To designate the narrative modes by which he works, James repeatedly uses four terms in the prefaces to the New York Edition: *picture, drama, story, plot.* He appears to use these terms interchangeably, favoring each and all by turns, yet usually reserving his highest praise for *picture*, which, as we commonly understand it, means narrative and intellectual reasoning removed from action. But this praise is misleading and also nervous, for the late novels show not only more honor given to the experience and heroism of action but a complementary shift away from James's favoring of the aesthetic and ethical bearing of *picture*. Under the surface of the employment of the terms in the prefaces—and from time to time even on the surface—a battle is going on among the narrative modes; and I argue that ascendancy in the battle belongs finally to *plot* and *story*, understood as founded on action more than on *picture* and on the still, contemplative reflectiveness of pictorial composition.

James matters immensely because of this transformation in his allegiances. The change seems the result of an urgent social judgment to the effect that modern life not only inhibits adequate reflection but inhibits even more crucially the transformation of intelligent consciousness into the form of externalized, adventurous acts. To James the inhibition of goodness as a realizable and realized form of activity is a great human sadness; and by means of a new commitment to plot and story, the late James insists on the necessary conversion of the good glimpsed by him and his characters into a form of active life. As James comes to see them, both American and English social experience have almost broken down even the possibility of such a form. With the exception of Yeats, the contemporaries of James whom we have considered in Chapter Six exemplify this breakdown, for they make prestigious a rebellious, amoral quietism, a dissociation of sensibility or human fineness from the creativity of action. The mature

James is characterized by a stubborn struggle against this dissociation—one that much of his earlier great work actually honors.

The shift of allegiance occurs most clearly at the thematic level—in what is represented. But in the prefaces we can see clues to the shift in the usage of the terms designating the modes of representation. As James uses the word *picture*, it seems to mean a striking composition of mere appearances that begins (at least) to lend the appearances form and significance, especially by means of their reflection in a personal center of consciousness. A reflective narrative mode, which explains and amplifies both subjectively and objectively what goes on under the surface of appearances, *picture* appears to be analytic and contemplative narrative reasoning rather than dynamic presentation of acts. Unlike *picture*, *drama* (referred to also as the "scenic" mode) seems exclusively objective representation of appearances. If it is reflective or analytic, it presents the immediate surface simultaneous with analysis, it "make[s] the presented occasion tell all its story itself, . . . shut up in its own presence." *Drama* seems to be a middle term between *picture*, *story*, and *plot*, capable of being synonymous with each of the others (except when *picture* is exclusively subjective). What, then, are *story* and *plot*? James uses them to suggest dynamism and development, the unsettling, uncomposed, and very possibly unreflective presence of will and of "headlong," transformative agencies. He calls *story* "action," does not—as the Russian Formalists do—distinguish it from *plot*, and comments on both honorifically by saying that "story *as such* . . . is ever, obviously, the prime and precious thing."[2]

Just how "prime and precious" is it? Such a comment is at odds with how, in the preface to *The Portrait of A Lady*, it is picture that looks prime and precious, although James ends the discussion of Isabel Archer's story by transubstantiating picture into the other modes. Outside of the prefaces, in the novels themselves, this conversion is not typical of James's mature practice of composition; but the play on the terms in regard to the early novel is instructive as a measure of what happens to the use of the modes later. James begins the discussion of *The Portrait of A Lady* with an organic metaphor: he calls the origin of the novel a germ, suggesting that the subject is a seed in life's garden and that its development is a spontaneous blossoming. James seems only to have to gather the blossom, not to make it grow by a plot, by an active, willful construction of relations. The germ is also, James says, a "fictive picture" of the heroine. The picture

> must have consisted not at all in any conceit of a "plot," nefarious name, in any flash upon the fancy, of a set of relations, or in any of those situations, that by a logic of their own, immediately fall, for the fabulist, into movement.

But what would Isabel Archer *do*, her author remembers wondering.

> Without her sense of [her adventures], her sense *for* them, they are next to nothing at all; but isn't the beauty and the difficulty just in showing their mystic conversion by that sense, conversion into the stuff of drama or, even more delightful word still, of "story?"

Difficult as it is to keep hold of a process undergoing mystic conversions, does this mean in effect that the "fictive picture" remains "picture," even though it also becomes "drama" and "story?" Apparently so, if one understands James to mean that Isabel considered as a fictive picture is an intense center of consciousness, a commanding sensibility. Her sensibility converts adventures—the equivalent in external deeds of mere appearances—into intellectually and ethically *significant* actions. In this instance James identifies significant action with drama and drama with story, calls them by the collective term "portrait," and makes them significant by internalizing them.

Yet the interidentity of the terms, their transubstantiation into picture, true as it is for *The Portrait of A Lady*, is not true for all of James. In late James there is more adventure than his characters' *sense for* it. The important question becomes, "What will picture and plot *together* 'do'?" Late Jamesian story can be seen as the effort at a further conversion. It becomes the attempt to turn purely reflective consciousness (merely contemplative narrative reason) back into meaningful activity as a test and a consummation of *all* meaning and significance and not as only a *means* to significance. If plot, the ally of story, is "nefarious," this is because it demands that consciousness act—and activity is threatening and dangerous. It unbalances and may even betray the insights of composed reflection. A *sense* for adventures does not guarantee that the adventurer will act out the story in the reflective narrative picture easily, honestly, cogently—or at all. Yet, for the later James, the enactment is necessary and supremely creative. Of course once the story is worked out and acted, it amounts to a new picture for the reader who contemplates it. And by means of picture, at the end of a tale James too may stand outside action rather than in it, containing activity within his pictorial frame. Yet the movement of story is less lucid than this transcendent stance. We sympathize with pictorial appreciativeness and lucidity, and need it. But would either reader or author be interested or moved if the activity of the characters and the story did not put lucidity and detachment under attack?

I have been arguing in this book that the ultimate test of significance in narrative reasoning is how significance withstands this attack and how it re-forms itself as action in terms of deed as well as of appreciation and thought. Viewed solely as speculative thought or appreciation, narrative intellectual and moral reasoning is a thematizing of experience that separates what happens from perspectives on what happens—a separation that I believe humbles narrative reason and dangerously separates signs from their referents. The young James saw in this separation only intellectual and moral richness, whereas the mature James comes to believe in a union of signs and referents with action, in a closer wedding of theme and plot; hence, in his later years James comes to favor plot and story, to think them more prime and precious than picture, even at the risk of having to allow the narrative modes to be at war with one another. He acknowledges the conflict explicitly: in the preface to *The Wings of the Dove*, he admits "the odd inveteracy with which picture, at almost any turn, is jealous of drama and drama . . . suspicious of picture." It is not only suspicion but open conflict: "Each baffles insidiously the other's ideal and eats round the edges of its position; each is too ready to say 'I can take the thing for "done" only when done in my way.' " Do plot and story also attempt a further insidious baffling of picture and even of drama? The question is important because James is talking about conflicts among presentational techniques, and yet he is also talking about more. Even "drama" can present the absence of action, but the battle James speaks of is ultimately a conflict over what is more privileged: a way of life characterized by reflective consciousness that is not expressed, or is violated, by action; or a way of life that features action, demands the realization of consciousness as act, and may even demand the temporary loss of clear consciousness for the sake of an act. The battle among the narrational modes is a battle between the ways of life on which the modes are ultimately based.

Although the prefaces name the conflict among the modes, they hide the way the conflict increasingly transforms the content of James's work. The James who writes *The Portrait of A Lady* does believe that a sense *for* adventure is greater than adventure; the James who writes *The Awkward Age* and the late novels thinks the adventure of action makes the most significant sense. If we look briefly at *The American*, *The Awkward Age*, and the stillborn experiment, *The Sense of the Past*, we can see more clearly how the transubstantiating of the terms does not remain possible for James except in the prefaces, how *picture* in his novels themselves gives way to the priority of *story* in thematic as well as in formal terms.

In the young James there is a characteristic identification of virtuous behavior with a denial of action. Indeed in his early work James insists that the creativity appropriate to Americans is located in their ability to keep free of deeds, in their aloofness from any temptation or provocation to enact plot. The American innocence and the American virtue is a sense for adventure that keeps adventure itself outside and at a distance, framed by a personal consciousness that is itself a shy romance, a subjective satisfaction in the intrigues of others. This kind of consciousness is a personification of Jamesian *picture*, and an examination of James's character, Christopher Newman, offers much insight into this particular pictorial mode of narration.

The crisis in *The American* turns on what Newman will make of the Dickensian plot and intrigue revealed to him as the true history of the Bellegardes. How can Newman's picturing consciousness accommodate itself to the dynamic twists and turns of action initiated by the Bellegardes and written down in the narrative of their misdeeds, which their servant Mrs. Bread offers Newman? Newman first wants to expose the story, even if it is not true. He thinks this will force the family to sanction his marriage to Claire Bellegarde, who is being driven into a convent as a result of her older brother's tyrannical opposition to her wedding with the American. The first person to whom Newman decides to tell his story is a noble friend of the family. But as he sits in this duchess's drawing room, he feels more and more confused. He cannot fit his story anywhere into the conversation, and he abandons his intention: "Whether or not the duchess would hear his story, he wouldn't tell it. Was he to sit there another half hour for the sake of exposing the Bellegardes? The Bellegardes be hanged!" He drifts off to England, then back to America, all the while unsure about what he feels or believes. Hearing that Claire has taken her final vows, he rushes back to Paris, looking like a man "with a plot in his head." Yet he does not know what to do, and at last a few moments in Notre Dame resolve him.

Somewhere in his mind, a tight knot seemed to have loosened. He thought of the Bellegardes; he had almost

forgotten them. He remembered them as people he had
meant to do something to. He gave a groan as he remembered what he had meant to do; he was annoyed at
having meant to do it; the bottom, suddenly, had fallen
out of his revenge. Whether it was Christian charity or
unregenerate good nature—what it was, in the background of his soul—I don't pretend to say; but Newman's last thought was that of course he would let the
Bellegardes go. If he had spoken it aloud he would have
said that he didn't want to hurt them. He was ashamed
of having wanted to hurt them. They had hurt him, but
such things were really not his game.[3]

He burns the narrative Mrs. Bread has given him.

But it is not so much vengeance as the alliance of conscience with elaborate and determined plot that is not Newman's game. His "unregenerate good nature" finally resists
his ability to extend the story of the Bellegardes by means of a
plot in his own head. He cannot grasp the reality of their history as it has been revealed to him. To Newman all the Bellegardes have the look of adventurers, of characters who inhabit not life but complicated and fabulous tales foreign to
American assumptions and experience. Newman cannot
comprehend life as literally plotted or storied, and this in the
end keeps him from realizing the image of happiness he had
projected for himself. And he not only feels that decency and
intrigue are incompatible but that even a decency that must
be pursued by deliberate, intriguing action is not worth the
trouble.

The James who writes *The American* also does not believe in
intrigue—either as a fact of life or of novelistic form. Intrigue
seems identical with action, and both the innocence of
James's hero and the conviction of James himself testify to an
incredulity about action: it seems to young James a convention of old-fashioned plot, or it is identical with aggression,
deceit, and hurt. Like his character, James admits in his preface to *The American* his disbelief in his own plot, in the way

things happen in the novel outside the hero's consciousness.
"The way [real] things happen is frankly not the way in
which they are represented as having happened, in Paris, to
my hero." The novel's interest thus lies both in the consciousness of the hero and in picture—in the portrait of a subjectivity that, like its author's, curiously, appreciatively, and
at last antagonistically, pictures action but does not join or
participate in it, except in a reflective stillness. For James the
lasting value of the book resides in the "more or less convincing image of his hero's center of consciousness":

> The picture of his consistency was all my undertaking.
> . . . If Newman was attaching enough, I must have
> argued, his tangle would be sensible enough; for the in-
> terest of everything is all that it is *his* vision, *his* concep-
> tion, *his* interpretation.

In *The American*, as in *The Portrait of A Lady*, story is trans-
substantiated into the prime and precious thing of picture.

But the man who can picture complex relations and who
nevertheless will not enter the frame of the picture keeps
James's attention but not his allegiance. Similarly, James re-
tains picture as narrative mode, but commits himself to the
primacy of action (or, otherwise expressed, of story). We can
see this if we understand that one of Christopher Newman's
last emanations is Vanderbank in *The Awkward Age*; considered as the American's heir, Vanderbank is a measure of
James's later coldness towards the man who keeps himself
puritanically clear of plot and plot's "doings." Now "the
awkward age" means not only late adolescence but the era
James's novel describes. The modernity of this era is seen in
its bad faith about standards and its inhibited and incoherent
enactment of its impulses. The novel questions if there is any
genuine or significant action or heroism available to the
"civilization" of such an era. In this age can young persons
realize a decent and fruitful maturity? The vehicles of James's
questionings are Longdon, who belongs to an earlier and
supposedly better age; Nanda Brookenham, one of the young

who feels the need of a life other than that which modern society offers her; and Vanderbank, a young man whose
smooth intelligence, self-possession, and glamour have a
sinister edge, but who seems to represent the best distillation
of the era. Nanda tries to save her friend Mitchett from the
indeterminacy of modern values by advising him to marry
Aggie, a girl brought up in old-fashioned seclusion and en-
forced innocence by a modern noblewoman who hardly practices the virtue she preaches to her ward. The marriage is a
failure because as a wife the girl shows herself as deceitful as
her guardian. Longdon fails in turn to "save" Vanderbank,
the young man Nanda loves, by trying to arrange for him a
marriage with Nanda free from financial obstacles. In the end
Vanderbank rejects Nanda and Longdon's offer, apparently
because he does not love the girl enough. But he also may not
want to marry her because of the studied humaneness she
has adopted from Longdon and has applied with such bad
results in the case of Mitchett. The implication of Vanderbank's point of view is that a modern person cannot free himself from all his compromises by returning to expressions of
human goodness (Nanda's aid to Mitchett is a kind of out-
dated Dickensian rescue attempt) that have lost their prac-
ticability.

So for Vanderbank there is left finally only a kind of detached, lucid endurance of the age, a lucidity that is modern
especially because it is inactive and, in its opposition to the
doings of Longdon and Nanda, even opposed to action. The
novel begins with Vanderbank comparing a photograph of
Lady Julia, symbol of an outmoded form of human goodness,
with a photograph of Nanda, symbol of the goodness that
must find and enact a modern form for itself. He ends the
same way, clinging to the clarity of his pictorial comparisons
and appreciations, thematizing experience, having an imaginative sense for it, but making and keeping separate his fullness of speculation and his poverty of deed. Van's development is to only know more certainly, at last, how woefully
inept Nanda and Longdon have been in their attempts to put
their contemplative images of goodness to work in the world.

Yet unmistakably James admires Longdon and Nanda more than Vanderbank. For James, at this time in his career, it is better to be inept (even if this is the price of "doing") than to be perfect as a reflector. Narrative intellectual and moral reasonings must be attached to active practice. In many of the prefaces James admits his own ineptitude but with a kind of stoic pride, for it is the result of willfully making experience tell as action and as story, not just as picture. By adopting Nanda, Longdon risks an active marriage of past values and a decent—even if compromised—modern humanity. And in so doing he acts to create a community of past and present ways of feeling and acting, even though he recognizes that "everythings's different from what it used to be." There is an irony in Vanderbank's refusal to marry Nanda: because Nanda has been exposed to the knowing sophistication and promiscuity of "the age," Vanderbank considers her unacceptably prepared for marriage, but if Vanderbank thinks this way, then he—rather than Longdon—turns out to be puritanical and nostalgic, even sentimental, about the past. And at the same time his appreciative realization that everything has changed is tainted by his refusal to attempt or to execute a further transformation. For the social and historical change that has created "the age" is not humanly satisfying. "What comes out, on reflection" for both Longdon and Nanda is that something must be done about this change, that they must enact a further change; whereas Vanderbank refuses commitment to anything but the reflective comprehension of change.

Vanderbank's commitment is not James's. His withdrawal from action, his appreciativeness of the "doings" of *others*— that quality inherited from Newman—is, as his name keeps telling us, a vanity. In their final alliance Nanda and Longdon are a hope that creative action is not, as Van would have it, "long done." James admires even Nanda's mother, Mrs. Brookenham, who in her own insistently willful intriguing is more creative than Vanderbank. And although the other characters call Vanderbank a "sacred terror," his glamor and power may be "the force of stillness in which nothing happens." In Christopher Newman, James had seen the force of stillness as a redemptive human and American virtue; in Vanderbank he sees it as both fine and stagnantly quiescent. But its quiescence cancels its fineness. Such men as Vanderbank leave the social and historical world mired in confusion, and they are sadly inactive in the face of its incoherence. In *The American* the intriguing and plotting characters had been the symptoms and agents of social evil, the antagonists of goodness and of passive decency. By the time of *The Awkward Age* James's world is not so neatly divided. He relocates his hope for a new moral and social order in the agents and agency of plot.

Now it is possible that in *The Sense of the Past* (started in 1900 and then not resumed until World War I) James wanted to reverse his new emphasis and essay a novel in which his narrative modes would once again be personified and interidentified by felicitous mystic conversions as they had been in *The Portrait of A Lady*. But it is also possible that the novel remained—and remains—an odd fragment because James could no longer believe in the necessity or value of the transformation. The novel's hero, the historian Ralph Pendrel, loves Aurora Coyne, who is likened to a Renaissance portrait and who refuses Ralph's suit because she wants to marry a man of action. Ralph's success as an historian has arisen from his ability to render intensely the pictorial tone and feel of things past and not from his ability to narrate past deeds, events, and adventures. As he himself says, "I don't know what anyone is who leads the life of action." He then literally slips back into the past by means of becoming the man in a Regency portrait he inherits. What first entranced him in this picture, what "kept him on and on," "was precisely the force of the stillness in which nothing happened."

The projected ending of the novel seems to have been tailored to convince both Aurora and the reader that for a modern man "the life of action" finds its equivalent in picture. By becoming the figure in the portrait, Ralph becomes what Aurora wants: a man who has experienced "the prodigy of . . . adventure." Story and plot, action and adventure are thus again made synonymous with a picture; moreover, Ralph's moral fineness is projected as the fruit of modernity's denial of the importance of action in Aurora's sense of the word. And yet, even *The Sense of the Past* stirs up contradictions of the formal identities James had especially cultivated in his earlier work and seems to have wanted to cultivate once more. Pendrel was to have been rescued from entrapment in the past by the *strenuous and active doing* of both his Regency sweetheart—a double of Aurora—and Aurora herself. The picture would have been in some way damning, after all; so we can see that in *The Sense of the Past* James's mystic conversions are not working as they used to.

If we turn to a close reading of *The Wings of the Dove*, we can especially observe how the conflict of the narrative modes is both technical and thematic and how the primacy of contemplative picture gives way in later James to the priority of story and action. In this novel of 1902 James makes picture, albeit with one exception, almost synonymous with *unreliable* consciousness, and he dramatizes the moral maturation of his hero as his yielding of reflection to the need for willful action. "Have you seen the picture in the house, the beautiful one that's so like you?" With this question, in the novel's first self-reflexive use of picture, Lord Mark brings Milly Theale face to face with what he thinks of as her double, a Bronzino portrait. Milly bursts into tears. In the picture

> the lady in question . . . was a very great personage— only unaccompanied by a joy. And she was dead, dead, dead. Milly recognized her exactly in words that had nothing to do with her. "I shall never be better than this."

Does Milly recognize the Bronzino "in words that had nothing to do with" its subject because she thinks that she herself will never be better than dead, will always be "unaccompanied by a joy?" What Milly, still facing the portrait, thinks and says after her tears is unclear to the reader and to Milly's interlocuter, Mark. Apparently Milly wants after all to resist recognition that the portrait is her double. Pressed by Mark to clarify her words of "recognition," Milly says she will "never be better" than this particular day has made her feel. She is at a brilliant English house called Matcham, where the entire company has created for Milly "a sort of magnificent maximum, the pink dawn of an apotheosis." The portrait has just become part of the "maximum" for her. But "you're a pair," Lord Mark insists, stubbornly matching (at Matcham) portrait and lady. Surely Milly will admit the identity straightforwardly? But she resists: "I don't know—one never knows one's self." When Kate Croy spots the resemblance and brings other viewers, Milly is doubly uneasy. "Lady Aldershaw . . . looked at Milly quite as if Milly had been the Bronzino and the Bronzino only Milly."[4]

The live creature does not like being mixed up with art. Moreover, she refuses to be identified with what she *appears* to be. Thematically *The Wings of the Dove* worries over a number of problems implicit in the portrait episode. How is life to be made valuable? What is life's best form? How does one really have or hold onto "life" or "self?" But James goes out of his way here to put thematic issues in terms of "picture," and this shows that his feelings about *picture* are as mixed as Milly's. Through the Bronzino scene the pictorial moment is shown to be an unreliable composition of appearances, a misleading still reflection. In its arranged fixity and richness the portrait does not stand for what Milly believes herself to be, nor for what she wants. Already suspicious that she is dying, Milly feels she can never be better than *alive*. The portrait's very lifelikeness is deceptive—its fineness is that of a still life, *hence* unaccompanied by joy.

After Matcham the moments of picture in *The Wings of the Dove* are suspect. Milly herself acts like Lady Aldershaw, mixing up alleged representations and copies of life with truth. One of the reasons the picture of "Milly" at Matcham is false is that it has no story in it: it does not represent its subject by what she does. In the National Gallery scene in Book Fifth, Milly will mistake a picture of Merton for the truth by ignoring how his story, what he is enacting, defines him more truthfully than what he appears to be. Milly is at the gallery to escape truth altogether, of course: at home her doctor is delivering a final diagnosis of her disease. At the museum she feels too weak to look at Titians and Turners, which we are to understand is also a blinking of truth—for she finds herself curious only about the ladies who copy the real pictures. She wants, suddenly, to lose herself, to escape the agony and burden of what she and James call "the personal question." "She should have been a lady-copyist—it met so the case. The case was the case of escape, of living under water."

She feels embarrassed by her interest in the copyists, but instead of turning to the authentic originals, she muses next over the hordes of American tourists in the gallery. When three American women stop in front of her, she watches and listens to their reaction to what she supposes is a portrait "in the English style" (as the women say) hanging at her back. She turns around to see that only Dutch genre paintings are there. The Americans have in fact been looking at Merton Densher. Just returned to England, Merton is at the gallery to meet with Kate, who as suddenly and surprisingly as Merton appears in Milly's line of vision. How, Milly is frightened and anxious to know, is this mysterious composition, this living picture, to be read? Surely the sheer visibility of appearances is all or almost all of the story.

> Little by little indeed, under the vividness of Kate's behavior, the probabilities fell back into their order. Merton Densher was in love, and Kate couldn't help it—could only be sorry and kind: wouldn't that, without wild flurries, cover everything? Milly at all events tried it as a cover, tried it hard.

She asks herself too—the question acting as part of the cover—if Merton will have changed since her meeting with him in America. But the picture is deceptively indefinite; it can be read any way the individual desires. So Milly was to see her question itself simply go to pieces. She couldn't tell if he were different or not, and she didn't know nor care if *she* were: these things had ceased to matter in the light of the only thing she did know. This was that she liked him. . . . It was at this point that she saw . . . that all she had to do with was the sense of being there with him.[5]

Merton's pictorial presence (and Kate's behind his) "covers everything." Nevertheless, the questions that go to pieces matter the most. Kate Croy is one of the lady-copyists, forging a substitute picture for the real thing. Milly takes Kate's portrait of Merton for the truth. She passes it on to Lord Mark, and struggles not to recognize her own lie. We see that there is a grave potential of falseness in the privileged pictorial moment. Moreover, whoever works to *fix* his life in the form of privileged picture, of a beatific still composition, is deceived. Meaningful as the pictorial moment is, it either has too many meanings or not enough. The dynamic of story must seize this moment and define and enact its truth. Picture confuses or inhibits the process of active movement and precise definition.

But, we might think, surely action can be no less a forgery, no less a deceiving "act" than the deceptions created by the eye and the mind's eye. However generally true this may be, in late James the act is featured as the means whereby uncertainties are cleared and treacheries are at last routed. In relation to the doubtful and ambiguous authority of picture, action is a superior authority, a final arbiter of truth. Moreover, mature Jamesian picture demands that action realize what consciousness sees, and that consciousness execute vision in the form of act. In Merton Densher, especially, we see the process whereby the truth and action of story—the supplementary execution of vision as deed—overcomes arbitrariness and stillness, even a treacherous passivity, in the purely contemplative or speculative aspect of picture.

At the end of the novel another picture proposes itself—

this time to Merton—again as a magnificent maximum. Merton is shown fixating his life upon a final portrait of Milly, a positively sacred icon set up in his imagination. With Mrs. Lowder in attendance, he contemplates himself contemplating Milly:

> He saw a young man, far off, in a relation inconceivable, saw him hushed, passive, staying his breath, but half understanding, yet dimly conscious of something immense and holding himself, not to lose it, painfully together. The young man, at these moments, so seen was too distant and too strange for the right identity; and yet outside, afterwards, it was his own face Densher had known. . . . At present there, with Mrs. Lowder, he knew he had gathered all. . . . He had been, to his recovered sense, forgiven, dedicated, blessed; but this he couldn't coherently express. It would have required an explanation—fatal to Mrs. Lowder's faith in him—of the nature of Milly's wrong. So, as to the wonderful scene, they just stood at the door. They had the sense of the presence within—they felt the charged stillness; after which, with their association deepened by it, they turned together away.[6]

Merton has been mystically converted and possessed by a new version of the Bronzino, but the possession is disconcerting to him and to us. There is again, as at Matcham and the National Gallery, an unsettling arbitrariness in the pictorial phenomenon—and, as this passage emphasizes, an ethical unreliability. The stillness of the picture is charged with implicit demands that stillness be broken, that passivity of awareness be transformed into activity for the sake of a finer utterance of truth. Even Merton's identity, maintained by the force of the stillness in which nothing happens, is deceiving and deceived.

By what grace has Merton become supported and fixed by an image of exemplary human decency? The arbitrariness of pictorial significances—in spite of any tendency to sanctify them as absolutely reliable iconography—is reinforced if we remember that Merton, only a few months before the scene with Mrs. Lowder, had found himself—as the young man he now strains to recognize—experiencing apparently the same phenomenon when the presence and the image had been Kate's:

> What had come to pass within his walls lingered there as an obsession importunate to all his sense; it lived again, as a cluster of pleasant memories, at every hour and in every subject; it made everything but itself irrelevant and tasteless. It remained, in a word, a conscious, watchful presence, active on its own side, forever to be reckoned with, in face of which the effort at detachment was scarcely less futile than frivolous. Kate had come to him; . . . to stay, as people called it; and what survived of her . . . was something he couldn't have banished if he had wished. Luckily he didn't wish, even though there might be . . . almost a shade of the awful in so unqualified a consequence of his act. It had simply worked, his idea, the idea he had made her accept; and all erect before him, really covering the ground as far as he could see, was the fact of the gained success that this represented. It was, otherwise, but the fact of the idea as directly applied, as converted from a luminous conception into an historic truth.[7]

Merton had presented Kate with the sketch of a plot. When the sketch is realized according to his vision Merton is dazzled by the consonance of his "luminous conception" with "historic truth." Picture, story, and plot here look identical. And yet Merton is deluded. Other forces are turning his historic truth back into an idea, less consequential as fact or act than he realizes. Kate's "conscious, watchful presence, active on its own side" seems to enjoin Merton from further "working"—another Jamesian synonym for plot. Further work may expel the presence filling Merton's room. It is expelled. *Milly*'s "conscious, watchful presence, active on its own side" takes over. But although Milly's icon seems more blessed to Merton because it has not been made in the active, willful way he made Kate's, Merton is again mistaken. He must stop picturing Milly's goodness to himself in a way that keeps him still and passive. The sacred icon, the luminous conception whose values are ethical as well as pictorial, demands conversion once again into a form of action so that it may become a deed, and hence "historic." This is one step further in the articulation of "history" than the one suggested as necessary in Chapter Two, when it was argued that Carlyle, for example, could not make history feel actual to us if he did not picture it or frame it in terms of theory. James's Merton suggests that a theoretical formulation provides only the preliminary formulation of an act. The act is greater, that is, more valuable and more truthful and definite than the theory.

Fixed before the icon of Milly in his scene with Mrs. Lowder, Merton is adhering to theory, to *that* "stillness"; but his story will not end until he exchanges contemplation—purely speculative narrative reasoning about Milly—for an act that supplements speculation and is initiated by himself. How does Merton at last succeed as an actor, giving up the passivity, quiescence, and arbitrariness of relation with which the picturing consciousness in late James seems doubtfully intertwined? Merton's success in making Kate come to him is the first step of his transformation from passive watcher to active maker of the story that is his, Kate's, and Milly's ; but no sooner has he taken the step, than he returns to passivity. At this point in the novel we are given a double sense of picture—reminded of its potential for truth as well as for falsity. By having consummated sexual relations with Kate, Merton makes himself more false to Milly; but "it was only on reflection that the falseness came out." "Reflection," the characteristic and fruit of picturing consciousness, is here a touchstone of truth and genuine conscience, and is being favored by James. But although the deed enacts the truth of Merton's relation to others, thus defining and mastering what reflection can bring out, reflective consciousness also resists such mastering definition. Consequently Merton can use reflection, in spite of what he undeniably does, to picture a false and happy composition of relations among Kate, Milly, and himself: Are they not each getting their just deserts? Everything is all right, that is—if Merton will just *see* it that way. And it helps Merton to see it that way if he does not commit himself to any further defining action, if he lets his action sink back into a felicitous composition of appearances.

> Action itself, of any sort, the right as well as the wrong—if the difference even survived—had heard . . . a vivid "Hush!" the injunction, from that moment, to keep intensely still. . . . His wisdom reduced itself—to the need again simply to be kind [to Milly]. That was the same as being still—as creating, studiously, the minimum of vibration. He felt himself, as he smoked, shut up to a room, on the wall of which something precious was too precariously hung. A false step would bring it down, and it must hang as long as possible.[8]

Is not the picture hanging here the falsely composed affair with Milly? Reflection is not bringing out the truth, after all, and the "precious" picture must be brought down, by the clarifying agency of what Merton will do.

But it is Mark who acts first, pushing Merton out of falsity and quiescence. The picture is brought down the moment Merton sees Mark, the evangel of truth, sitting behind the plate glass of Florian's café on the Piazza San Marco with the *Figaro* on his knee, with an unfinished drink on his table, and staring at a rococo wall. This is, curiously, a replacement of one picture by another; but now the picture is incontrovertibly "true." The vision of Mark is the supreme pictorial moment in *The Wings of the Dove*, realizing once more James's old ambition to have a reflective moment tell the entire story for both the fictional character and the reader—a moment reconciling the presentational ideals of the narrative modes and conveying an absolute of truthful perception through the reconciliation. Seeing Mark, Merton takes two turns around the square in order to see him twice more. The terror of this appearance compels him to repeat the sight. Merton literally envisions a reversal of his fortune and his life, for he immediately understands that the truth of his relation to Milly has just been revealed to her. And simultaneously he knows he can no longer cover up from himself the truth of his relation to her. What happens to Merton here echoes James's remark in another preface:

> One never really chooses one's general range of vision:
> . . . this proves ever what it has *had* to be, this is one with
> the very turn one's life has taken; so that whatever it
> "gives," . . . we regard very much as imposed and inevi-
> table.[9]

In the scene in St. Mark's square, Merton's physical vision is unified with the fatal turn the reality and significance of his life have taken. And picture, drama, plot, and story are also unified because here Merton's apprehension of Mark's appearance does not have to await unfolding and testing by time, by action, or by "work." The image is at once one with definitive historic truth.

Yet it is not enough for the late James—and for Merton—to "see" story this way. In the café window Mark's image is story, imposing itself visually as truth and picture. But story's form of "doing" is not identical with vision, either physical or speculative. What is anyone—what is Merton—to *do* with "one's general range of vision?" Consciousness, pervaded by awareness and "vision," presses for a further conversion, a transformation into action, a making of a novel difference to itself through an externalizing of what it knows, in the form of an overt deed. When Merton hangs his precious picture of *Milly* on his wall, it too must be brought down—and by his own willful agency, not by passive acquiescence. For the revelation produced by Mark in Venice is again a passive reflective experience for Merton; so is his being held by Kate's design, then by Milly's icon, then by Milly's will.

In the last pages Densher struggles against passivity. Milly's will makes her an ally of Kate. It composes the fate of all three persons in—apparently—the happiest terms. But Merton refuses to accept this final composition. For him his internalized pictures of Milly, her will, and his will, do not match. The document from New York is a picturing of herself that Milly hands on to her survivors. Merton refuses to take this image for the truth: he rejects it as incompatible with his feelings and with goodness. Milly must be better than this. Merton says he will marry Kate on condition that they reject Milly's legacy. This condition subordinates and even annuls Kate's creative agency; it makes Merton the superior actor and intriguer. Merton will now do more than recognize he has cherished Milly and has regretted deceiving her. Recognition could be appreciative of Milly and could still be "covered" by acceptance of the legacy, but Merton's accession to intrigue is to interpret his sacred icon of Milly by enacting his sense of its value with a deed that wipes out Milly's last picture of herself as well as Kate's entire design. Densher does offer Kate the appearance of a marriage with him, but she knows as well as he the absolutely defining nature of the act rejecting the legacy.

What Densher wills and does, not merely what he appreciates, sees, or feels, makes definite Kate's judgment about his transformation. And Merton's act defining the transformation closes the novel, breaking him and Kate apart at the moment when Merton has become, as an *enactor* of a perception of values, most like Kate. His similarity to Kate at this point is of course easily available to detached pictorial consciousness, but the break with Kate might be said to underline how action tells more than the identities available to picture. And for the most proper appreciation of Merton's telling action, it is necessary to emphasize and reiterate that Merton contravenes Milly as well as Kate. For this means that Merton himself is picturing goodness without a clear, available, external model (Milly's will is obviously not one) and insisting that he make himself the model of this goodness by an action attempting concretely to define and embody the value he "sees." What he sees may be only awkwardly embodied in action (just as in *The Awkward Age* Nanda and Longdon are awkward actors), but the vision *must* be followed through with a deed. Merton's final move against Milly and Kate features Merton as actor by cancelling the heroines' self-picturings and their speculative designs. The novel ends its narrative reasoning emphatically as story.

Merton is thus not a Newman or a Vanderbank, withdrawing from action either for the sake of a superior quiet goodness and intelligence or for the sake of avoiding something compromising of or frustrating to lucidity in the form of action in the modern era. Merton's act is a sort of risk of moral creativity that neither Newman nor Vanderbank could manage. Moreover, the morality or goodness of Merton's action is complex: his deed does not simplify experience, nor does it make experience conform to innocence. The goodness or fineness in Milly to which Merton's act testifies is not Milly's innocence or kindness. It is as if James identifies Milly's goodness with an integrity of passionate desire in her, with what she wants most: we can assume that Merton feels this integrity betrayed by the self-effacing kindness of the will. Merton's own last willful action testifies to the identity of his self with his transformed *desire*: he has come to love Milly more than Kate. In Merton's case, as in Milly's, James ultimately portrays goodness as fidelity to one's desires and truth to the transformations they create. Merton's action thus does not instance an abstract morality of love or kindness but a goodness that is truth: truth to one's essential reality. Through Merton James is willing to risk the idea that such truth is preeminently moral, no matter what is the object of desire or the nature of the character to which the actor is morally true. Of course, neither the desire nor the essential nature and reality is seen by James as possessing integrity if it is not witnessed by and as action.

In this risky notion of what is good or moral we can see James's imagination of Merton, like his imagination of Kate, looking forward to the achieved apotheosis of intrigue and plot in *The Golden Bowl*, where the morality of action leaps beyond reflective pictorial composition and conventional good and evil, beyond easy discriminations of innocence and betrayal. And, in looking forward to *The Golden Bowl* and its princess, we must not underestimate "princess" Milly's address to goodness and to action. Milly matures by becoming an intriguer. How else can she really *have* her life: when she marches through Regent's Park, fresh with the news of her approaching death, she is as fiercely purposeful and grasping, as committed to an intrigue and action that leave behind conventional good and evil as Kate is. Thus, we have followed James's lead in involving his characters with his technical modes, for as we have seen in citations from *The Wings of the Dove*, the characters are often figured as live symbols of *picture* or of *story*, in such a way as to dramatize the differing weights and values of primarily contemplative or primarily active ways of life. But we must now ask, what is the good of Merton's and James's enactment of their version of good? And what is the good of James's cultivating a battle between ways of life that turns out to disrupt and even sacrifice his aesthetic transubstantiations of picture, drama, plot, and story?

The featuring of act in the late James is the result of his growing conviction that the inhibition of action, either by passive, still, and quiescent life or by a limitation upon action's intellectual and moral diversity and risk, is a blow to civilization, to the fortunes of human community. Since the shift in James's technical and thematic interests is so motivated, it is necessary to consider further what the sense of plot means to James in terms of the fate of society. The young James presents the withdrawal from plot and active intrigue as an American and social virtue, not merely as a private one. And beginning with *The Awkward Age*, the elder James shows the active intrigue of Longdon and Nanda as an honorable attempt to redeem a blighted social state. But in what way are the actions "social" whereby Kate or Merton execute their purposes and values? The fruit of Merton's break with Kate can only be satisfaction with his own will and act. It creates nothing happy or blessed for Kate; it contravenes Milly; it leaves him utterly alone. Kate's activity too has left her penniless and destitute. Is the fruit of action only desolation and solitude? No wonder human happiness and good, even human interrelation, may seem more available to contemplative narrative consciousness than to the consciousness that transforms "picture" into action. The active plotter is true to himself, but appears also to do himself harm and to do no one else any good.

Bleak as this prospect is, James's most valued late characters find that they must embrace it. Merton may create nothing for himself but an isolation, but paradoxically this represents hope for a decent form of human interrelation—even if the form can exist only as an act of hope. Human relation as it already exists is far from happy. Kate once exclaims to Milly with great pathos and envy: "You're an outsider, independent and standing by yourself; you're not hideously relative to tiers and tiers of others." In many of the novels both early and late, James's characters begin their stories without sufficient independence. An excess of relationship, crowded with presences and possibilities of connection, demoralizes and even terrifies them. Kate's activity is finally sadder than Merton's, perhaps because she cannot think of alternatives to the closeness of relation that characterizes her family. She describes her "narrow little family feeling" as a "small stupid piety." She insists on honoring it, though, when "face to face . . . with the bond of blood," she finds it neither uplifting nor sweet. Unfortunately she reproduces these relations among herself, Merton, Mrs. Lowder, and Milly. Her family feeling becomes a literally bloody bond. But if Milly becomes quickly relative—hideously so—to tiers and tiers of others, it is not just because Kate plots or "works" her into relation. Kate only uses the connection already existing between Milly and Merton.

All the characters of *The Wings of the Dove* are hideously relative to each other, through family ties, love, or financial need. The bonds of connection are almost instantaneous. Lord Mark and Milly agree not to be intimate, but, despite the agreement, Milly feels "a perverse quickening of the relation [with Mark] to which she had been, in spite of herself, appointed."[10] When Mark seems to exchange with Kate looks that comment on Milly, Milly feels the onset of a "relation into which she was sinking." Indeed Milly's consciousness is "crowded" with "the various signs of a relation," and this is a kind of suffocating terror to her. In the face of relation as crowded, bloody bond and passive sinking, the activity that achieves isolation (such as Merton's last act) is thus an honorable and creative check to the bondage of passive interrelations. In their place, the act puts a hope of interrelations that are freely created. This hope suggests what positive social relations, rather than "sinking" ones, would be.

Here is an interesting difference between James, his predecessors, and his Victorian contemporaries, for in Scott, Dickens, or Eliot the characters are originally isolated, and they plot in order to achieve a final close, even crowded, state of connection. But when the reverse happens in James, it is nevertheless motivated by social intention. Of course we are speaking not of a passive withdrawal of the individual from the crowd of relations but of an active plotted assertion against them. Not surprisingly, in the prefaces James talks of relations constituted by passive sinkings in terms of "pictorial" metaphor, so that it seems plot or story can be actions moving against relations associated with the contemplativeness of picture. For example, when James says that "really, universally, relations stop nowhere," the famous sentence has an ominous side. The expansiveness promises the novelist and his characters unlimited developments, but it simultaneously threatens confusion and entrapment. Just after the famous sentence James says that connections and continuities frighten him. Even as "a young embroiderer of the canvas of life," he "soon began to work in terror, fairly, of the vast expanse" of surface before him. Since James speaks here in terms of a pictorial figure, we may take him to mean that picture's relations stop nowhere. This fecundity is a hazard for James the mature storyteller. The immense quantity of such relations needs to be checked by plot, which for the sake of a significant action must sacrifice some of them. Otherwise, James will find himself in the situation of Milly, for whom, in a moment of picture, relations seem to "stop nowhere" and are a matter of passive sinking. With emotional and moral urgency, James intervenes against the passivity, and shows the characters of his later work doing the same for their lives and for others. Art demands, James says,

> a dire process of selection and comparison, of surrender and sacrifice. The very meaning of expertness is acquired courage to brace one's self for the cruel crisis from the moment one sees it grimly loom.[11]

Story, plot, action: these are other names for the "dire process" that brings the storyteller, his story, and his characters to an emphatic end. The relation stops somewhere, for good and for ill. If this process sacrifices possibilities of picture on the aesthetic and reflective level and passive communities of relationship on the ethical and social level, it is for the sake of "the cruel crisis" of action. For the late James, without active plot or doing, no form of goodness substantiates itself. This means a willful self-bracing, an acquired and even brutal courage on the actor's part. The price and the fruit of this is the radical alteration of the actor's social being, whether he is the novelist or the novelist's fictive agent. The possible or probable isolation that results *may* do the actor harm and may not—in practical and immediate terms—do much good for anyone else. Yet, as James sees it, his braced sacrificial deed can be the hope of any human and aesthetic state in which relation is characterized by only passively received givens or by a consciousness that can reflect upon its discriminations but cannot fulfill its narrative reasonings by enacting them.

There will be advocates of James who will resist this account of him, who will insist that the narrative modes receive no individual featuring or favor earlier or later in the career, and who will find in work as rich as James's numerous exceptions to my argument. But these advocates will sadly have little or no sense of what James believed was at stake in an American storyteller's relation to action at the beginning of this century. In *The American Scene*, we find James once again using the pictorial mode—this time in nonfiction—and we find him simultaneously perplexed and frustrated by "scenic" impressions. James decides that America has devoted itself to something like a parody of Jamesian picture: the country basks in monstrous self-reflections of its economic and physical grandeur; it insistently matches its identity with a portrait James at first assiduously scrutinizes and then rejects as uncreative and probably uncivilized. What damages America for James is that it resists story and history, that it denies the narrative motions of consciousness, especially insofar as those motions feature acts. In one sense, of course, James's America does favor action by the primacy it assigns to the "work" of business, but it inhibits and overlooks action of every other kind. In *The American Scene* James's prescription for American civilization is not contemplation or withdrawal from the action of business but a finer cultivation of will and adventure, a broadening of the possibilities for significant human deeds. Because James's recommendation has obvious bearing on his mature thoughts about story, *The American Scene* deserves attention here. And to focus the sense of plot especially brought out by this last of James's examinations of American culture, it will also be fruitful to take a long look backward at the attitudes towards the relations of picture and story, of contemplative composition or reflection and action in Nathaniel Hawthorne, the novelist who most inspired James's lifelong pictorial technique as well as the type of Jamesian "drama" represented by *The American*. Hawthorne's presence and achievement must inevitably frame a consideration of Jamesian story; and the older James's difference from Hawthorne is one of the best gauges of transformation in James's sense of the value of story and action for American civilization.

Jamesian *picture* seems to have sprung directly from *The House of the Seven Gables*, the drama of which concerns a hero whose photographic pictorial art is identified by Hawthorne with truth and quiescent speculation and with the absence of manipulatory intrigue and will, and whose storytelling art—in direct contrast—is identified with lying and coercion, with mastery of others, with plot and action considered as evil. Through Holgrave Hawthorne gives storytelling a nefarious name, for the photographer plots to put a mesmeric spell on Phoebe Pyncheon by reading her his story of Alice Pyncheon. He all but succeeds, and Hawthorne tells us that "to a disposition like Holgrave's, at once speculative and active, there is no temptation so great as the opportunity of acquiring empire over the human spirit." Holgrave's kind of storytelling is this great temptation to acquire empire over the reader and the listener by spellbinding them with the tale's proximity to reality and by using the tale to incite action rather than reflection. Fortunately, we are made to think, Holgrave cedes his intriguing ambitions for the sake of Phoebe, who represents natural truth free of story's alleged magics and artifices. Hawthorne follows Holgrave's example. He deauthorizes the truth of his novel, insisting that the reader *not* suspend disbelief in the tale. It is not magic or metaphysical evil that *The House of the Seven Gables* attacks but fictive fabling, which according to Hawthorne curses experience by manipulating its shape and calling it truth. The legends of the house are spurious superstructures of plot and will. The novel's authentic story, its only real or important truth, lies in picturings available to natural light or to non-manipulative reflective light. In a remarkable early instance of the modern sense of plot, Hawthorne juxtaposes his characters in a variety of combinations for the sake of speculative comparisons and contrasts. When these combinations of pictures bring the characters to the threshold of a fable or a plot, Hawthorne lingers and draws back, anxious *not* to fable but to remain on the threshold of story. Indeed what Hawthorne seems to want in *The House of the Seven Gables* is to replace story with Phoebe's "easy and flexible charm of play," with "a succession of kaleidoscopic pictures" like those in Maule's Well, whose water provides "a continually shifting apparition of quaint figures, vanishing too suddenly to be definable." Where plot is concerned, in *The House of the Seven Gables* Hawthorne has the detachment and the innocence of Newman confronting Mrs. Bread. And Hawthorne's emphasis upon Phoebe deauthorizes the life and fact of action: the heroine represents a suspension of will and act, a reproof to the prestige and definiteness of deeds.[12]

Hawthorne's reluctance to master appearances by means of plot and his conversion of story and action into indefinite picture and play are taken up by James and made the essence of much of his career. But *The American Scene*, although it is nonfiction, shows as significantly great a difference from the narrative and moral values of James's master as *The Wings of the Dove* or *The Golden Bowl* show from the narrative and moral values of *Roderick Hudson* and *The American*. In *The American Scene* James's pictorial moments, although he has committed himself to their use, are all questionable: their lack of reliability makes him feel "pricked by thorns," "impotent," and "poisoned." "The lone visionary" finds himself "betrayed and arrested in the very act of vision." He finds some relief from the betrayals of picture, however,

> in that blest general drop of the immediate need for conclusions, or rather in that blest general feeling for the impossibility of them. . . . [The spectator] doesn't *know*, he can't *say*, before the facts, and he doesn't even want to know or say: . . . it is as if the syllables were too numerous to make a legible word. The *il*legible word, accordingly, the great inscrutable answer to questions, hangs in the vast American sky, to his imagination, as something fantastic and *abracadabrant*, belonging to no known language.

But this relief is momentary, and creative initiative passes from reflective composition to willful making of relations. In the face of nonsense James must *make* sense. "The high honour of the painter of life [is] always to *make* a sense," even when he surmises that "the cluster of appearances can *have* no sense. . . . The last thing decently permitted him is to recognize incoherence—to recognize it, that is, as baffling." Does not Hawthorne's narrative playfulness allow experience to be recognized by the storyteller as baffling, even incoherent, in no way that he can correct? As a descendant of Holgrave, James cannot be content with bafflement; he wants "empire" over appearances. By emphasizing his own resistance to passive spectatorship, James shifts the vehicle of his analysis to willful exertion: "the painter of life" remains a visionary, but in response to the scene he becomes a purposefully shaping actor. James thus highlights one of his principal definitions of civilization: it is "the capture of conceived values," and the means of realizing this capture are the enactments that supplement conceptions. Thus, the famous identification of the "hotel-spirit" as *the* modern American hallmark is not a condemnation on James's part: by the time he reaches Florida, he realizes that the American hotel is, after all, a "capture" of the "inordinate desire for taste." The activity is all to the good, for it transforms the conception of taste into a definite and realized form. The only pathos of this desire, James explicitly says, is that it will "remain a mere heartbreak to the historic muse" by not transforming itself into a greater variety of realizations or enactments—especially by confining its "capture" to a pictorial and visible form of business activity:

> The human imagination, . . . the collective consciousness, in however empty an air, gasps for a relation, as intimate as possible, to something superior, something as central as possible, from which it may more or less have proceeded and round which its life may revolve—and its dim desire is always, I think, to do it justice, that this object or presence shall have had as much as possi-

ble an heroic or romantic association. But the difficulty is
that in these later times . . . the heroic and romantic elements, even under the earliest rude stress, have been all
too tragically obscure, belonged to smothered, unwritten, almost unconscious private history: so that the central something, the social *point de repére*, has had to be ex-
temporised rather pitifully after the fact, and made to
consist of the biggest hotel or the biggest common
school, the biggest factory, the biggest newspaper office,
or, for climax of desperation, the house of the biggest bil-
lionaire.[13]

The pictorial presences and grandeurs are mere blanks if
they are cut loose from the diverse and complex actions and
stories that make them. James is most shocked to note the national absence of reference to the Civil War. But although the
War's increasing obscurity would be reversed by an American renewal of consciousness and reflection in relation to its
past, James is also arguing that America has "unmade" the
complex ideological and spiritual activity it represented. If
there were room again for a spectrum of activities other than
business and the pursuit of material grandeur, America
might be able to imagine the War again, and might become
more civilized by broadening the scope of action whereby
values are captured. Now James, as I have said before, never
gives up his pictorial mode; nor does he ever equate it with
vulgar visibilities, as America equates her own self-picturings; nor does he even suggest that America can dispense
with reflective self-awareness. But he wants to insist on both
the value of the narrative realities that America has made secret and on the value of the stories and actions she inhibits or
hides. What James calls "the great social proposition" is a
matter of cultivated and captured diversity of character, and
character itself is "developed to visible fineness only by fric-
tion and discipline on a large scale, only by its having to
reckon with a complexity of forces." True "visible fineness"
develops out of the frictions and forces that in America be-

long to the "smothered, unwritten, almost unconscious" private histories, relations, and acts that it is the storyteller's vocation to designate and express.[14]

James ends his book on modern America with an act of rejection that typifies the late Jamesian sense of plot: reflective consciousness must fulfill itself by a supplementary determined enactment. To collect pictures is not enough; what the pictures show must be matched by a deed. James's definitive deed is the break with America announced at the end of *The American Scene*. This is his proud and willful resolution of the meaning of the illegible word hanging in the vast American sky. Hawthorne, who far more than James is to be associated with ambiguities, would not have pressed the American questions to so definite and active a conclusion; but James *will* show his empire over the "abracadabrants" of experience. He shows his empire by breaking off his relation: "one's supreme relation . . . was one's relation to one's country," but to carry on the hope of community implicit in that relation and to show his own personal capture of conceived values, James resolves the story of his ties by an act of rejection that undoes them. What this act constitutes in the actor is a form of the goodness we have seen in Merton: a complex integrity, discrimination, and enactment of desire. Civilization needs such resolving, constitutive acts, by means of even "nefarious" plots and plotters, since such resolutions create the stories— the testimonies of conceived *and enacted* discriminations—for which humanity hungers. Might I suggest in closing that James's surrender of American citizenship in 1915 is another measure of his final distance from Hawthorne and Christopher Newman, is an instance too of his late favoring of the story in complex intrigue and overt action rather than of the story in picture? In his change of nationality, whatever claims are to be made for its sheer convenience, James designates as his country the one whose novelistic tradition shows, at least in the last century, relatively more trust than America's in plot, story, and the representation of action.[15]

EIGHT

The Family Plot: Conrad, Joyce, Lawrence, Woolf, and Faulkner

> There are some families and any one can be married in them and some in them are not married and some in them are married and any one of them almost any one of them can have some children and some of them have some children and some of them do not have children and some of them do something, do anything again. . . . Family living is being existing.
>
> —Gertrude Stein, *The Making of Americans*

I have contended that the late James is a novelist who thinks it is not enough only to know life and to have fine impressions and imaginations. Consciousness and imagination must make a difference for practice, and they do so for James by their "capture" in action. Through action the capture of intelligence and imagined values gives knowledge and imagination empire, so that they may rule and newly shape the context of their "captor." We have seen the same commitment in Dickens, for the rescue is the archetype of action that captures—and liberates—knowledge and desire, gives them practicable sway in the world, and sets them free from confinement in a purely theoretical, unrealized sphere. The turn of James's sense of plot to the story in action rather than to the story in picture occurs, however, just at the onset of the major phase of the modern sense of plot. As we have seen in earlier chapters, the modern sense of plot subverts not only the idea and fact of action but the idea and the possibility of truthful, valuable, authoritatively shaping intentions in verbal art; it subverts the *authority* of contemplative designs of life, whether or not they are realizable or practicable as action. In a closer examination of this subversion in the greatest modern attacks on the positive sense of plot, on action, on narrative intellectual and moral reason, on willfully shaped and unifying perspectival functions, we will find that the novelists focus on one persistent thematic object: the family.

In Dickens, family—at least in its ideal emanations—is not the "nuclear" family but a spontaneous community of kindred identities whose creative interaction is the model for the dynamism of the various strands of Dickensian narrative relations. David Copperfield's genuine kin—not only his mother, but his aunt, Mr. Dick, Mr. Peggotty, and others— are his rescuers from immaturity, his makers for the better rather than for the worse. David's storytelling—his making of narrative relations—also makes him for the better. It forms him at last—as his kin have been trying to form him—as the hero of his life. Now we have seen that, in contrast to Dickens, James fears the crowded closeness and passivity of existing human relations. But we have also seen how this fear stimulates James to favor action that counteracts passive crowding, that is hopeful for the close and authoritative kinships such action can embody. Longdon and Nanda have valuably plotted a new familial relation between them; and Maggie Verver's renewal of her marriage and of her familial authority derives from her mature commitment (like her author's) to magisterially plotted action.

Unlike Dickens and James the great modern novels are not only about families but in one way or another they are antagonistic to the action whereby life is formed as family structure. They are especially antagonistic to the parental actor, to his creative power and shaping authority. In Hardy, Conrad, and Ford, in Gertrude Stein, Joyce, and Lawrence, in Woolf and Faulkner, the parent is a merely alleged author, one who stupidly refuses to admit that genealogical relations or family lines are factitious structures or "creations," that family is a misleading name for anarchy, and that generation and filiation are substitutes for significance. This antagonism to family as a fact and ordering of life is accompanied by a resistance to any kind of story or plot that seems formally to imitate family relations. If a story has a line in which one event is causally dependent upon another in a filiative way, if the major parts and minor details of what the story represents and what it narratively reasons are all hierarchically shaped by any mastering meaning or intention, then to the modern novelist this story needs breaking down and its will-to-meaning needs thwarting and dispersing, for the story's plot is miming as form a family order that is false and nefarious as fact.

There is indeed an analogy between family line and story line in the modern novel: and the modern novelist and his sense of plot subverts both lines. I will now consider this subversion in Conrad, Joyce, Lawrence, Woolf, and Faulkner. But I want to consider it not just to applaud or flatter it, for I would like to bring to bear on our great modern classics considerations inspired by the sense of plot in Dickens and late James. This may be all to the good, for in writing about and in teaching modern literature we have been applauding antagonism to the family and calling it modern or modernism for a long while. And while the modern novel *does* complement its antagonism to family with a novel form of plot, the complementarity is not the whole story, or even the most telling one.

We have recently applauded the *partial* story of family in the modern novel in our reception of Edward Said's *Beginnings*. *Beginnings* very clearly and usefully contrasts the old and familial narrative structure and sense of plot with a new antifamiliar novelistic discourse characteristic of the modern negative and wary senses of plot. Said lists the familiar conventions that "the [traditional] novel employs . . . in its plot, subject matter, and development," and he concludes the list by describing the familiar convention the modern novelists most oppose:

> The fifth and final convention is that the unity or integrity of the text is maintained by a series of genealogical connections: author-text, beginning-end, text-meaning,

reader-interpretation. . . . Underneath all these is the imagery of succession, of paternity, of hierarchy.

A handy illustration of the modern prestigious disruption of "succession, paternity, hierarchy" is offered by Said via *The Interpretation of Dreams*. In Freud "the key-step" in each dream-analysis "is the abandonment of quasi-natural continuity—continuity as paternal authority, as the dream's 'plot,' as Freud's narrative history of his experiences, as the . . . logic of consecutive explanation." What, then, supersedes parental authority in narrative and explanation? A "discourse" characterized by unresolved openness. Its parts may repeat each other but in such a way as to resist dynastic or hierarchical dependence on each other. Indeed these parts are disrupted and disruptive, without any necessary filiation or connection either to themselves, to a "parental" origin, or to an engendering end. Said calls this a condition of "mutuality." It represents "the mutuality between men which ensues when a repressive central authority is removed."

For novels, presumably, the repressive central authority is the plot shaping life, differentiating and reproducing life as a significant specific truth or as a definitive external form. Without the "repressive central authority" of what we may call the family plot (a narrative form of parenthood), without any "genealogical" relations, the parts of a fictional discourse become adjacencies, juxtapositions. These adjacent parts are fraternal, but they are kin without parents. And since in their mutuality they do not either couple with or sire one another, they are figuratively celibate, even sterile. What truth the parts of such discourse reveal or uncover is not deliberately formed; their truth results from a disclosure rising up from the mutuality and adjacency of the parts.[1]

Thus, to take six examples of the modern novel, in *The Secret Agent*, *The Rainbow*, *Women in Love*, *Ulysses*, *To the Lighthouse*, and *The Sound and the Fury* genealogical forms of narration—strictly dependent and interdependent lines of continuity—are replaced by mutuality and adjacency of parts.

This is immediately obvious if one thinks of the disruptions of linear and of hierarchically causal narrative sequence in *The Secret Agent*, *To the Lighthouse*, and *The Sound and the Fury*. And although *The Rainbow*, *Women in Love*, and *Ulysses* are strictly chronological in their storytelling, the novels saturate the reader with intensities of feeling that make their strict chronology and their causal relations and continuities recede from sight. In these latter novels we feel the juxtaposing of feelings and events in a way that confuses our consciousness by disrupting its sense of causal order and form. What is confused is our sense of a story being purposefully shaped to *tell about* the intensities these novels communicate. We do not feel as we read Lawrence or Joyce that they are authoritatively plotting experience towards the definitive shaping of an all-consuming goal or significance.

We must remember, as Said points out, that these attacks on family and plot were no mere "espousal of nihilism." There is creativity, the novelists claim, even in sterility, whether it be biological or narrational; life and significance even where there is no parenthood and its analogous forms of discourse. Arguably, then, these moderns welcome what we can call the end of filiation by emphatically saying farewell to the family plot. But the present remarks mean to point out what is equivocal in both the welcome and the farewell. In the classic modern fictions about these family matters uncertainty and self-division have not been sufficiently realized or acknowledged. The subversion of the family plot as fact and as form in the modern novel is unquestionable. But just as unquestionable is a countertendency, a deep frustration with the very need to break the form that features the creativity and shaping authority—the significance—of the parent considered as both a biological and cultural agent and as a plotting narrative agent. Of the five novelists to be considered here, at least Conrad, Lawrence, and Faulkner are in the position of having exploded parenthood, only to look, perhaps in spite of themselves, as if they wanted the family plot reinstituted—although in a new way and on a new foundation.

They are not nostalgic for what they have discredited: the vigor of their disillusion with families as they have existed prevents them from merely looking backward. But Faulkner especially stands for an impulse to find or to create what will be called here a new and adversary parenthood.

In the main this chapter will examine the end of filiation and the farewell to the family plot in all of these moderns, to make clear in a fresh way the emotional and moral impact of the attack on parenthood, to suggest the needs this attack stimulated or suppressed, and to point out its self-divisions where they seem to exist. To do this most conveniently the six novels will not be treated chronologically. *Ulysses* and *To the Lighthouse* will be considered first, for they are the most singlemindedly devoted to the end of filiation. Lawrence comes next; in our study of self-division on family plot and family matters, he is a kind of pivot because he most insistently denies his mixed feeling. In order to illustrate the sense of plot especially motivating *my* part of the argument from the study of Lawrence onward, I might point out that the more Lawrence struggles against family and against the mere idea of parenthood, the more he puts himself, contrary to his own intention, of course, in the position of undermining or negating his creative power. For I assume that Lawrence's creative power—any novelist's, for that matter—has to do with his ambition to be the parent of his text in such a way as to demonstrate that his parental authority is not repressively masterful or deadening but authoritatively shaping and life-giving. We cannot understand *Women in Love* unless we see it as a "gladiatorial" between the two woefully opposed sides of its author, the Lawrence who *will* be the absolute father of the novel's content and meaning and the Lawrence who must destroy all fathers and all forms and meanings associated in his mind with family plot.

Now Joyce would flatly oppose the assumption that the novelist's power derives from his will to be the authoritative parent of a text whose parts he strictly, genealogically interrelates. This version of Joyce may have little in common with the conventional estimate of him as a godlike all-controlling artistic authority. Notwithstanding the conventional estimate, it is more accurate to claim that for Joyce the novelist's authority is purely "deconstructive"; that is, his authority comes only from his ability to play with and to break down all the structures of plot and story—not just filiations but narrative reasonings and relations and featurings of act—to make them all appear pointedly (and pointlessly?) factitious. The episodes of *Ulysses* illustrate by their variety the artificial and provisional nature of all narrative order, especially the order that is the family plot. The counterauthority licensing Joyce's deconstructions resides in the consciousness he assigns Molly. In relation to all of the preceding episodes, the last episode of *Ulysses* is meant to be a touchstone of truth, of nonmanipulated and nonfactitious form and feeling. In Joyce's mind Molly stands for the authority and satisfaction of a play with and dissolution of forms—although her relative formlessness has a form of its own: the nonparental mutualities and adjacencies (although perhaps not the discontinuities) that Said speaks of. Joyce wants to identify this "form" with the female, who exemplifies for him an essence (perhaps too a complete actual presence) that has not yet been sufficiently expressed in history or in fiction because it has been male-dominated and forced to utter itself entirely through male assumptions and male forms.

We must not think of Molly as symbolic of matriarchy: this would only give us a female version of the family plot. Joyce certainly emphasizes woman's intimacy with child-bearing as the mark of an intimacy with creation superior to man's; but the family structure in *Ulysses*, whether paternal or maternal, is being presented as a passing historical fact. Indeed we must read *Ulysses* as a late specimen of the historical novel, as an attempt to clarify an historical change (one that has special consequences for narration) through a study of the men and women who enact the change: what is undergoing historical transformation is family life, while what is undergoing formal change is the life-structure of story. Leopold Bloom desires to author a son; Stephen Dedalus desires to author a literary monument. In this they both show a favoring for patriarchal life, and Joyce presents their narrative motions of consciousness as saturated by what he thinks of as male, patriarchal forms of story. But these forms are passing away, to make room for the sense of life and plot that belong to Molly. Joyce seems to write *Ulysses* to cede his own male originating authority and its traditional narrative sense to Molly's allegedly disorderly mutualities. The future, like Joyce's future in *Finnegans Wake*, belongs to Molly's "form," to the end of the privileging of filiation both in and out of fiction.

In order to better see Joyce's intention to identify a new form of story and of "telling" with a female consciousness free of male form, we must not underemphasize how Bloom watches for his own cuckolding throughout the single day of *Ulysses*—a suicidal watching of his death as husband and father, echoing the suicide of his own father. Of course it is part of Joyce's greatness to make us feel intense sympathy with Bloom's passing patriarchal temperament. But we must not be misled by the idealization of paternities and filiations, of father-son relationships and needs for each other imported into *Ulysses* by nostalgic commentators. Joyce is writing to cool this nostalgia. More important than his sympathy for Bloom is Bloom's sympathy for woman: as Molly says, he "understood or felt what woman is," and Joyce aspires to the same understanding. So just as Bloom, to understand woman, must accept Boylan and must confine his patriarchal ambitions to daydreams, Joyce, wanting to exalt what woman is, must take Molly for female archetype, must know and reveal the narrative form appropriate to woman. In a kind of transvestite spite of his own gender, Joyce thus throws the weight of his book against paternities and filiations.

This is why Stephen's brillant discourse on Shakespeare in the library deserves far more serious attention than it has yet received: because it is negative about paternity and authority, it is *the* key to *Ulysses*, both thematically and formally.[2] It cannot be overlooked or minimized by calling Stephen

sophomoric or by taking John Eglinton's point of view when
he says, "What do we care for [Shakespeare's] wife and
father? I should say that only family poets have family lives."
There is nothing *but* family life in *Ulysses*. But what Joyce tries
to tell us through Stephen's biography of Shakespeare is that
the authentic center of family, life, and art is—or ought to be
recognized as—somehow solely woman, not man-and-
woman and certainly not man, either in himself or as parent.
The stimulus to Shakespeare's plays is Ann who, Stephen insists, did not die "for literature at least, before she was born."
We might even say that Ann is in fact the creator of the plays,
as if after God—to paraphrase Eglinton on Shakespeare—
woman has created most. But "created" in this sense means
"generated," and to use this word is to assign to the female a
process the male has made up, in effect, for the sake of his
self-aggrandizement. Stephen wants to identify authority
and creativity with his sex, not with woman's, but in his own
life and in Shakespeare's he bitterly perceives that the male
claim to creativity and generation is factitious. As Stephen
sees Ann, she destroyed Shakespeare's belief in himself, in
his engendering, creative initiative as a male; he wrote his
plays as a defense and as a lie against Ann's effect. The death
of paternity and of paternal authority finds its summary
statement when Stephen says:

> Fatherhood, in the sense of conscious begetting, is un-
> known to man. It is a mystical estate, an apostolic suc-
> cession, from only begetter to only begotten. On that
> mystery and not on the madonna which the cunning Ital-
> ian intellect flung to the mob of Europe the church is
> founded and founded irremovably because founded, like
> the world, macro- and microcosm, upon the void. Upon
> incertitude, upon unlikelihood. *Amor matris* subjective
> and objective genitive, may be the only true thing in life.
> Paternity may be a legal fiction.[3]

Stephen suggests here that paternity generates only fictions—that even the process of generation is factitious.

Shakespeare's plays seem to be his offspring; yet since Stephen has already made them Ann's more than Will's, the link between artist and his work now seems no more definite than the link between father and son, which is not a sacrosanct or even a real succession. "What links them in nature? An instant of blind rut."

If succession in nature is only an instant of blind rut, then successions in narrative ("plot is the element of sequence") have no truthful ground; like paternity, these successions are founded upon male fiction. Authority and truth lie in disruption of the family line, as Ann disrupted it, adding insult to Will's injury by committing adultery with at least one brother-in-law. Defending himself against female disruption, the male insists that creativity is identical with the authority of clearly linear, filiative order in life, plot, and story. In Stephen's discourse the characteristic note of nostalgia ascribed to Shakespeare merges with the terminology of dramatic narrative structures: in Shakespeare's life the "note of banishment . . . doubles itself, repeats itself, protasis, epitasis, catastasis, catastrophe." Joyce has Stephen use these formal, rhetorical terms to imply that these are the terms and structures of plotting order and sequence that the male creates under the curse of distance and exile from the female center. The structures of the fictive order Stephen names are identical with the male's paternal will; and his claims to creative paternity rest on the maintenance of such linear logics. They are analogies of the succession through which the male wants to dominate life and to avoid seeing that all his sequences, even the generational ones, are blind. In contrast, Molly's consciousness is not clearly successive or sequential. It cannot be structured in terms of "protasis, epitasis," etc. Moreover, it is neither a nostalgic nor a searching, questing consciousness. In *Ulysses* forms of quest and search are also male: the sections of the novel dominated by its men are all quests. Does this mean that the male favors quest because it is a process that enacts getting and begetting, as if they were conscious and purposeful and not merely blind instants? Once we are inside Molly's mind, anxieties over parenthood and family plot, over the quests for relation that have all but controlled the novel, vanish.

Molly's monologue must be read as the complement of Stephen's lecture—in fact as the proof that what he thinks *may be* true *is* true. By the time Molly voices her disgust with men by exclaiming "why don't they go and create something," Joyce has persuaded us that she is closer to creation (in spite of the coincidence of her monologue with her menstruation) than they. But Molly does not create by any kind of willful fabrication, by any active construction, *ex nihilo*, in the manner producing novel differences that is characteristic of the God of Genesis. *He* too, it seems, is a male plot. "*Amor matris*," Stephen says, "subjective and objective genitive, may be the only true thing in life." But, in spite of the mother's rather than the father's closeness to children, is the mother's "genitive" generative in the same way that the male defines generation? Molly's power is that she does not need to make or create but that she inhabits and is creation, substantially. Experience for her is a plenum; if it has gaps or voids, she is careless of them, trusting truth to arise out of discontinuity. As it is, Molly seems to lack nothing, not even the past. Her desires satisfy her as much as their fulfillment. The unmoved mover of the novel and its men, she is not the maker of things and forms but the presence of things and forms.

In contrast the men feel life to be absence more than presence; their consciousness is frustrated, forever curious and searching; they insist that they will make gaps "tell," but they are forever baffled. The males need plot and story to realize life as "point," to "make" creation "significant" by reproducing it in some form they can grasp. But the male is not at home in life, nor can he make a home in it; whereas the female is already at home, fulfilled. Unlike the men, when Molly is puzzled by a discontinuity, she gives in to it, without searching for and plotting a relational link. Spontaneously a link arises; the relation is already there: metempsychosis is "met him pike hoses," base baritone is "base barreltone." The author of *Finnegans Wake* wants us to consider these answers as accurate and satisfying, even if they do not meet traditional standards of the search for truth and for the adequate making of relation. The male believes that truth is not immediate, so he makes another fiction, another story, out of it. And of course the male insists on the mediacy of all experience, on the necessary intervention of memory and foresight in all truthful comprehension. He thus makes even time a puzzle, needing stories to understand or "tell" it. Molly, in contrast, is as full of time as of creation. She feels "not a day older than then." Her sorrow over Rudy is as genuine as Leopold's, but she does not hold tightly to it; she accepts the break in continuity that is Rudy's death. But because she accepts, the sorrow seems less past, less in need of compensation by an obsessive return to attempts at developing successions. Molly pursues no generative quest, and paradoxically her world is fruitful.

The narrative of Molly's monologue is thus without a positive sense of plot: it is not shaped by male purposeful direction or by structures of willful creation. The satisfaction and fulfillment of Molly's kind of consciousness may be gauged by comparing it to a self-destructive element in the male commitment to purposeful creation, epitomized by the narrative quest and the desire to father sons and significances. What is this self-destructive element? The male in *Ulysses* never allows his quests to realize their promise. Stephen understands this because he knows that "the sun [sic] unborn mars beauty," but "born he brings pain." The male authority is self-destructive because it quarrels with what it engenders. To the male genius "the images of other males of his blood will repel him. He will see in them grotesque attempts of nature to foretell or repeat himself."[4] The male certainly does not want mutuality with what it creates; it wants creation ruthlessly hierarchized. Thus in reaction, sons rebel against their fathers, wanting the paternal power exclusively for themselves. Hence the men of *Ulysses* sire forms of filiative order identical with forms of frustration: their nostalgia looks willful, as well as self-frustrating.

In his persistent pride and vanity the male even attempts to remake woman in his image. In Gerty MacDowell's feelings and thoughts we see what the male plotting of life makes of the female enslaved to it. Gerty is the madonna engendered by the fiction of paternity. She flatters the male forms by adopting them; hence Gerty too thinks and feels in terms of quest. And to think in terms of quest means commitment to and secret worship of absence and postponement, of enticing and frustrating distances. Joyce sees plot as a tease. Gerty's thoughts are among the easiest to read in *Ulysses* because she is devoted to syntax and to conventionally clear narrative. But through Gerty Joyce identifies this clarity with censorship, with the male desire to prove its potency by teasing and frustrating life's spontaneity. All of Gerty's syntax serves prudery ("Gerty MacDowell bent down her head and crimsoned at the idea of Cissy saying an unladylike thing like that out loud"). The episode itself has the narrative syntax Stephen names: the catastrophe is the fireworks display ("O!") and Gerty's and Bloom's masturbation ("O!"). But this is Joyce laughing at point and climax as form. Joyce's judgment is patent, especially when Gerty gets up and walks: the organization of experience by means of conventional syntax or by the narrative syntax and the sense of plot leading from epitasis to catastrophe to point of reversal (when Gerty walks) is masturbatory and lame because it is the creation of the male.

The satire of the Gerty episode is thus directed against male form—or, more accurately, against male reform. Gerty reforms experience by structures she shares with Stephen and Bloom, not with Molly, whose relative narrative disorder is genuine or authentic form. Joyce makes this point partly by setting Gerty's episode against the background of the Virgin's novena, dedicated to the reformation of intemperance. More importantly, Gerty is the victim of the male will to form life over again in its image, as the domestic dynasty that is the male-dominated family. Hence Gerty devotes herself to home (she "was womanly wise and knew that a mere man liked that feeling of hominess"), and also imagines her marriage in the male terms and forms of quest and distance ("she could see at once . . . that he was a foreigner . . . her dreamhusband. . . . They both knew that she [herself] was something aloof, apart in another sphere"). Yearning for her "dreamhusband" to crush her body against him, Gerty is already crushed: the granddaughter of the raging patriarch Giltrap and the fantasy-beloved of the patriarch Bloom, she is the male-formed female, coerced into testifying that life is a romantic male quest-story, one not founded upon a void.

Thinking about "stupid husbands jealousy" Molly wonders, "why can't we all remain friends over it instead of quarreling." She wants to satisfy all her desires: "what else were we given all those desires for I'd like to know I can't help it." Gerty could not admit or say this or allow the thought to form her life. The narrative reform Joyce is promulgating through Molly and locating in the spontaneous flowerings of her thoughts and feelings is the form of "all those desires," given full play as perpetual mutuality and adjacency, uncensured by hierarchizing narrative reasonings, either intellectual or moral. Gerty wants to be crushed by a father because she feels orphaned and hopeless. She has suffered because "that vile decoction which has ruined so many hearths and homes had cast its shadow over her childhood days." Yet fathers are intoxicated by their own assumed power. For Gerty to look to father-dominated family hierarchy as a remedy for disorder is hopeless. Perhaps the disorder—if that is the right word for what Molly stands for—is irremovably there, "in the home circle" itself, beyond the control of fathers. In fact Joyce wants to argue that this disorder—when it is not organized by fathers—is really not so bad—that it is not bad at all. As Molly represents it, relative disorder (of feeling, of thought, of narrative), not order is the solution to our familial woes. The approach to Molly lies through the cabman's shelter, where Parnell's adultery and the Irish anarchists are compounded in the general conversation. Molly's adultery, her competition with Milly, her fantasy of Stephen as at once a son and a sexual partner—if these mean an end of filiation in consciousness and in form, a disorder and anarchy, then they are represented as attractive, harmless, vitally substantial. Upsetting differentiations and distinctions, caring little about control of self or others, Molly has a presence that makes the male plots raging about her small and pointless.

But Stephen and Bloom do sense the freedom and fulfillment of Molly's form—or relative formlessness—of life. She is at home in creation as they are not for all their striving to domesticate the world by means of dynasty or dynastic thinking. Yet Joyce points out that the male has, after all, a more direct connection than he knows with Molly's vitality, with her freedom from male structures. At the end of the library lecture, Stephen announces that "we walk through ourselves . . . always meeting ourselves." The gist of the paradox appears to be that self-definition does not depend upon the engendering of others or of one's self. Bloom believes his identity would be consummated if he fathered a son, as if his identity needs a willful and plotted reproduction and mirroring for its existence. But Stephen's idea implies that the self at one point in time, doing any kind of thing, does not beget its own extension or its own transformation. The self is not sired or authorized or fulfilled by engenderings. Stephen perceives that the self rises free of generation. "I, entelechy, form of forms, am I by memory because under everchanging forms . . . I, I and I. I."[5] Bloom, at the end of Gerty's episode, has the same thought. "So it returns. Think you're escaping and run into yourself. Longest way round is the shortest way home."

This thought brings Stephen and Bloom closest to the rationale of the form underlying Molly's consciousness. The self does not need to make a home for itself by engendering relations—familial, filial, or otherwise. Its persistent subsistence shows that "the note of banishment" is not its essence. The duration of identity, the at-one-ness of "I, I and I," is what Molly and her kind of narrative repose on. In contrast to her male associates with their repressive, central plotting authority, Molly does not center on the ambition to plot and reproduce life in her image. Although a mother, she is not obsessed with mothering, as male-formed Gerty would be. Molly does not need mystic successions in consciousness, family, or narrative. By replacing the father's authority and organization with her monologue's form of forms, Molly—and Joyce—recreate domestic order and narrative so that they transcend family plot. This does not mean, incidentally, that the last episode of *Ulysses* is the product of automatic writing on Joyce's part; it is the intentional product of one sense of plot undoing for the sake of truth the factitiousness it sees pervading another sense of plot. Because Joyce's males hold fast to this other sense of plot, they think they have lost a world in which they were once at home; they believe they will be at home again if they can become biological and cultural sires. But the lesson Joyce's men undergo in our eyes, if not in theirs, is that they are at home in the world even if they do not conform to the received notions of what males most stand for and do in order to be at home. The male consciousness can find itself embodied in the female, Joyce argues, as soon as it ceases attempting to wrest power from her, as soon as it gives up favoring fatherhood and the nostalgias and fictions about creation induced by the pursuit of filiation.

For Joyce, then, the narrative forms of parental authority are repressive and deadening, but Molly's consciousness and form are the essence of vitality. Insofar as story and plot hide this vitality, Joyce wants to strip them away. Since the spontaneous life Molly stands for is not matriarchal, she is not obsessed with the idea that creation means production or reproduction. In this regard it is not surprising that the ascendancy of Molly in Joyce's mind does not lead to a greater development of realism in his work. The family plot is addicted to another genealogical connection, "reality-novel"—that is, reality reproducing itself as the novel, its reflector. By arguing that males identify creativity with the pursuit of reproduction, Joyce enables Molly in contrast to stand more clearly for creation as nonreproductive process and presence, as substance and plenitude already made. The artist reveals this presence rather than makes or plots it. Now in turning from Joyce to Virginia Woolf's farewell to the family plot in *To the Lighthouse*, we find an even more powerful and almost chillingly impassive commitment to the idea that neither creation nor life mean production or reproduction. In Woolf the subversion of family and the end of filiation are attached to a notion that life itself is a misleading name for an essential sterility or waste that even the artist's creation must exemplify. The novel begins by identifying fatherhood with what it calls "the fatal sterility of the male," and it ends in alliance with this sterility—although presented in a tone finer than "fatal" suggests.

What Woolf wants to say about life as a curious sterile process is obscured if *To the Lighthouse* is read as either an attack on the patriarchal male or as an elevation—even nostalgic—of the matriarch. Both Mr. and Mrs. Ramsay are doomed; there is something as wrong with Mrs. Ramsay's mode of order and relation as with her husband's. Together the husband and wife represent two faces of family plot, one harmful, the other helpful. Mr. Ramsay, representing "the fatal sterility of the male," is an "arid scimitar"; his control of life wounds life. James Ramsay hates his father's "tyranny, despotism . . . making people do what they did not want to do, cutting off their right to speak." Mrs. Ramsay, on the other hand, "this delicious fecundity, this fountain and spray of life," has no apparent tyrannic ambitions. Whereas the father uses the family plot for domination and aggression, the mother uses it to guard both father and children from the injuries and repressions of shaping impulse and order. The stocking she is knitting represents her function as a protective sheath. Grown-up James can still feel his father's "beak on his bare legs, where it had struck when he was a child." Mrs. Ramsay has knitted to counteract this harm. The knitting is also symbolic of the fact that "the whole of the effort of merging and flowing and creating" rests on her. She links the members of the family into relation, and she knits them onward, not just together. Mr. Ramsay, who as a philosopher represents the possibility of plotting life as a logical, linear succession, worries that he cannot really move forward. He believes he has the power "to repeat every letter of the alphabet [of philosophical thought] from A to Z accurately in order. Meanwhile, he stuck at Q. On, then, on to R." Mrs. Ramsay supports and stimulates the movement on to R. In this way she abets both familial and spiritual continuity. Woolf links Mrs. Ramsay's role as a muse of family plot in life with her role as a symbolic muse of family plot in narrative by having Mr. Ramsay look to his wife for the living possibility and practice of continuity, while simultaneously having him look to Walter Scott for the narrative reproduction of continuity. When Charles Tansley, the philosopher's spiritual son, exclaims that Scott is no longer read, Mr. Ramsay thinks, "That's what they'll say of me." He retreats to the library— and takes down a volume of Scott. He thus propitiates a spiritual father, hoping to insure his own dynastic continuity. Reading Scott he is also reassured about intellectual progress and continuity: at least "somebody would reach Z." But Mr. Ramsay and Scott are both male and have that odd, fatal sterility; if one of their sex reaches Z, whether in life or philosophy or story, it will happen because of the fecund power of their mothers and wives.[6]

So, at least, the first part of *To the Lighthouse* seems to argue. Yet at the very moment of the father's confidence about reaching Z, Mrs. Ramsay doubts her fecundity. Is she really any less sterile than the male? The brilliant dinner of "The Window" does not go "on." Mrs. Ramsay understands that it "was vanishing even as she looked. . . . It had become, she knew, giving one last look at it over her shoulder, already the past." Mrs. Ramsay has been arranging the marriage of Minta Doyle and Paul Rayley; she has also been promoting a union between the spinster Lily Briscoe and the widower William Bankes. Now she asks herself: "Why is it then that one wants people to marry? What was the value, the meaning of things?" Mrs. Ramsay's two questions fit together, possibly, because marriage appears to be the matrix of value—and of meaning—since it continues and reproduces life in the face of death. In terms of family plot, for life to be a significant story there must be marriage: it guarantees continuity and a fixed point whereby to understand and measure beginnings and endings, repetitions and renewals. Perhaps some such logic gets Mrs. Ramsay over the doubt that stimulates her question. Yet *To the Lighthouse* does not surmount that doubt. The *novel* goes on only in order to question the continuity that Mrs. Ramsay's "fecundity" generates: death takes Mrs. Ramsay and her son Andrew; the Rayley marriage fails; Cam and James league together against their father, attempting to disrupt his line. The most important and lasting consequence the Ramsays have seems to be in Lily Briscoe's mind. Yet Lily is at once the Ramsays' heir and a confirmed orphan and celibate. She feels a malicious triumph over Mrs. Ramsay's "saying, of all incongruous things, 'Marry, marry!' " And when she feels a tender need for the older woman, she twice cries out to her for help—and "nothing happened. Nothing! Nothing!"[7] By the end of *To the Lighthouse* Mrs. Ramsay, like marriage, is remembered; but with what consequence? Not even female fecundity has a sure issue or success.

Life in *To the Lighthouse* is shown as powerless to represent or reproduce itself in *any* familial form. For the narrative artist it is therefore untruthful to reproduce life in any familial form of plot—in any form that stresses continuity rather than disruption, mutualities with clear relations rather than without. As story the form of *To the Lighthouse* is disrupted; it juxtaposes its three *nominally* related parts rather than strictly connecting them. Story cannot articulate connection if life is a darkness, an obscurity, that not even sexual differentiation or generation can plot or articulate. Something like this must be understood by Mrs. Ramsay's sudden lapse from her matriarchal function and identity in "The Window," Chapter 11:

> To be silent; to be alone. All the being and the doing . . .
> evaporated; and one shrunk, with a sense of solemnity,
> to being oneself, a wedge-shaped core of darkness. . . . It
> was thus that she felt herself . . . when life sank down for
> a moment, the range of experience seemed limitless. . . .
> Our apparitions, the things you know us by, are simply
> childish. Beneath it is all dark, it is all spreading, it is un-
> fathomably deep; but now and again we rise to the sur-
> face and that is what you see us by.

Family, family plot, and filiation are perhaps especially "what
you see us by"; but, if so, they are only at the surface naive
appearances that are not life's essence.

In withdrawing from the family, Mrs. Ramsay identifies
the mysterious darkness with "peace, rest, eternity." Is this
identification conditioned, in spite of her withdrawal, by her
matriarchal ordering of life? It is if Lily Briscoe's response to
the core of darkness is weighed against Mrs. Ramsay's. Lily
seems to inherit the older woman's vision, for the wedge of
darkness turns up on her canvas—on the picture she cannot
get right, which she abandons and ten years later resumes.
William Bankes asks Lily: " 'What did she wish to indicate by
the triangular purple shape, just there?' 'It was Mrs. Ramsay
reading to James,' she said." Yet Lily has made no reproductive or representational likeness of the two persons. She has
introduced the dark wedge to balance a bright corner. Of
course the abstract form, Lily argues, can pay "tribute" to
family: "A mother and child might be reduced to a shadow
without irreverence. A light here required a shadow there." It
is arguable that Lily's pictorial formalism is the analogue of
Mr. Ramsay's progress from Q to R or of Mrs. Ramsay's knitting; her abstraction may also be Lily's mode of fecundity or
her version of "this peace, this rest." But Lily also knows that
neither mother and child, nor abstract form, nor peace and
rest can represent or reproduce the essence of life. For life in
To the Lighthouse is (ironically) the darkness that resists all re-

production in terms of plotted shape, form, or stability. Even the dark triangle is too orderly and ordering a form. This is why Woolf makes Lily struggle so long with her picture. Lily realizes that her commitment to picturing cannot represent "the fluidity of life." "Phrases came. Visions came. Beautiful pictures. Beautiful phrases. But what she wished to get hold of was that very jar on the nerves, the thing itself before it has been made anything."[8]

Does the line with which Lily finishes her painting plot or achieve its form by definitively representing a subject, by re-producing life? Does that line somehow get hold of "the thing itself, before it has been made anything?" The novel raises these questions, but does not answer them. Lily perhaps "centers" or "finishes" her painting by a line which shadows all that *cannot* be achieved, all that *cannot* be represented or reproduced. If we read this final stroke as a nonrepresenta-tional, nonreproductive "presentation" of life, then we can understand why the novel should end with the celibate Lily paying homage to the sterile Mr. Ramsay. For Lily under-stands that, although the family plot makes Mr. Ramsay ag-gressive, aggression is not the truth of life—sterility is. The novel ends as an ally of sterility, not of any harsh, aggressive, familial kind but of the kind observed by and embodied in Lily Briscoe. She, the principle heir of the Ramsays, pays tribute to family relations, yet also "reduces" them, no matter how reverentially, because she knows that children—like the products of artistic reproductions—do not carry on or sub-stantiate the bond between their parents or origins any more than do strangers to family like herself.

And like the family connections that *To the Lighthouse* describes, the novel's narrative connections are achieved by juxtapositions that disconnect: its continuity is established in discontinuity. Moreover, privileged or stable moments in the discontinuity do not generate others. They are repeated again only by a mysterious grace. "Family" itself is only a privileged moment. Its claims to be anything more (it can scarcely claim even so much because of its inherent instability) make it one among many fictions: like the progress of philosophy to truth, or the abstract formalism of Lily's pictorial art, or Mrs. Ramsay's story for James about the relations between the fisherman and his wife. These fictions are norms for the plotting of life and art *within To the Lighthouse*, a work that encloses these instances in an alternative, nonnormative plotting. The source of this alternative is, as Woolf sees it, the essential sterility of the world.

The world for Woolf is barren because for her creation and reproduction are names for indefinite and illusory phenomena. What *difference* do "acts" of creation, family plots, productions of continuity really make for life? Lily's celibate life and abstract art stimulate these questions. They are posed by Woolf in order to make them an essential part of ordinary experience. When Lily thinks she sees Mrs. Ramsay, long dead, she feels how it is "to want and want and not to have." But she accepts discontinuity, frustration, and their fruitlessness. "That too became part of ordinary experience." Virginia Woolf attempts to domesticate sterility for narrative, to make it part of the ordinary experience of novelistic story. Thi. means presenting story itself as nonproductive and as nonreproductive, barren representation. Because she attempts this, *To the Lighthouse* ends with Cam and James as well as Lily in touch with Mr. Ramsay, each paying tribute to *him*. Woolf, achieving her own literary production in much the same way as her father-figure achieves the lighthouse, nevertheless movingly emphasizes the truth she believes is behind the achievement: it is the product of a character whose essence is sterile because life's essence is sterile. Such an interpretation may not sit well with conventional or feminist views of *To the Lighthouse*, but whatever Woolf's general feelings about family or feminism, in this work they do not serve to idealize or celebrate any human fecundity, male or female, familial or artistic. Yet Woolf bravely has no nostalgia for life as a process of fruitful continuities or productions. With a courageous, doubtlessly suitable neutrality, *To the Lighthouse* accepts the sterilizing of human and artistic experience, the paradoxical fruitlessness of creation, the unhousing of life from a generative center and process.

Now I might do well to remind the reader of what has already been said (especially in regard to Eliot and Melville) about the imitative relation of plotted form to the content it conveys. The relation is complex: to imitate life a novelist may use narrative reason, emphasizing its intellectual or moral aspects, while at the same time casting suspicion on narrative reason; likewise he may use the idea or appearance of action, as Eliot and Melville certainly do, yet make the reality of action doubtfully identifiable or meaningful. Joyce's form imitates what he thinks of as a male sense of plot in the male-dominated episodes, yet he does this with the intention to subvert what he imitates. He uses the form to subvert the form because he plays it off against an alternative form—Molly's—the one he believes must control his sense of plot. Now Virginia Woolf attempts formally to imitate the world's sterile discontinuities. Yet I must say again, as I have said of writers treated earlier, that Woolf obviously cannot just imitate meaninglessness. Even to show the passing of the fecund origin and spray of life, she must shape language and form meaningfully. She therefore does not simply imitate sterility; and she uses the forms fruitful for meaning—in her first section she even uses family plot formally—to convey the fruitless nature of life. Yet her form, however positive, *means* this fruitlessness, as Eliot's form, however determinate, means indeterminacy, and Melville's, however authorially shaped, means passivity and accident.

The use of forms meaningful in themselves or by tradition is not therefore identical with the writer's featured content. And where that content determines a hostile or wary sense of plot, the writer uses the forms of meaning to humble them, to show their provisional and essentially illusory nature. The hostile or wary sense of plot always uses narrative reasonings in this humbling way; whether it be to divorce narrative reason from action (as in the young James) or to cast suspicion on the certainty of all definite distinctions or truths (as in Eliot and, especially, Melville). In Joyce and Woolf this humbling of narrative forms—this use of them to convey an antinarrational truth—is so much subordinated to that truth that we scarcely feel a conflict between content and form or between a hostile or wary sense of plot and any intrinsically antagonistic, positive forms used to convey the hostility or wariness. But in Lawrence we come to our first modern case of a sense of plot desperately engaged with the narrative forms it seeks to humble. It is a sense of plot therefore dynamically and intensely at odds with itself—most so in the "gladiatorial" of *Women in Love*.

For their relevance to the "gladiatorial" we must glance first at Lawrence's *Study of Thomas Hardy* and *The Rainbow*. Although the study of Hardy is about Lawrence's spiritual father, its doctrine is poppyhood—that is, another (this time exuberant) version of Woolf's essential sterility of the world. For Lawrence the poppy flower stands for an antigenerational, antifiliational order of things that Lawrence says is recklessly, shamelessly, glamorously "wasteful." Nature does not exist for generation, for parenthood. "The red of the poppy, this flame of the phoenix, this extravagant being, even its so-called waste" tells Lawrence that marriage and procreation and also the cultural procreation represented by work and the dissemination of knowledge are "active in the immediate rear of life"; they are "settled into an almost mechanized system of detaining some of the life which otherwise sweeps on and is lost in the full adventure."[9] The full adventure is the spontaneous and glamorous waste. We can see at once that the poppy challenges the family plot as form. If Lawrence is to be a storyteller at all, he must find a form that will represent human or cultural reproduction but that will then also subordinate these to "extravagant being, even to so-called waste." This suggests that Lawrence must simultaneously tell a story and break down the means of telling. And if Lawrence chooses a plot concerning family, then he will have to show how the breakdown of family is not tragic but an ultimate creative step, possibly creative even be-

cause it is a step into sterility. It is just this kind of step forward into poppy-extravagance that Lawrence illustrates in
the family history of *The Rainbow*.

In *The Rainbow* the Brangwens are always searching for a
step forward into a "beyond," a widening circle of life that
means a matter of finer civilization. The way "beyond" seems
to be through biological generation, but this is only an appearance; for from the first step forward taken by Tom
Brangwen, the family plot as structure of life is used simply
for the sake of consuming that structure. So Ursula's completion of the venture into the beyond is her "waste" of
Skrebensky's baby, her refusal to connect self-development
with parenthood. Of course Lawrence knows civilization depends upon spiritual fruitfulness, not upon the fruit of the
body. But Lawrence also knows that it is virtually impossible
to separate culture from biology; and he knows that in the
changing historical character of culture there are epochs
when culture is as uncreative as mere procreation.

Such an uncreative epoch closes *The Rainbow*. Ursula's
escape from motherhood is an escape from what Lawrence
presents as a repellent modern intertwining of physical and
cultural parenthood. It is repellent because both are forms of
a destructive will to control life by manipulating life's shape
and by mastering it, and in Lawrence's mind this will to control experience is the foundation of modern industrial democracy. Lawrence rather overlooks the fact that Ursula's final,
"wasteful" venture "beyond" owes itself to the democratic
industrial expansion whose vehicle is the willfulness he condemns. It is because of industrial democracy that Ursula oc-
cupies the "distance" prohibited to her grandmothers. Yet
insofar as resistance to parenthood resists just this form of social organization, whenever we find the Brangwens despair-
ing of or willfully resigning the authority and shaping power
of parenthood, Lawrence points out a moment of genuine
growth, even if this means an anguishing disappointment of
the desire to be a parent. Tom Brangwen must admit the
powerlessness of the family plot. At Anna's wedding he asks

himself: "What right had he to feel responsible, like a father? He was still as unsure and unfixed as when he had married. . . . His wife and he! With a pang of anguish he realized what uncertainties they both were."[10]

We can assume that Lawrence feels the same anguish, for the author-father of the plot must realize how uncertain he is in the making of his own story, how uncertainly he makes the connections among its parts and the connection between itself and *its* world "beyond"—the world of readers. But Lawrence can face his own uncertainty by reminding himself and us that the certainty Tom Brangwen cannot possess belongs to the mastering will, to the ugliness of mastery. And therefore Lawrence can turn his own uncertainty into the virtue of a new narrative mode. If family life, like marriage, industrial democracy, and most selves in *The Rainbow* are, as Tom Brangwen also understands, "always . . . unfinished and unformed," then Lawrence will use narrative to oppose finish and form both in storytelling and in culture.

The alternative narrative form that replaces the finish and form of the family plot and of mastering intentions serves surrender, a letting-go, an opening to what is unwilled, unplanned, and indeterminate. This leads the author to make use of a narrative mode he described in a foreword to *Women in Love* as a "continual, slightly modified repetition" and as a "pulsing, frictional, to-and-fro which works up to culmination," but which, we must add, never arrives at it. For the consummation would be arrival at finish and form, against both of which Lawrence must defend himself. This defense makes *The Rainbow* a shimmering haze of pulsations and repetitions, a matter of adjacent experiences and mutualities not bound together by an authoritatively shaping will but duplicating on the narrative level Lawrence's thematic opposition to the manipulative generations of plot and plan. It is true that, as the father and originator of his work, Lawrence must make a difference for life rather more than the extravagant poppy makes a difference. As author Lawrence is generative, productive. In his way he takes the step Tom Brangwen took in pursuing Lydia or the step Ursula took in competing with her schoolmaster, Harby: by an act of willful self-engendering and mastery he takes his place in the world. But he must take his place as the father of a story and must then surrender or negate attachment of any value to his power to originate or to shape the narrative.

In *Women in Love* Lawrence *looks* more reconciled to this surrender and negation of fatherhood and of a familial form of story, but after *The Rainbow* his self-division grows rather than lessens. Thus, in *Women in Love*, far from easily surrendering fatherhood, Lawrence is obsessed with the imagination and the pursuit of fathers, and he is arguably more obsessed as a result of the vehemence of his antagonism to them. Gerald Crich and his father are the next versions of Anton Skrebensky in Lawrence's fiction, and they are the scions of what is nothing less than an English House of Atreus, whose hereditary crime is unparalleled willfulness (of Gerald, for example, we know he was "that willful, masterful—he'd mastered one nurse at six months"). But in reading *Women in Love* we have always been misled by insisting that Rupert Birkin is Lawrence. Lawrence is no less Gerald's father and Gerald than he is Birkin; indeed he likely enough wants to be and feels that he is the *novel*'s "repressive central authority," the equivalent of the industrial magnate and the father-apparent of the Crich household. The power of *Women in Love* is harrowing because the struggle between Rupert and Gerald is Lawrence's struggle to subdue his own family plotting and to subdue and even destroy the Gerald in himself.

The Crich-figure, the allegedly repressive central authority, is analogous to the fathering (or mothering) authority in any novelist or storyteller because of the way the father shapes spontaneous appearances of the world into telling and objectified order. The vehicle of this shaping is an analytic arrangement that masters the world's appearances and produces or engenders those appearances as plot and story. (We are again considering narrative reason, of course—a willful, active, relation-making component in it rather than a passively reflective component.) In the senior Crich, productive and reproductive shaping of the world is combined with unremitting paternalistic attention and personal sympathy: and unlike Tom Brangwen, Mr. Crich never questions his right to feel responsible, like a father, for ordering the world according to a shape he believes will best express and interconnect its parts. But Lawrence is afraid the productivity and sympathy of this fathering authority is a mask for a terror of death, for a will to master dread and vulnerability, for a panic in the face of meaninglessness and negation. Mrs. Crich sees this panic as her husband's "armor," his refusal to surrender not just to death but to life. Yet the senior Crich has so successfully exerted his shaping parental force that he is physically untouched by death. In one of the novel's most neglected but significant scenes, Mrs. Crich is roused to hatred by the resistance to vulnerability and death expressed by the face and flesh of her husband's corpse. She cries out to her children with "a strange, wild command from out of the unknown, . . . 'None of you look like this, when you are dead! Don't let it happen again.' "[11]

We ought to read this remarkable scene as a projected panicky desire on Lawrence's part to dissociate himself from the father he identifies as the repressive central authority because he fears that he wants to be that authority himself. In fact, the scene is symbolic of Lawrence's anxiety that storytelling—narrative reasoning (even when humbled by being dissociated from imitation of action)—is implicated in democratic industrial forms of mastery. Mrs. Crich's command is that *storytellers* not "look like this," that they not give a vivid impression of life as the result of reproducing its contingencies and disruptions or its spontaneous absence of filiation in a form and in a reasoning that controls and masters these diverse phenomena, producing their meaning and making them tell in a hierarchized, centrally organized way. Such mastery gives an impression of life, but is indistinguishable from death. We always take Lawrence at his word, acknowledging that he wants no such mastering parenthood.

But does Mrs. Crich's hysteria come from a resistance that is purely disengaged? If Lawrence's shaping authority in the novel is analogous to the will of the male Criches, can he surrender his own will to sire order and meaning through life's reproduction in the form of the novel? In wanting a brotherhood with Gerald—the master of a family and a social order of masters and slaves—Birkin (Lawrence's alleged spokesman) wants a brotherhood, a mutuality, that uses a family term to transcend both family and the intertwining of mastery with physical and cultural parenthood. Birkin's author wants this transcendence as a narrative form to write by and as an ethic to live by. Can he wrestle down and negate the Crich-figure in himself?

We can examine how the wrestling works out in two adjacent incidents in the "Continental" chapter of *Women in Love*. Among a crowd of Germans in their Alpine lodge, Rupert and Ursula and Gerald and Gudrun are dancing the *schuhplattel*. The dance becomes powerfully erotic, and Birkin takes his wife to bed to perform an unspecified sexual act that is new to her. "Wasn't it rather horrible," Ursula thinks, "a man who could be so soulful and spiritual, now to be so—she balked at her own thoughts: then she added—so bestial?" Ursula winces, but then she exults. "She exulted in it. She was bestial. How good it was to be really shameful! There would be no shameful thing she had not experienced." At the same moment, still below at the dance, Gudrun is ashamed to admit that Gerald is not monogamous, but, as she says, "naturally promiscuous. That is his nature." Later, in their room, Gerald, whom Lawrence describes as "glistening," asks Gudrun, "Who do you like best downstairs?" The motive of this question is not clear, and it begins a powerful and similarly unclear "strange battle between her ordinary consciousness and his uncanny, black-art consciousness."

What is this juxtaposition of the two couples about? What is its plot; what is the story that makes it tell? Lawrence appears to inhibit himself from *making* it tell. The licentiousness of the two men and the differing responses of the sisters to what they take to be male sexual brutality exemplify the narrative adjacency that puts a premium on the absence of ties, causations, motives, defining connections. Lawrence communicates here a texture of being prior to any ordering of it: an extravagance of blood, a random and momentary human flowering, a haze and shimmer with which even brutal eros glistens. And is not this moment of juxtaposition, in the haze that leaves connections open and disrupted, characteristic of the entire form of *Women in Love*? To answer affirmatively is to agree that the Lawrence who writes the novel *is* like the Birkin who does not want to shape life or to master its meaning by producing meaning out of the world or out of his darkly shimmering self. Yet to read *Women in Love* this way is to evade the truth behind each of these juxtaposed blood-flowerings of Lawrence's characters. We know as soon as we step back from the juxtaposition that not a single spontaneous shimmer is here without its conditioning cause or purpose, without its telling filiative connection assigned it by the author. Lawrence makes us know that Gerald is not "naturally" promiscuous, as Gudrun self-defensively wants to think; Lawrence insists we recognize that Gerald is promiscuous because he is the product of a society artificially willful and obsessed with production and mastery. His licentiousness comes from his inherited democratic-industrial fear of vulnerability and death. Lawrence insists we recognize as well that Ursula can freely bless her own shamefulness because she is free of Gerald's fears and also because she is free of the productive industrial complex Gerald controls and is also controlled by. Indeed Lawrence's plot forces upon us the idea that Birkin's lusts are due to his absence of defensiveness and that Gerald's are due to *his* protective armor. The sociological and psychological analysis of *Women in Love* is inalienable from its distinction; and its distinction is founded on the storyteller's authoritative use, analysis, and manipulation of causes and effects. And this is to say that the story and its power are founded irremovably on the shaping, narratively reasoning purpose of a storyteller who hierarchizes experi-

ence by designating its origin and its filiated strands and who
fathers meaning by making life speak not randomly and
spontaneously but under a compellingly purposeful direction.

   Yet this fatherhood of analytic narrative reason and plot so
troubles Lawrence that he must hand himself over to the defeat and negation of his own authority. It is not an exaggera-
tion or distortion to speak of negation. Remembering Birkin's
ethic of polarities, we may claim that Lawrence's narration is
a polarized balance of the paternal-masterful mode and the
mutual-yielding mode. But were Lawrence balanced between
two narrative modes and not torn between them, not convinced that one must negate the other, we probably would
not have *Women in Love*. We would certainly not have the
grief and terror of the last chapter of *Women in Love*. The negation and the intense desire for it is clearly spoken in that
chapter, in a passage completing a much earlier thought of
Birkin's. The earlier thought is that

> at moments it seemed to [Birkin] he did not care a straw
> whether Ursula or Hermione or anybody else existed or
> did not exist. Why bother! Why strive for a coherent,
> satisfied life? Why not drift on in a series of accidents—
> like a picaresque novel? Why not? . . . Why form any
> serious connections at all? Why not be casual, drifting
> along, taking all for what it was worth?

   The immediate but not the final answer to these questions
comes from Lawrence the storyteller: "And yet, still, he was
damned and doomed to the old effort at serious living." This
means that Birkin is doomed to making serious connections,
to engendering relations if not filiations, just as Lawrence
feels himself "damned and doomed" to the old effort at seriously mastering life by connecting and interrelating its experiences in the form of family plot. But in the last chapter of
Women in Love this old effort is negated by Birkin's admission
that to care for any form of connection rather than any form
of drift is not worth the damning and dooming effort; the

image of the glamorously wasteful poppy is now tragically darkened. Rupert turns away from Gerald's corpse. "Either the heart would break, or cease to care. Best cease to care. Whatever the mystery which has brought forth man and the universe, it is a non-human mystery, it has its own great ends. Man is not the criterion. Best leave it all to the vast, creative, non-human mystery."[12] Lawrence adds, "it was very consoling to Birkin to think this."

The final wisdom—and consolation!—of *Women in Love* is the powerlessness of humanity, its distance from the creative engendering of relations, especially filiative ones. The one parent Lawrence can acknowledge in *Women in Love* is the nonhuman one. Humanity fathers nothing and masters nothing—and *this* absence and negation of fatherhood is the tragedy of *Women in Love*. Our applause of mutualities in discourse covers up the fact that the end of filiation is *the* central misery in Lawrence's novel. We are used to thinking of the novel as presenting the end of filiation as a misery only because, from Birkin's point of view, humanity will not recognize the need to end the family plot. But this is not the truth. There are two stories about family plot in *Women in Love*, and we keep reading only one. The one we habitually read tells us that at the level of form the family plot is finished: we have instead of its hierarchizing action and narrative reason a fictional discourse founded on mutualities and adjacencies. At the level of content Birkin represents this new form turned into a moral ideal: he wants the end of hierarchy in family and marriage, he wants the end of the family plot as fact. But at the formal level the end of filiation, the humbling of that kind of meaningful form, is a screen, hiding the desire that the creative mystery be human and be made compatible with an organization of plot that is as bent on the authoritative mastery of life and meaning as are Mr. Crich and Gerald.

It is not mutualities and adjacencies of form but family plot as form and narrative reason that gives us the *story* of *Women in Love*; if we take away that form, we are left with the adjacencies of vivid sensations and of Birkin's rhetorical insistencies, but then neither of them will be telling or significant. Birkin insists that genuine love is brotherly or brother-and-sisterly, and Lawrence hopes both the familial and the narrative structures of filiation will be moved aside for this kind of love. But the hope has persuasive force and meaning only because it is not a spontaneous poppy-like flowering. Without the exercise of fathering authority that in Lawrence compels experience to speak as he sees and shapes it, we would not be moved to consider the urgent need for a new mutuality in life and in narrative. But it is clear that Lawrence wants to accept the negation of his own creative and analytic power. The fathering impulse in Lawrence becomes a secret agency of plot, and he mourns it the more deeply in secret, the more openly he denies it. Just as we are used to identifying Lawrence with Birkin, we are used to talking about *Women in Love* as the product of repressed homosexuality. *Women in Love* is more likely the powerful product of a repression of a desire for fatherhood that will not be appeased by either the morality or the form of the end of filiation.

Now when we turn to Conrad's *The Secret Agent* and consider the descriptive relevance of *mutuality, adjacency,* and *discontinuity* to Conrad's story, we see that the story line of *The Secret Agent* supports their application, especially if we point to the striking narrative discontinuity between Chapter Seven, when the relatively strict chronology of the story ceases, and Chapter Eight, when a flashback occurs dramatizing the trip of Stevie's and Winnie's mother to the almshouse. And yet *The Secret Agent* presents problems of interpretation or of response that these terms may obscure rather than clarify. Mutuality, adjacency, and discontinuity appear in Conrad's novel as the reflex of a horror, and as *experienced phenomena* in the novel they are horrible. When Conrad's story line, translated into a newspaper report of Winnie's death, breaks up again in Ossipon's mind, the repetitious mutuality and adjacency of the parts are maddening. And they are not only maddening, but have a dynastic effect theoretically at odds with their form. For, by reproducing wildly perplexed and mentally dismembered Stevie as Ossipon, they engender in Ossipon, the man, the state of the idiotic child.

But we can put aside for now the emotional bearing of Conrad's narrative strategy for the sake of emphasizing that *The Secret Agent* certainly subverts the family plot as fact and form. "From a certain point of view," reads a sentence in the novel, "we are here in the presence of a domestic drama." The discontinuity and breakup of the story line must be understood from this certain point of view, although the all-consuming presence of domestic drama in *The Secret Agent* has not yet been rightly commented on. What Conrad's Assistant Commissioner of Police (reporting the Verloc case to the Home Secretary) says in the sentence just quoted could serve as a motto for Conrad's novel because Conrad insistently dramatizes his characters in response to domesticity: all of the novel's politics are literally domestic issues, and virtually all of the domestic issues are parental.

But what exactly is the "certain point of view?" For Conrad this viewpoint resists narrative syntax and articulation. The sequential disruption in *The Secret Agent* begins with the advent of Chapter Eight because it is at this point that the novel begins to be burdened by more than it can tell clearly. And by the time the newspaper report of Winnie's death announces that "an impenetrable mystery seems destined to hang for ever over this act of madness or despair," for Ossipon, Conrad, and ourselves the mystery *is* impenetrable in spite of our acquaintance with the facts. The mystery behind the facts is that of the domestic drama itself. The breakdown of family plot, the breakup of narrative filiation, is carried out by Conrad because the domestic drama can be conveyed only through discontinuity, only through the power of disconnected speech. And this is because Conrad believes that domestic family life—the apparent protector of the sources of existence—in fact menaces its springs and is a symptom that the sources of human order are themselves injurious. Conrad wants to express through his novel the idea that parenthood and family structure are explosively irrational. They are the mask of an essential anarchy of intense feelings, of excitements that—like Stevie's—can only stutter their intensity, confusion, and disorder no matter how much they try to articulate themselves as clarity and order. It is from *this* point of view that Conrad sees the human domestic drama. And to underwrite as well as to convey his perception, Conrad reduces his book to a new form of subversion of the family plot, a form of narrative stuttering.

There is a chain of domestic dramas underlying the broken continuities, repetitions, and adjacencies of the narrative stutter. Conrad makes sure we know how Chief Inspector Heat, the Assistant Commissioner of Police, and the Secretary of State (whom Conrad in the preface calls the Home Secretary, and whom he identifies with Winnie by making him not want to look into "details") are all principally motivated by their home lives. And Conrad shows us how this motivation makes these men no less ruthless than anarchists: the Chief Inspector loves having "a sense . . . of evil freedom" in his work; Heat, "a kind man, an excellent husband, a devoted father," knows Michaelis is innocent, but wants him destroyed and Verloc exploited; the Home Secretary, as his wifelike male secretary Toodles says, is himself a revolutionary. Through this presentation of the politicians and the police, Conrad builds up the interidentity of domestic man and anarchic man in a way that identifies "the blameless bosom of the average married citizen" as an untrustworthy secret weapon of violence. This secret weapon becomes more and more significant in the novel until it becomes "the domestic carving knife" with which Winnie kills her husband. This weapon, this carving knife, is the most familiar of agents—domestic order itself. But the familiar agent is no more reliable than Conrad's Perfect Anarchist, the Professor, whose attempt to invent a perfect weapon is rather pointless. The perfect weapon has been long invented and established: it is family man and family plot; the parent who creates literal filiations and the parent-author who creates narrative filiations for the sake of the doomed effort of ordering life. By the end of Conrad's novel, family man and plotting man are synonymous with what they are supposed to be defenses against: aggression and violence, disruption and anarchy. Sympathy with Winnie hides this identification. Winnie kills her husband partly in rage at his veracity. "Don't you make any mistake about it," he says. "If you will have it that I killed the boy, then you've killed him as much as I."[13]

We come now to the component that more than any other underlies the mystery and the breakup of Conrad's narrative. The step determining the stutter is the step Conrad takes in identifying parenthood with what the Assistant Commissioner of Police calls some species of authorized scoundrelism. The interidentity of domestic and anarchic man in the novel is meant to underwrite this crucial identification. We can define the passion of parenthood as the intense desire to create conditions favorable for the growth of a child. It is the will also to shape a line of growth for the child such that the child's life matters or "tells," for the better rather than for the worse. To crush or kill the child is scarcely a deliberate intention of this passion. Yet the title of Conrad's novel cites Winnie Verloc. She is the secret agent of the death of three persons: Stevie, Verloc, and herself. Since there are no fatalities in the novel except those she originates, she is certainly more destructive than the Perfect Anarchist, the Professor.

To clarify Winnie's destructive agency and its bearing on the stutter, we return to the disruptive narrative adjacency of Chapters Seven and Eight, to consider the grotesque maimed cabman and Stevie's response to him. The maimed man has a corporeal and vocal similarity to Verloc that is clinched when—with thematic inevitability—"he talked to Stevie of domestic matters." "I've got my missus and four kids at 'ome," he declares. And Conrad adds, with black humor, that "the monstrous nature of that declaration of paternity seemed to strike the world dumb." The silence that reigns after this declaration does not explain why it is monstrous—

nor what is monstrous in its nature. The cabman himself is physically monstrous, of course, as perhaps is his old horse, "the steed of apocalyptic misery." But it is not the physical aspect that has Conrad's interest. The explanation of the monstrosity comes a few pages later when Stevie perceives "the human and equine misery in close association." Long before this we perceive in *The Secret Agent* not only the close association of anarchy and domestic average order but also the proximity of the human and the equine. With a kind of witty idiocy, as if Conrad were a more clever Stevie, the author has written the intimacy of horses and humans into the names in his book. *Winnie* puns on *whinny*; Verloc combines *fetlock* and *wedlock*. Behind these puns stand the saints of rational domesticity in English literature, the Houyhnhnms, most pacific of the horses of instruction. The cabman's monstrosity has to do with the close association of the human and equine, and it enters Stevie's mind with an emphasis that clarifies the dumbfounding essence of the cabman's paternity:

> The contemplation of the infirm and lonely steed overcame [Stevie]. Jostled, but obstinate, he would remain there trying to express the view newly opened to his sympathies of the human and equine misery in close association. But it was very difficult. "Poor brute, poor people!" was all he could repeat. It did not seem forcible enough, and he came to a stop with an angry splutter: "Shame!" Stevie was no master of phrases, and perhaps for that very reason his thoughts lacked clearness and precision. But he felt with greater completeness and some profundity. That little word contained all his sense of indignation and horror at one sort of wretchedness having to feed upon the anguish of the other—at the poor cabman beating the poor horse in the name, as it were, of his poor kids at home. . . . It was a bad world. Bad! Bad![14]

At the upper levels of society, as Conrad sees it, the Home Secretary can beat the nasty kids, the anarchists, in the name of the wife and kids at home; and this beating can be done to preserve the opposition between anarchy and domesticity. It can also be done to preserve the notion that parental passion is solely nurturing, that it is not itself intertwined with destructiveness. When the poor cabman patriarch beats the horse, the close association of the equine and the human makes the violence an emblem of the cabman beating his wife and kids—and in their own name. Stevie is seeing the parental passion as essentially not differentiated from the destructive one. The secret theme of *The Secret Agent* is that parents, the domestic horses of instruction, are in fact the wrathful tigers who inadvertently consume their children. The same theme is exemplified in stuttering, spluttering Stevie, whose tenderness is in close association with rage:

> The tenderness of [Stevie's] universal charity had two phases as indissolubly joined and connected as the reverse and obverse sides of a medal. The anguish of immoderate compassion was succeeded by the pain of an innocent but pitiless rage.[15]

But the compassion and the rage do not so much succeed each other, as they are indissolubly joined, simultaneous, and undifferentiated.

Thus the hoarse cabman (who is likened to Silenus) beating the humanlike horse stands for the pitiless rage tangled with immoderate compassion that Conrad presents as characteristic not of idiocy but of parenthood or, we might say, of the idiocy that is the passion of parenthood and the idiocy that is the passion for family plot and genealogical filiation. Of course this idiocy is not only the male parent's. This same disruptive Chapter Eight gives us a portrait of Winnie's mother. The old woman is joined to Winnie's agency in the murder of Stevie; by moving out of Verloc's house she attempts to protect Stevie, but in effect throws him together with Verloc much more than ever before. "Heroic and unscrupulous and full of love for both her children," the mother is "sacrificing Winnie" for Stevie, in order to settle her son permanently in life.

But I will not dwell on this "settling," for we must turn at last to Winnie, since she is the central specimen of the secret idiocy of parental plot. Winnie's murderous effects have been mentioned, but consideration of her in one more aspect will prepare a final assessment of what Conrad feels about her relevance to the plotting of a novel. She and Stevie are sister and brother. But the sibling relationship gets blurred, especially when their mother withdraws. In effect Winnie turns into Stevie's mother. Who then really is Winnie's spouse? The Verloc pornography shop no doubt sells prophylactics, and the Verloc couple no doubt practices birth control, perhaps even sexual abstention. On Winnie's part this is for Stevie's sake, but it also keeps Winnie emotionally mated to their father; and when the mother moves out, it is as if she were resigning her place to a daughter-rival. It does not matter that the father, "the licensed victualler," is dead: the confusion of relationships in the Verloc house keeps him emotionally alive. And there is more confusion. The living person whom Winnie treats as a spouse is Stevie: she feels for her brother-son as for a lover. Stevie remembers his sister taking him as a child into a "bed of compassion," "the supreme remedy" for pain. In nursing her brother with all "the force of her protective passion," Winnie long ago had wedded him. Winnie Verloc is thus wedded to father, husband, brother, and son. No wonder her father used to call her "a wicked she-devil": if we are to judge from her multiple weddings, she is anarchic in her desires.

Her father seems to have been similarly anarchic. He strikes at Stevie as if at a rival; he breaks down doors to get at Winnie, and throws a poker at her. Stevie's idiocy looks like the fruit of an incest uncommitted but wished for. Of course Winnie appears to be moral, self-suppressing, and "purely" parental. Her maternal passion and compassion have been intended to shield herself and Stevie from "all these scenes of violence . . . accompanied by the unrefined noise of deep vociferations proceeding from a man [their father] wounded in his paternal pride."[16] Winnie's father had beaten the kids at home in the name of "paternal pride," and she had justly defended her brother against the patriarch. She went so far in her defense as to give up her romance with the young butcher—for the sake of Verloc's protective domesticity.[17] But her pure maternal morality becomes the immorality from which it flees. Her relations are psychological incests; and having given up "the butcher," she marries another one, and butchers her husband and her own flesh and blood.

Now why does this disorderly and destructive creature concern Conrad? Does he make a terrible black comedy out of her parental passion for the sake of justifying his form's innovative cultivation (characteristically Conradian, of course) of mutualities and adjacencies? It does not seem anything so willful. Conrad dramatizes Ossipon's confusion at the novel's end to show the way the destructiveness of parental or domestic passion has come upon Conrad himself as a truth he has not wanted to see but cannot escape. And Conrad *still* does not want to see it; and he admires Winnie for her blindness. In spite of the fact that the fraternal mutuality of brother and sister might well have been left alone by Winnie, Conrad appears to admire her because she attempts to become a parent—a cultural parent rather than a biological one. Damned and doomed as her effort is, Winnie's mothering of Stevie seems an attempt to overcome the absolute confusion and simultaneity of her desires, their racking mutual adjacencies. In his "Author's Note" Conrad asserts that Winnie, whom we know as anarchic and destructive, is the muse of his novel. Having wanted to tell a tale of London, Conrad could not find a story line that would make the blank undifferentiated mass of the city matter. To make it tell, "it would take years to find the right way," Conrad thought. But "slowly the dawning conviction of Mrs. Verloc's maternal passion grew up to a flame between me and that background [the town], tingeing it with its secret ardour. . . . At last the story of Winnie Verloc stood out complete. . . . *This* book is *that* story." Winnie and her secret ardor are thus the agent of Conrad's *storytelling*. Is she then the muse of adjacencies and repetitions, of the stuttering frictional to-and-fro of a new narrative form represented by the breaking lines that madden Ossipon? She is, and she is not. We must thus consider how she can be another kind of muse.

What Conrad sees in *The Secret Agent* resists not only the tradition of the family plot but resists seeing altogether. In a moment of truth in which Winnie comprehends the horrible undoing of her parental passion, she sees that there is nothing left to see, only "a blankness to run at and dash your head against." How ironically we may remember the famous comment by Ford Madox Ford about his own and Conrad's narrative experiments: their purpose was above all "to make you see." What the experiment in *The Secret Agent* communicates is a blankness that blinds. The demonstration of the idea that parenthood kills is blinding to sight and sense. It leads us to the conviction that nothing matters and that nothing tells. But Conrad leads us to this conviction and also makes a heroine of Winnie. What value or heroism can her parental passion possibly represent if the menace to human life is at the source of generation and nurture?

The first answer to this question is that for Conrad parenthood is a constructively shaping illusion that averts the suicidal vision of the blank wall. He presents us simultaneously with a farewell to family plot and with a muse of filiation to show how parenthood that is genuinely nurturing and fruitfully shaping is in truth a fiction and a factitious plot, while at the same time making us desire the fiction and the plot in spite of the truth. The reason why Conrad makes us desire the fiction may be derived from the moment in *The Secret Agent* that most poignantly exposes Winnie's willfully-made seven years of parenthood as in fact an analogy of a storyteller's story. In creating a home for Stevie, Winnie has authored and housed him securely, and has authored and housed her own maternal passion. Conrad writes about what Winnie authors in terms of "continuity of feeling and tenacity of purpose," the characteristics of sequence and intentional filiation in the traditional form of family plotting. Thus we see Winnie viewing Verloc and Stevie in the following way:

> She stared at the vision of her husband and poor Stevie walking up Brett Street side by side away from the shop. It was the last scene of an existence created by Mrs. Verloc's genius; an existence foreign to all grace and charm, without beauty and almost without decency, but admirable in the continuity of feeling and tenacity of purpose. And this last vision had such plastic relief, such nearness of form, such a fidelity of suggestive detail, that it wrung from Mrs. Verloc an anguished and faint murmur, reproducing the supreme illusion of her life, an appalled murmur that died out on her blanched lips.
>
> "Might have been father and son."[18]

"Plastic relief," "nearness of form," "fidelity of suggestive detail"—all of these terms intensify the suggestion that Winnie's "genius" is novelistic. And the supreme illusion of her life has been reproduction of the family plot—a form of "might have been mother and child" or "father and child," a filiative order characterized by unbroken, linear "continuity of feeling and tenacity of purpose." The narrative analogy in "might have been father and son" makes the phrase stand not only for a parental intention but for a sense of sequential and hierarchical family plot.

The muse of filiation projects on the blank wall of undifferentiated life the shadow of an idea that life matters because of parenthood and that the family plot as fact and as form might yet rise free of the illusion and the destructiveness tangled in its roots. The discontinuity and mutuality of parts in Conrad's form—his narrative stutter—represents a maddening contradiction and its maddening effects, and there must be a rescue from this madness. Winnie matters for Conrad because she is the muse of desired rescue, of an alternative narrative form, and of a highly traditional one. In welcoming the "new" antitraditional mutualities and adjacencies of discourse, we must be careful of making Winnie's desire for parenthood and for family plot even more secret and inhibited a creative agency than Conrad's novel shows it to be.

Sympathy for Winnie does not implicate Conrad in nostalgia. He seems to convince himself that authentic domestic order or parenthood has never yet existed, that such order remains an ideal, a possibility for the *future*. There may yet be a parental authority and concern, like Winnie's, that does not explode itself. And there is in Conrad the suggestion that plotted narrative also has not ended, that in fact it has not yet been adequately constituted. Conrad refuses to be homesick for a lost family past that in truth never existed, and his openness to the possibility that Winnie represents a valuable ideal of desire seems to stem from the fact that his attention is fixed more than is obvious on the child-figure who needs the shaping and forming purpose of the parent just as life may need the shaping and forming purpose of the positive sense of plot—so that *life* may articulate itself without stuttering.

This persistent need is what Faulkner writes of in *The Sound and the Fury, his* story about an idiotic child, and his version of formal stutter. The puzzling temporal derangement of the four sections of the novel apparently takes its inspiration from the disorder and anarchy of the Compsons;[19] or, if the four parts do not have such an imitative intention, they may once again represent the mutuality appropriate to the discourse of modernity. Nevertheless Faulkner ends his novel with an image remarkable for the challenge it poses to theories about our modern sense of the predominance of fraternity in life and of mutuality in discourse. At the end of *The Sound and the Fury,* Benjy, on his way to visit the family plot at the cemetery, howls when his driver moves him in a direction reversing the normal flow of his vision and his progress. The proper order for Benjy means movement to the right of "the monument" from the left. The left-to-right eye motion is the condition and convention of Western literacy, and Benjy is crying at a disruption the reader analogously experiences in Faulkner's narrative sequence. The novel's time and line of sequence do not move, as it were, from left to right. But Faulkner seems to want satisfaction for Benjy. And in the last pages of the novel Jason—for the first time—rescues Benjy, making Luster drive so that each object will be "in its ordered place." This is the first time Jason has acted like a father. As a brother he is inevitably spiteful to the idiot and a torturing rival of all his siblings. Thus, his "fraternity" with Benjy consists of disorderly mutuality or adjacency, like the disorderly adjacency of Faulkner's first three narratives. But the objective and sequential last section of the novel returns us to a parental narrative authority, an hierarchic and filiative order of narrative discourse.

Jason ratifies this return of the form to its traditional norm by a protective assumption—even if momentary—of paternal care. But since Faulkner has already illustrated the inadequacy of the traditional familial form, and since he has rejected intelligible sequence until the fourth section, it is as if he were looking *ahead* to a familial authority and a plotted narrative that will resolve the novel's human sorrows and its own formal disorder. Like his author, Benjy too looks forward. What he desires on the way to the graveyard (where his grandmother, father, and brother are buried) is not just a fixed souvenir of the past, like Caddy's slipper. Rather, he wants motion, an active process in which one part of the sequence engenders another. Since Jason has had Benjy castrated, he has thus reinforced the sterile fixity of Benjy's life. But when Jason helps Benjy to read the signs of motion correctly, he is putting Benjy back into an order of meaningful engenderings—back into a moving process. We are invited to feel that this is what a successful, genuine parent would do. The process looks forward, not nostalgically backward; it momentarily undoes castration; it is a hint of progress toward a family plot and toward a filiation that will not be explosive or destructive.

There is no parenthood or family plot to look backward to. What has been wrong with the Compsons as parents? The Compson father, Jason III, distrusts all authorities and refuses to assert his own. He will not plot his children's lives; he seems rather to want to entrust them to the spontaneities of growth. His wife sums up his treatment of the children: "He was always saying they didn't need controlling, that they already knew what cleanliness and honesty were, which was all that anyone could hope to be taught."[20] Mrs. Compson speaks bitterly, but the father's saying seems wise, as do his thoughts at the end of the second section about the temporary nature of all of life. The father impressively argues that the very nature of time resists or deauthorizes all human efforts to control it. We can assume family to be one of these efforts; family plot another.

Yet Faulkner keeps the debate about the plot and the family open. What is the best form for the family to take? Is it the father's or the mother's? Caroline Compson's attempts to "control" what happens may be more destructive than her husband's quietism. One way of forming life or family is to plot or expect definitive culminations and apotheoses from them. Quentin wants such an apotheosis—as the father recognizes—in his fantasy of incest with Caddy. But Quentin's desire for apotheosis is an inheritance of Caroline's desire for "control." Renaming Maury, insisting that Quentin go to Harvard, banishing Caddy, the mother is committed to plotting her children's lives with a vengeance. Through his presentation of the death of Damuddy Compson in the first section, Faulkner symbolizes the inadequacy of both kinds of parental authority: neither daddy's nor mummy's way, neither the absence of control nor its apotheosis is vital either to plotting life or to caring for children.

Nevertheless, Faulkner insists that there must be a constructive and creative side of the child's need to be taken care of as well as a constructive response to the need. The child's need is simultaneously the parent's, as the ending of the first section makes pointedly clear when the father asks Caddy "to take good care of Maury." In the next section Caddy will ask Quentin "to look after Benjy and Father"; Caddy marries Herbert both to take care of the child Dalton Ames will not care for and to take care of Jason by getting a job for him; Jason's life is then centered on his promise to care for Caddy's daughter; and of course Dilsey takes care of them all. In the fourth section Jason bitterly complains to the sheriff: "Care, hell. Is this what you call taking care of me?" Here Jason is receiving his just deserts; but Faulkner obsessively repeats the theme of care even at this moment.

The concern for care is not just for feeling it, but for the discovery of a practice or of a practical design whereby to enact it. And Faulkner clearly links the desire for a practical parental design of care with the desire for design of narrative. He compounds the confusion over authoritative parental design with the children's constant need to "tell" something about themselves or others. As grown men, Quentin and Jason are still obsessed with telling Father about Caddy or telling Mother about Quentin. This "telling" is motivated by spite or coercive will, but Faulkner also presents this narrative motif to point up the children's clamor for justification of their lives and for wisdom about them through tales or stories about themselves. Mr. Compson tells his suicidal son: "You are blind to what is in yourself to that part of general truth the sequence of natural events and their causes which shadows every mans brow even Benjys." The truth Mr. Compson means is finitude and the temporariness of any state or event: "a love or a sorrow is a bond purchased without design and which matures willynilly and is recalled without warning to be replaced by whatever issue the gods happen to be floating." Such fluidity and arbitrariness apparently make experience not narratable in terms of genealogical filiations, of family plot. But Mr. Compson overstates. The sequence of natural events and their causes shadows every man's brow with a structure that *can* be *told*. Quentin's desire to make his and his sister's life a definitive moral fable also leads to overstatement, true enough. Quentin desires too intensely that his life be narratable in content and form; like Winnie's, his intense need for a housing structure drives him to suicide. But the suicide is especially poignant and wasteful, precisely because Quentin, on the day of his death, shows himself to be a better parent than either of his own. The immigrant "sister" who more or less adopts him and who unwittingly gets him arrested is not a stand-in for Caddy. Faulkner inserts this episode to show a child needing care and successfully getting it in Quentin's authoritative but feeling response. Without recognizing his own success, Quentin hits upon a reconciliation of the desire for a form of parental care with the desire for "telling" design.

"Philoprogenitive" means "fond of children, especially one's own"; or it means "fond of producing offspring, or of reproduction." Quentin very obscurely uses this word in *The Sound and the Fury*, where it occurs only once.[21] The word has special relevance to Faulkner as a narrative artist. His thematic interest in the care of children and his desire to find an active form for their care—a parental or familial order or design that is also comprehensible as a narrative design, as plot and story—is philoprogenitive. This desire of Faulkner's is not homesickness for a family life or for a successful paternity or maternity that has never been. Rather, Faulkner cares for the formation of children: for their growth and fulfillment. At the same time he has little trust that growth can be achieved by substituting brotherhood for parenthood as the exclusively fulfilling goal of development. The sort of brotherhood Said idealizes, which results from the removal of oppressive paternal authority in discourse as well as in life, does not look chaotic in *Beginnings*, but it does look chaotic in *The Sound and the Fury*, whether the removed authority is oppressive or not. In Jason the absence of parenthood looks cruelly uncaring as well as chaotic. In his funny but mean cowardice and his lack of generous feeling, he may be allowed to stand in our minds for the possible fate of the human character that is not philoprogenitive and that is careless of family plot and filiation.

Judging by the sterility of Jason's ungenerous character, we can understand why of all the modern masters Faulkner persisted after *The Sound and the Fury* in plotting and telling stories. To do so was to be essentially at odds with the antiparental and antifiliational modes of discourse that for Faulkner are Jason-like. Out of antagonism for what Jason stands for there is a rebirth of story and plot in Faulkner, even though his experiments borrow narrative devices used by artists— Lawrence, Ford, Stein, Joyce, Woolf—antagonistic to family plot. At the same time, because the parenthood of the past appears to Faulkner to have been no less sterile than Jason, he imagines what I have spoken of as adversary parenthood. The imagined parenthood is adversary in the sense of being critical of the past and present parenthoods that the novel portrays. And it is adversary too in its suggestion that no past or present order of society can fulfill the need of parents and children (symbolic of the need of plotting agents in general) for the active shaping of life, for the generation of any telling difference out of life's indifferent chaos, for the transformation of life's spontaneity into captured forms of value.

The full bearing and practice of what would be a new family plot will become clear of course only when art and life together solve what is problematic in the nature of the family. In its classical tradition the novel always made fathers, mothers, and heroes out of orphans and bastards; and it is interesting to think of parental figures now in exile from the novel, as if waiting to return.[22] Meanwhile, until the old family plot is replaced and reembodied by a new parenthood and by a storytelling whose renewal of filiation will loom as authoritative and genuinely novel, we will continue to feel uncertain and self-divided about the value of plotting stories and making families, about the repressions and specious superstructures of reason and morality they may imply, and about whether or not telling a story or enacting the passion of parenthood makes a difference worth our concern.

☙ AFTERWORD ☙

The narrator of Samuel Beckett's *How It Is* thinks there may be a person or presence who "must sometimes wonder if to these perpetual revictuallings narrations and auditions he might not put an end without ceasing to maintain us in some kind of being without end and some kind of justice without flaw." Does the "maintain" here mean that in perpetual narrations, as well as in their abolition, there is being without end and a trace of justice without flaw? Does it mean that a narration is itself the sign of flawed being, and the flawed sign of a never more than partial justice? The latter meaning is more likely, in the light of our ordinary understanding of Beckett. And it would show a strict continuity with Beckett's 1931 essay on Proust, where Beckett says that Proust's characters "solicit a pure subject so that they may pass from a state of blind will to a state of representation. Proust is that pure subject. . . . Will, being utilitarian, . . . is not a condition of the artistic experience."[1] Under the inspiration of Beckett's novels, one might extend this to say that plot and story are allies of will, and hence are conditions only of flawed artistic experience.

Yet narration does not die in Beckett. Plot and story seem always to be pushing themselves forward into his writing. His novels are not about the end of either life or narrative but about the obstinate intrusiveness and will-to-form of both. In *Malone Dies*, Malone speaks of "the plan I had formed, to live, cause to live, at last, to play at last and die alive." Malone, waiting to die, planned to tell stories that he here asserts as an activity *causing* life. He ducks his assertion when he says he plans the stories to be "almost lifeless, like the teller." But Malone—and Beckett—are duplicit. On the one hand Malone "clings" to his storytelling as to "putrid mucus"; on the other, he feels it is an exuberant "swelling." He feels himself

swelling, saying, got it at last, my legend. . . . Why this
sudden heat, has anything happened, has anything
changed? No, the answer is no, I shall never get born
and therefore never get dead, and a good job too. And if
I tell of me and of that other who is my little one, it is as
always for want of love, well I'll be buggered, I wasn't
expecting that, want of a homuncule, I can't stop.[2]

As in this passage, Beckett is always invaded by continuity,
by a surprising narrative motion of consciousness. One goes
on reading him because plot and story are always about to
arise and appear in him in some loving and renewing emanation.

But it is true that Malone's life is only a prospective possibility, just as his life in the form of narrative story and of significant action is also only prospective. Tzvetan Todorov,
writing about grail narratives, explains that the object of romance quests, the grail itself, is the very possibility of narrative. Perhaps all narration, all plotting and storytelling, promise or search for their possibility of realization more than they
achieve it. Plot and story are thus present to us only as absences. Beckett's and Todorov's way of understanding this is
more tender than Gertrude Stein's. They construe story's absence optimistically, as a complete actual presence always
about to be.[3]

But if plot and story exist always as only partially achieved
quests for their own essence, then we have been surveying a
formal issue that transcends historical change and any narrative's specific content. For if in one set of authors we see narrative form realized and in another set we see it questioned,
we can surmise that each set has hold of only half the truth.
The full truth would be that every plot is pervaded by a coun-
terforce that undoes plotting, and that every attempt not to
plot or tell a story is pervaded by a stubborn narrative impulse. Therefore it is arguable that with a wide enough vision
we can see that the struggle for and against narrative is always with us, in any plot and story, at any point in history.

I can certainly agree with this point of view. At the same time I believe that this struggle for and against narrative can have an historically new salience that is more important than the struggle's timeless aspect. After the preceding pages I hope that even the ultraformalist reader can grant the possibility of this belief. If he does so, he will have to allow that content determines form and that form is not its own exclusive content.

All novelists have been formalists insofar as they have been preoccupied with the imitation of life seeking or resisting form. The novel's changing narrative forms represent and answer this search and resistance. But in so doing the novel gives life and its most general content as much attention as the forms that life seeks and questions. If the novelists of one era represent life as impatient with or oppressed by plotted form (as Moore, Stein, Joyce, or Beckett represent it), or unfulfilled by forms of story (as Eliot or Lawrence represent it); or if they think life incompatible with narrative, which in turn becomes the artist's province and seems more interesting than life (as Poe's case seems to show); or if, moreover, the novelists represent life and life's meanings in one era as not consummated in action or in narrative reason that imitates action, then surely there is room to argue that the novelists care about a content that is not merely formal and that gives the timeless narrative struggle an historical urgency and reference. Even the fact that the tendencies for and against plot and story exist side by side in one era does not argue only their atemporal formal nature, for the coexistence of the two structures is itself historical, the product of a transition between an era dominated by one social content and an era dominated by another.

We inhabit an era in which differing narrative forms do not merely coexist but seek to dominate each other because of their differing contents. George Eliot seeks to dominate Dickensian narrative form because she wants the representation of life "as it is" to pervade art. The classic American storytellers want to experiment with or subvert plot for the sake of

an ethos that they identify with their nationality and its alleged alliance with general human novelty. It is a mistake to
underestimate the conflict over narrative by playing down
the values and pressures of the changing human experience
that informs it.

It would be a further mistake to play down the varieties of
experience, feeling, and form that can be found on both sides
of the narrative issue. Poe is a storyteller, yet he is not at all a
storyteller like Dickens. The difference between them, represented by their use of reversal, makes it possible to class Poe
with plot's antagonists more than with its proponents. Yet
Poe delights in his fabrications in a way very different from
Melville; Poe's enjoyment of the willfulness of storytelling is
quite unlike Melville's distrust of will in any form. Thus, in
his revision of the sense of plot Poe is not an ally of Melville in
any simple manner. And while Hawthorne's antinarrative
impulses may be much like Melville's, Hawthorne's Phoebe,
considered as an antinarrative muse, is in her fruitfulness
very different from an antinarrative muse like Woolf's Lily
Briscoe, who is depicted as a paragon of sterility. Gertrude
Stein opposes story for the sake of complete actual presence;
Beckett opposes story because he does not believe in presence. These representative differences among the novelists
impatient with story are complemented by differences among
story's champions. Dickens shows action to be the creative
overcoming of isolation, a happy forging of community;
James shows action to be the hopeful sign of a community
that remains tragically absent in spite of that sign.

But all of these particular cases and differences do line up
for and against one significant claim and issue, which is now
the historical substance of the formal struggle. The claim is
that we have no significance, meaning, or happiness as actors. The narrative controversy centers on the profound
change in consciousness and value implied by this claim. The
writers who implicitly or explicitly approve it do not identify
it with human frustration, as committed storytellers would.
The further bearing of this claim is that meaning or value do

not depend upon action, and that meaning or value of any
definite and unqualified kind are either not identifiable or are
not important to human well-being. The novelists we have
considered who in effect side with this claim and with its further bearing are Poe, Hawthorne, Melville, George Eliot, Pater, the young Henry James, Moore, Wilde, Adams, Hardy,
Lawrence, Joyce, Woolf, Conrad, Faulkner (in part), and
Beckett. The inclusion of especially George Eliot in such
company may outrage conventional opinion, but what has
been said about her in Chapter Four, along with the recent
interpretations of *Middlemarch* by J. Hillis Miller cited in the
text, adequately withstands the critical pieties that need to be
offset.

Scott had a profound prophetic sense of the narrative divisions that were to follow him. His knowledge derived from
the historical change his stories represent. He understood
modern society would be organized and characterized by
men of speculation and feeling who would not be able—
easily or at all—to enact what they thought or felt. Scott's
mixed responses to this cannot be underestimated. But his
heroes inevitably do transform their intense sensibilities into
action, and this transformation marks their maturity. Scott
stands behind my chapter on Dickens and Eliot. He initiates
for the nineteenth-century English novel the rescue motif and
action. And Edward Waverley, for example, becomes a real
hero to himself and others, not by turning the Scottish past
into a library of sentimental speculations but by his rescue of
his uneasy ally Talbot from behind Jacobite lines. This rescue
is a reenactment of the active heroism of the fading past.
Modern social structure and rationality, as Scott sees them—
and accepts them—constrain this heroic action. Yet the modern world hungers for some version of this heroism, and
Scott suggests it must find a renewed form of this conduct.

As I have presented it, the history of the novel after Scott is
a long unravelling of Scott's suggestion. Dickens and the later
James are great exceptions in a novelistic tradition more and
more dedicated to the undoing of human deeds. Scott would

have been saddened to see the heirs of *Waverley*'s men and women of feeling—from Felix Holt to Christopher Newman to Lily Briscoe—justify their passive isolation, their inhibited consequence, and their inability to affect the world as a mark of their superior intelligence and sensibility. Nevertheless, perhaps the novel's long-lived and ever more powerful attempt to undo the fact and the prestige of action is coming to an end. Faulkner's fertility and popularity have yet to be fully assessed in the light of the novel's history since Scott. We may have in Faulkner an American Dickens whose moral values will appear, as time passes, increasingly more like those of the nineteenth-century proponents of plot and less like the modernists' narrative antagonisms and experiments. Moreover, to return to Beckett, we must not underestimate the remarkably positive aspects of narrative that appear in *his* novels. The narrator of *How It Is* insists there is a "natural order" of beginning, middle, and end to life. It is an insistence that story's traditional order and structure are not artificial, *not fictive* but spontaneously living. And although every attempt in *How It Is* to plot the "justice" of life, to argue "we are regulated thus," is answered by the refrain "something wrong there," life still registers in *How It Is* (as it does in *Molloy*, too) as a maddeningly puzzling but incontrovertible *act*, a "quaqua" that imposes itself upon sense and feeling not as "presence" or thought but as raw yet magisterial event.

The heroes in this book have been those writers who have made central "the featuring of act" or event. Our acts are not our only thoughts, but I believe they are or can be our most authentic and our most creative thoughts. We can be moved to this belief by Dickens's demonstration that life is the urgent occasion for those enactments by which we create our interidentity, our growth, our decency. We can be moved to it by James's conviction that although the genuine hero enacts himself into isolation, in the face of the world's vain indifference to action his clear capture of a deed is the germ of social beauty and value. It is not that the writers opposed to story do not value growth or decency or even community.

But Dickens and late James make us think that valuations that leave out the dimension of the act are vainly speculative.

In what way are acts themselves not vainly speculative? How are they at least the supreme tests of speculation? An intellectual structure is a differentiation that responds to variations in perception and experience. The origin of these variations is change, the daily revolution or reversal with which intelligence must come to grips. To put change or reversal at the heart of both intelligence and plot is to insist that thought always recall its genesis in change. And change, the emergence of novelty, the transformation of one condition into another, is the primal act, hence the primal story. In a novelist who minimalizes action—Woolf, for example—the ability of thought to differentiate experience becomes perplexed. Change then makes no difference to such a novelist; paradoxically, it is the same as changelessness, just as continuity appears, from such a point of view, identical with sterility. *To the Lighthouse* tells us of the decay and renewal of the Ramsay house. But how much do we feel this as definite transformation, compared, let us say, to the ineluctable change of things brought about by Merton's act at the end of *The Wings of the Dove*? James's ending makes change palpably definite, not paradoxical. In contrast, in writers such as Poe and Melville, we see the attraction to paradox and indefiniteness, the same collapse of differences accompanying their suspicion of action as the archetype and test of meaning. The novelists who break down story are full of these collapses. But Dickens and James find changes and differences that they cannot evade. And where opposites have merged they differentiate them, for they insist that action, story, and plot arise out of difference and that they must repeatedly make a difference to make sense, and vice versa.

I probably do not need to repeat at this point the fruit of such insistence. In the course of this book I have not been polemically in favor of the positive sense of plot and story and of the value of the motions of narrative consciousness as the positive sense defines them. I have sympathized with

varieties of antinarrative feeling in order to be fully respon-
sive to all sides of the narrative issue. But if changes in the
sense of plot do represent a human transformation, an era of
transition in which one form of life is seeking to dominate
another, this study's committed allegiances are unqualifiedly
on one side rather than the other. I have written as a partisan
of story because without the narrative representation of action life cannot be apprehended or cared for as continuous,
purposeful, or creative (as I believe life can be in *fact*) and
values that measure and determine conduct cannot be fruitfully discriminated or even distinguished.

⚡ NOTES ⚡

INTRODUCTION

1. Aristotle *Poetics* 6.5.
2. Walter Benjamin, *Illuminations*, ed. Hannah Arendt and trans. Harry Zohn (New York, 1968), p. 83.
3. Kenneth Burke, *A Grammar of Motives* (New York, 1945), p. 65.
4. See Tzvetan Todorov, *Poétique de la prose* (Paris, 1971), especially Chapter 10, "La quête du recit." The American translation by Richard Howard is *The Poetics of Prose* (Cornell, 1977).
5. Poe initiates an antinarrative tradition that includes Stein as one of its inevitable products. An antinarrative impulse appears in all the Americans treated here, except for the late James and except for the Dickensian aspect of Faulkner's narrative.
6. In fact the length of the book has made it necessary for me to skimp treatment of Scott, to merely mention Cooper and Hardy, and to eliminate consideration of Thackeray, Trollope, Twain, Howells, and Dreiser. I would have argued that the five last-named figures oppose plot.

CHAPTER ONE

1. E. M. Forster, *Aspects of the Novel* (New York, 1927), p. 152. The most interesting attack on story and plot in the novel remains the second essay in José Ortega y Gasset's *The Dehumanization of Art and Notes on the Novel*, trans. Helene Weyl (Princeton, 1948). For a summary of the prevailing prejudice of "culture" against story, see Lionel Trilling, *Sincerity and Authenticity* (Cambridge, 1972), pp. 134-139.
2. Robert Scholes and Robert Kellogg, *The Nature of Narrative* (New York, 1966), p. 207.
3. Ernest Fenollosa, *The Chinese Written Character As a Medium for Poetry* (New York, 1936), p. 11. This was first published in 1920.
4. For the difference between "relation" in narrative story and poetry, see Geoffrey H. Hartman, *The Unmediated Vision* (New Haven, 1954), pp. 38-39, 76.
5. Kenneth Burke, *A Grammar of Motives* (New York, 1945), pp. 14, 227.

6. Barbara Hardy, "Towards a Poetics of Fiction: 3) An Approach Through Narrative," *Novel* 2 (1968): 5-14. See also Barbara Hardy, *Tellers and Listeners* (London, 1975), pp. 3-4.

7. Georg Lukács, *The Meaning of Contemporary Realism*, trans. John and Necke Mander (London, 1963), pp. 54-55.

8. Lee T. Lemon and Marion J. Reis, trans., *Russian Formalist Criticism* (Lincoln, 1965), pp. 57, 67-68, 116. See also Roman Jakobson, "On Realism in Art," in *Readings in Russian Poetics: Formalist and Structuralist Views*, ed. Ladislav Matejka and Krystyna Pomorska (Cambridge and London, 1971).

9. The word "writeable" is taken from Roland Barthes. See Robert Scholes, *Structuralism in Literature* (New Haven and London, 1974), p. 151.

10. Tony Tanner, *The Reign of Wonder* (Cambridge, 1965), p. 195.

11. Gertrude Stein, *Lectures in America* (New York, 1935), pp. 185, 118-119, 94-95, 100.

12. Ibid., p. 125.

13. Ibid., p. 180.

14. Gertrude Stein, *Narration* (Chicago, 1935), pp. 19-20.

15. Stein, *Lectures in America*, p. 161.

16. Part 3, Chapter 1. Since there is no uniform or standard edition of Orwell's novels, I refer to them by citing chapters only.

17. Sonia Orwell and Ian Angus, eds., *The Collected Essays, Journalism and Letters of George Orwell* (London, 1968), 1:426.

18. Ibid., pp. 446, 442-443.

19. Alvin Kernan, *The Cankered Muse* (New Haven, 1959), p. 30, and *The Plot of Satire* (New Haven, 1965), *passim*; Stephen Jay Greenblatt, *Three Modern Satirists: Waugh, Orwell, and Huxley* (New Haven and London, 1965), pp. 111-112.

20. Scholes and Kellogg, *The Nature of Narrative*, p. 239.

CHAPTER TWO

1. José Ortega y Gasset, *Toward a Philosophy of History* (New York, 1941), pp. 214, 227-228.

2. Thomas Carlyle, *Sartor Resartus*, ed. C. F. Harrold (Indianapolis and New York, 1937), pp. 78-79.

3. J. B. Schneewind, ed., *Mill's Essays on Literature and Society* (New York, 1965), p. 190.

4. Thomas Carlyle, *The Works of Thomas Carlyle*, ed. H. D. Trail, The Centenary Edition (London, 1896-1901), 4:248.

5. René Wellek, *Confrontations* (Princeton, 1965), pp. 105-106.

6. George Levine, *The Boundaries of Fiction: Carlyle, Macauley, Newman* (Princeton, 1968), p. 46.

7. Wellek, *Confrontations*, p. 104.

8. Carlyle, *Works*, 3:145-146.

9. For an exposition of the Dionysian element in Carlyle's history, see Albert J. La Valley, *Carlyle and the Idea of the Modern* (New Haven and London, 1968), *passim*. Especially relevant to narrative reason and action are pp. 135-139 and p. 151.

10. Wellek, *Confrontations*, p. 109.

11. E. T. Cook and Alexander Wedderburn, eds., *The Works of John Ruskin* (London, 1903-1912), 9:21.

12. See the brilliant psychological reduction of Ruskin's method in Richard Ellmann, *Golden Codgers* (London, New York, and Toronto, 1973), p. 48. Later in this chapter I am indebted to Ellmann's remark on Pater in the same source, p. 51.

13. Cook and Wedderburn, *The Works of John Ruskin*, 11:209-210. My use of "system of reserve" is borrowed from traditional Biblical exegesis, but distorts the phrase's traditional sense and usage. The phrase "the optic of narrative reason" is not connected with the title of John D. Rosenberg's *The Darkening Glass: A Portrait of Ruskin's Genius* (New York and London, 1961).

14. Cook and Wedderburn, *The Works of John Ruskin*, 36:465.

15. Walter Pater, *The Works of Walter Pater* (London, 1900-1901), 3:218, 219-220.

16. See Anthony Ward, *Walter Pater: The Idea in Nature* (Worcester and London, 1966). For what Pater means to the narrative practice of a present day English novelist, see especially Ward's Preface.

CHAPTER THREE

1. Steven Marcus, *Dickens: from Pickwick to Dombey* (New York, 1965), pp. 175, 204.

2. See Donald Davie, *The Heyday of Sir Walter Scott* (London, 1961). I am especially indebted to Davie's reading of Scott and to Georg Lukács's *The Historical Novel*, trans. Hannah and Stanley Mitchell (London, 1962). I endorse and amplify Lukács's criticism of *Barnaby Rudge*, pp. 243-244.

3. See the essay by Jack Lindsay on *Barnaby Rudge* in *Dickens and The Twentieth Century*, eds. John Gross and Gabriel Pearson (London, 1962).

4. Northrop Frye, *The Stubborn Structure* (Cornell, 1970), pp. 220, 240.

5. Northrop Frye, *Anatomy of Criticism* (Princeton, 1957), pp. 344, 346. In the previous paragraph, quotations are from *Anatomy of Criticism*, p. 93; Frye's *Fables of Identity* (New York, 1963), p. 37; and Frye's *The Stubborn Structure*, p. 218.

6. Philip Collins, ed., *Dickens: The Critical Heritage* (New York, 1971), p. 473.

7. See Marcus, *Dickens: from Pickwick to Dombey*, Chapter 3, "The True Prudence."

8. My argument here derives from what I take to be an interpretation of Poe in "Death and the Compass" by Jorge Luis Borges. See Jorge Luis Borges, *The Aleph and Other Stories 1933-1969* (New York, 1970).

9. For an exposition of irony and comedy in Poe, see G. R. Thompson, *Poe's Fiction* (Wisconsin, 1973).

10. William Carlos Williams, *In the American Grain* (Norfolk, Conn., 1956), p. 230.

11. G. R. Levy, *The Gate of Horn* (London, 1948). For another interpretation of labyrinths in their relation to narrative, see J. Hillis Miller, "Ariadne's Thread: Repetition and the Narrative Line," *Critical Inquiry* 3 (1976): 57-77.

12. D. H. Lawrence, *Studies in Classic American Literature* (New York, 1923), p. 93.

CHAPTER FOUR

1. George Herbert Mead, *The Philosophy of the Act*, ed. Charles W. Morris (Chicago and London, 1938), pp. xxx, xlix.

2. The quotations are from Roland Barthes, *S/Z*, trans. Richard Miller (New York, 1974), pp. 80, 82-83; the essays by J. Hillis Miller are "Narrative and History," *ELH* 41 (Fall, 1974): 455-473, and "Optic and Semiotic in *Middlemarch*," *Harvard English Studies* 6 (1975): 125-145.

3. See George H. Ford, *Dickens and His Readers: Aspects of Novel-Criticism since 1836* (Princeton, 1955), p. 182. The documentation relevant to the later novelists' adversity to Dickens is in Ford, especially Chapters 7 and 10; see also Kenneth Graham, *English Criticism of the Novel 1865-1900* (Oxford, 1965), and Richard Stang, *The Theory of the*

Novel in England 1850-1870 (New York, 1959). In preparing this chapter I have also been stimulated by Harold Bloom's "The Internalization of Quest Romance" in *The Ringers in the Tower: Studies in Romantic Tradition* (Chicago, 1971). The Victorian novelists as well as the postromantic poets must carry forward the project Bloom describes as Shelley's, p. 24.

4. The connection between *Bleak House* and *Felix Holt, The Radical* was pointed out to me by Robert Newsom, author of *Dickens on the Romantic Side of Familiar Things: Bleak House and the Novel Tradition* (New York, 1977). Newsom has generously allowed me to make use of his insight here.

5. Stephen Wall, ed., *Charles Dickens: A Critical Anthology* (Penguin Books, 1970), p. 202.

6. See Barbara Hardy, *The Novels of George Eliot* (London, 1959), pp. 135-136. For remarks on coincidence and Eliot's plots, see Hardy's Chapter 6. In Hardy's *The Moral Art of Dickens* (New York, 1970), we find a contrast of Dickens's treatment of moral action with George Eliot's. Dickens, Hardy says on p. 55, is "too interested . . . in melodramatic intrigue and mystery to give more space to moral action." But the intrigue and mystery adequately carry the moral action. Hardy insists that "it is as if [Dickens] were committed to the imposed external action of some eighteenth-century novels." Why "imposed?" Our modern sense of plot invariably sees plot as imposition. A variation of this viewpoint is the idea that the novel's plots or actions "displace" their true subjects. See Taylor Stoehr, *Dickens: The Dreamer's Stance* (Ithaca, 1965).

7. Erich Auerbach, *Mimesis*, trans. W. R. Trask (Princeton, 1953), p. 135.

8. George Eliot, *Felix Holt, The Radical* (Edinburgh and London, 1866), 3:199 (Chapter 45).

9. See F. R. and Q. D. Leavis, *Dickens, The Novelist* (London, 1970), p. 166.

10. J. Hillis Miller, *Charles Dickens: The World of His Novels* (Cambridge, 1958), pp. 217-219.

11. Charles Dickens, *Bleak House*, The New Oxford Illustrated Dickens (London, New York, and Toronto, 1948), p. 740 (Chapter 54).

12. D. H. Lawrence, *Psychoanalysis and the Unconscious and Fantasia of the Unconscious* (New York, 1960), p. 220.

CHAPTER FIVE

1. Charles Olson, *Human Universe and Other Essays*, ed. Donald Allen (New York, 1967), pp. 114-115, 118-119, 122. See also "Some Good News" in Olson, *The Maximus Poems* (New York, 1960), pp. 120-127.

2. Gregory Bateson, *Steps to an Ecology of Mind* (New York, 1972), pp. 319, 445, 451. I am indebted to Roy D. Skodnick for suggesting that Bateson's work illustrates Melville and Olson.

3. Daniel G. Hoffman, *Form and Fable in American Fiction* (New York, 1961), pp. 261, 270, 274, 235.

4. Ibid., pp. 277, 262.

5. Ibid., p. 277.

6. Robert Scholes, *Structuralism in Literature: An Introduction* (New Haven and London, 1974), p. 108.

7. Herman Melville, *The Writings of Herman Melville*, Northwestern-Newberry Edition (Evanston and Chicago, 1968-), 5:320 (Chapter 75).

8. Ibid., p. 151 (Chapter 36).

9. Melville, "The End," in *Writings*, 5:398.

10. I might note here that Edgar A. Dryden's intelligent exposition of *White Jacket* in *Melville's Thematics of Form* (Baltimore, 1968), pp. 67-79, differs from mine in that it does not emphasize the *political* "thematics of form." Dryden treats the *Town-Ho* story perceptively, but does not explain Steelkilt, as is also the case in Warner Berthoff, *The Example of Melville* (Princeton, 1962), especially Chapter Six, "Melville's Story-Telling."

CHAPTER SIX

1. Kenneth Burke, *A Grammar of Motives* (New York, 1945), p. 16.

2. Edmund Gosse, *Father and Son: A Study of Two Temperaments* (New York, 1907), pp. 77, 91, 147, 349.

3. See Georg Lukács, *The Historical Novel*, trans. Hannah and Stanley Mitchell (London, 1962), p. 103.

4. E. T. Cook and Alexander Wedderburn, eds., *The Works of John Ruskin* (London, 1903-1912), 35:115.

5. John Stuart Mill, *Autobiography of John Stuart Mill* (New York, 1924), pp. 79, 32, 77, 170, 100.

6. Gosse, *Father and Son*, pp. 114, 355, 324, 35.

7. I quote from William Barrett and Henry D. Aiken, eds., *Philosophy in the Twentieth Century* (New York, 1962), 1:360-361.

8. Oscar Wilde, *Complete Works*, introd. Vyvyan Holland (London and Glasgow, 1966), pp. 915, 957.

9. Barrett and Aiken, *Philosophy in the Twentieth Century*, 1:341.

10. See Walter Pater, *The Works of Walter Pater* (London, 1900-1901), 1:231. "Natural laws we shall never modify; . . . but there is still something in the nobler or less noble attitude with which we watch their fatal combinations."

11. Wilde, *Works*, pp. 891, 920, 957.

12. George Moore, *The Carra Edition of the Collected Works of George Moore* (New York, 1922-1924), 9:361, 304-305.

13. Ibid., pp. 299, 464, 414, 397, 368.

14. Ibid., 10:282-283.

15. Ibid., p. 226.

16. William Butler Yeats, *The Autobiography of William Butler Yeats* (New York, 1938), pp. 373-374.

17. Ibid., p. 390.

18. Ibid., pp. 400-401.

19. Ibid., p. 470.

20. Ernest Samuels, ed., *The Education of Henry Adams* (Boston, 1973), p. 511.

21. Gertrude Stein, *Narration* (Chicago, 1935), p. 59.

22. Gertrude Stein, *The Autobiography of Alice B. Toklas* (New York, 1933), p. 83.

23. Paul Goodman, "Politics Within Limits," *The New York Review of Books* 19, no. 2 (10 August 1972): 33.

CHAPTER SEVEN

1. See Laurence B. Holland, *The Expense of Vision* (Princeton, 1964).

2. Henry James, *The Art of the Novel: Critical Prefaces*, ed. Richard P. Blackmur (New York and London, 1934), pp. 111, 314-315. See also pp. 252-253 and *passim*.

3. Henry James, *The New York Edition of the Novels and Tales of Henry James* (New York, 1907-1909), 2:534 (Chapter 26).

4. Ibid., 19:217, 221, 223 (Book Fifth, ii).

5. Ibid., pp. 288, 298 (Book Fifth, vii).

6. Ibid., 20:342 (Book Tenth, ii).

7. Ibid., pp. 235-236 (Book Ninth, i).

8. Ibid., pp. 252-253 (Book Ninth, ii).

9. James, *The Art of the Novel*, p. 201.

10. James, *The New York Edition*, 19:163 (Book Fourth, i).

11. James, *The Art of the Novel*, p. 6.

12. Nathaniel Hawthorne, *The Centenary Edition of the Works of Nathaniel Hawthorne* (Ohio State University Press, 1962-1977), pp. 212, 82, 319, 88 (Chapters, 5, 6, 14, 21).

13. Henry James, *The American Scene* (Bloomington and London, 1968), p. 290. The previous quotations are from pp. 307, 121-122, 273, 102, 446.

14. Ibid., p. 427.

15. Leon Edel emphasizes the most superficial of James's reasons for becoming a British citizen: convenience. See *Henry James: The Master, 1901-1916* (Philadelphia and New York, 1972), pp. 528-532. Edel seems to me out of touch with the strength and complexity of James's feelings in his letter to Henry James, Jr., 24 June 1915. See Henry James, *The Letters of Henry James*, ed. Percy Lubbock (New York, 1920), 2:477-479. I am attempting here to add another dimension to that complexity. In mentioning viewpoints at odds with my argument in this chapter, I should note my disagreements on the subject of picture and story with Percy Lubbock, *The Craft of Fiction* (London, 1963), *passim*; J. A. Ward, *The Search for Form: Studies in the Structure of James's Fiction* (Chapel Hill, 1967), especially Chapter 2, "Picture and Action"; and Viola Hopkins Winner, *Henry James and the Visual Arts* (Charlottesville, 1970), especially p. 60 and pp. 194-195.

CHAPTER EIGHT

1. Edward W. Said, *Beginnings: Intention and Method* (New York, 1975), pp. 162, 174, 351. See also pp. 133-137.

2. For a viewpoint similar to mine see Mark Schechner, *Joyce in Nighttown: A Psychoanalytic Inquiry into Ulysses* (Berkeley, 1974).

3. James Joyce, *Ulysses*, The Modern Library Edition (New York, 1961), p. 207.

4. Ibid., pp. 195-196.

5. Ibid., p. 189. See also p. 213.

6. Virginia Woolf, *To the Lighthouse* (New York, 1927), pp. 58-59, 53-54, 179-180.

7. Ibid., p. 79.

8. Ibid., pp. 95-96, 81-82, 287.

9. D. H. Lawrence, *Phoenix: The Posthumous Papers* (London, 1936), pp. 401-403. See also p. 471.

10. D. H. Lawrence, *The Rainbow* (New York, 1924), pp. 124-125 (Chapter 5).

11. D. H. Lawrence, *Women in Love* (New York, 1950), p. 383 (Chapter 24).

12. Ibid., p. 345 (Chapter 23), p. 545 (Chapter 31).

13. Joseph Conrad, *The Uniform Edition of The Works of Joseph Conrad* (London and Toronto, 1923), 14:258.

14. Ibid., p. 171.

15. Ibid., p. 169.

16. Ibid., p. 242.

17. Ibid., pp. 40, 243.

18. Ibid., pp. 243-244.

19. See Cleanth Brooks, *William Faulkner: The Yoknapatawpha Country* (New Haven, 1963), pp. 344-345.

20. William Faulkner, *The Sound and the Fury* (New York, 1956), p. 278.

21. Ibid., p. 141.

22. This emphasis on a genuine future family, this nostalgia *forward* (so to speak) puts Conrad and Faulkner at odds with the idea of the novel as nostalgic symptom of transcendental homelessness. See Georg Lukács, *The Theory of the Novel*, trans. Anna Bostock (London, 1971). That some modern novels should imply the need for an adversary parenthood makes their formal modernism compatible with Marxist revolutionary hopes. In this connection I refer back to Melville's Steelkilt, who might be compatible with the imagination of a new and radically republican form of parenthood. A novelist's implicit idealization of the cultural adversary who is also a parental figure rather than of the orphan or bastard child is also a challenge to Marthe Robert's brilliant *Roman des origines et origines du roman* (Paris, 1972).

AFTERWORD

1. Samuel Beckett, *Proust* (New York, 1970), p. 69.

2. Samuel Beckett, *Malone Dies* (New York, 1956), pp. 51-52.

3. For the same idea see Tzvetan Todorov, *Poétique de la prose* (Paris, 1971), Chapter 10. The American translation by Richard Howard is *The Poetics of Prose* (Cornell, 1977).

⬧ INDEX ⬧

Wilde, Oscar (*cont.*)
  Importance of Being Earnest, 178
will, 143-144, 155, 231, 256, 284
Williams, William Carlos, 83-84, 90
Winner, Viola Hopkins, 296n
Woolf, Virginia, xvii, xx, 96, 131,
  233, 234, 248-254, 255, 284, 285,
  287; plot and "sterility" of life in,
  248-254; *To the Lighthouse*, 235,
  236, 237, 248-254, 287

work, as form of plot, 9, 24, 120-
  122, 144, 147, 216

Yeats, William Butler, 188-191,
  195, 200; life as plotted drama in,
  190; *The Bounty of Sweden*, 190;
  Dramatis Personae 1896-1902, 188

Zola, Émile, 183

LIBRARY OF CONGRESS CATALOGING IN PUBLICATION DATA

Caserio, Robert L   1944-
   Plot, story, and the novel.

   Includes bibliographical references and index.
   1.   English fiction—History and criticism.
2.   American fiction—History and criticism.
3.   Plots (Drama, novel, etc.)   I.   Title.
PR826.C3   823′.009′24   79-4321
ISBN 0-691-06382-6